Philosophy for Life

Mel Thompson

For my daughter, Rebecca

Philosophy for Life

Mel Thompson

First published in Great Britain in 1995 by Hodder & Stoughton.
An Hachette UK company.

First published in US in 1995 by The McGraw-Hill Companies, Inc.

This edition published 2017 by John Murray Learning

Previously published as *Teach Yourself Understand Philosophy*

Copyright © 1995, 2000, 2003, 2006, 2010, 2017 Mel Thompson

British Library Cataloguing in Publication Data: a catalogue record for this title is
available from the British Library.

Library of Congress Catalog Card Number: on file.

ISBN 978 1 473 65788 5

eISBN 978 1 473 65791 5

1

Typeset by Cenveo® Publisher Services.

Printed and bound in Great Brit

John Murray Learning policy is
recyclable products and made fr
and manufacturing processes ar
regulations of the country of ori

Carmelite House

50 Victoria Embankment

London EC4Y 0DZ

www.hodder.co.uk

Also available
in ebook

Contents

Acknowledgements

The author and publishers would like to thank the following for their permission to use copyright material in this book:

The Observer for the newspaper extract on page 37; Chatto and Windus for the quotation from Iris Murdoch's *Metaphysics as a Guide to Morals*; Penguin Books Ltd for the quotation from Descartes' *Discourse on Method* and *Chambers Concise Dictionary* (2nd edition, 2009), for its definition of philosophy.

Taking it further

Many books, both classic and modern, have been referred to within the text, and they may serve as a next step for those wanting to deepen their understanding of the subject.

However, books, articles and websites are constantly appearing and changing, and it is therefore unrealistic to attempt to list here all the material that may be of value to those wanting to follow up on issues raised in this book.

Those wanting to explore the subject further should therefore visit the *Philosophy for Life* website, which provides a range of suitable material and web-links. It also gives you an opportunity to leave comments, ask questions or recommend material for inclusion. Just log on to: **www.philosophyforlife.co.uk**. You can also visit the author's website at: **www.philosophyandethics.com**

Meet the author

Welcome to *Philosophy for Life!*

We're all philosophers. When there's a tough choice to be made, when faced with the facts of birth, love or death, or simply when thinking about what we want to do with our lives or what we hold dear, we all tend to ask fundamental questions and to use our reason to try to make sense of our situation. Work is no escape from it; whether it's examining the logic of a business decision, sifting the relevance of scientific data, or trying to express oneself as clearly as possible in an email, we are exercising our philosophical muscles. To me, philosophy is doing what comes naturally, but doing it in a rigorous and systematic way, and not opting out when the mental going gets tough. It's a wonderful discipline for clearing the mind; a skill like no other. It's also a point of entry into the history of ideas, perusing the wisdom of the past to aid our decisions for the future.

That's why, for me, philosophy is 'for life'. It goes beyond taking an interest in academic arguments and the history of ideas, presenting us with an essential tool for rational living, sharpening up our ability to think, to listen to the arguments of others, to weigh evidence and to examine reasons. We live in a time (sometimes labelled 'post-truth') when emotional appeals and unquestioned assumptions too often dominate the media. Philosophy does not deny the power of emotion or intuition, but it sets it in context. To live life to the full requires balance, empathy, reason and the development of a purposeful sense of what life is for. Philosophy therefore contributes not just a body of wisdom, but an essential set of skills for living well.

Mel Thompson, 2017

Introduction: Thinking to Enhance your Life

In this Introduction you will:

- ▶ *Be aware that philosophy is a skill as well as a body of knowledge*
- ▶ *Consider how precise thinking puts you in control*
- ▶ *Explore different styles of argument*
- ▶ *Reflect on the therapeutic value of philosophy*

According to the *Concise Chambers Dictionary*, philosophy is:

1 The search for truth and knowledge concerning the universe, human existence, perception and behaviour, pursued by means of reflection, reasoning and argument

2 Any particular system or set of beliefs established as a result of this

3 A set of principles that serves as a basis for making judgements and decisions

To philosophize involves thinking clearly and accurately, considering evidence, reflecting on experience, sorting out arguments and testing out claims. Philosophy also probes the meaning of life; it examines morality, politics and religion; it challenges our assumptions and invites us to think again about our opinions.

Some overall sense of who we are and what life is for may enhance our appreciation of life in general. Where do we stand on the big issues that face us? How can we find contentment in a world that includes so much suffering and evil? How do we come to terms with our own fragility and mortality? What does it mean to be an individual, and how does that affect the way we treat others? What, if anything, can we know for certain? These universal and personal questions are not exclusively philosophical, nor are they necessarily issues with which professional philosophers wrestle on a day-to-day basis, but I want to suggest that most of the topics covered in courses in philosophy can be related to them, so that some knowledge of philosophy can yield immediate, personal benefits, quite apart from the intellectual stimulus that studying philosophy offers.

In order to enjoy and benefit from philosophy, it is important to remember that it is both *an activity* and *a body of knowledge*:

As an activity, it is a matter of asking questions, challenging assumptions, re-examining traditionally held views, unpacking the meaning of words, weighing up the value of evidence and examining the logic of arguments. It cultivates an enquiring and critical mind, even if it sometimes infuriates those who want an easy intellectual life. Philosophy clarifies your thinking, your way of expressing yourself, your way of examining arguments, and sharpens up your ability to make reasoned decisions. Philosophy is a tool with which to expose nonsense, and express ideas in a way that is as unambiguous as possible.

As a body of knowledge, philosophy is the cumulative wisdom of some of the world's greatest thinkers. It offers you a chance to explore fundamental questions and to see what philosophers in different periods of history have had to say about them. You can examine the philosophy of a particular period. The philosophy of ancient Greece, for example, is particularly important for understanding the origins of much Western thought and culture. You might look at the philosophy of the European Enlightenment, or of the twentieth century, each giving an insight into ideas that developed out of and shaped that particular period of history. This historical perspective on ideas is valuable, because it frees you from being limited by the unquestioned assumptions of those around you. To be able to think through issues from first principles is helped by having looked at the way in which philosophers have gone about their work in the past, so this second aspect of philosophy reinforces the first.

So we can see philosophy as a life-tool, a set of skills for engaging with any subject, but also as a body of wisdom that can serve as a guide and help inform our decisions and moral judgments.

Take back control!

In a lecture in 1854, Louis Pasteur is reported to have said 'In the fields of observation, chance favours only the prepared mind.' It is my view that, in life as in observation, the varied situations and crises that chance throws up present both hazards and opportunities. The person who is alert and sensitive to what life is about, and who has already considered the fundamental principles of what we can know or what we should do, will hopefully be better able to grasp and use each situation to the full. It has always been appreciated that information is needed in order to make good business decisions. At one time, an advertisement for the *Financial Times* said simply 'No FT; no comment.' To me, the same thing applies to life in general: 'No philosophy; no comment.'

We are constantly bombarded by facts, arguments and people wanting to influence our decisions and shape the way we look at life. Whether it comes from religious groups, political parties or commercial enterprises, we are all vulnerable to being influenced in ways that might not reflect our own best interests.

In 2016, 'post-truth' was added to the Oxford English Dictionary, defined as:

> 'Relating to or denoting circumstances in which objective facts are less influential in shaping public opinion than appeals to emotion and personal belief.'

Living with a mixture of truth and post-truth is now a feature of life and the reason we need smart thinking. Understanding life has always been a matter of balancing facts against hopes, aspirations, emotions and traditions. Nobody can be completely objective because we all have a particular perspective and intention behind all that we say, think about or do. But the art is to be aware of that balance, and particularly to be *in control* of that balance.

Key idea for life

Are you content to live on the basis of other people's ideas and values? At his trial, Socrates is said to have claimed 'The unexamined life is not worth living.' Not everyone would go that far, but it is at least worthwhile giving one's life a mental workout once in a while, to find out whether the examined life is more purposeful than the unexamined one, and whether it genuinely encourages you to think for yourself rather than to be influenced by whatever appealing post-truth is being offered. Whatever the limitations of your circumstances, and whether you are eventually shown to be right or wrong on any issue, at the very least, the examined life is genuinely *your* life, not one that you have borrowed from the media.

Different styles of argument

Philosophy can be presented in different ways. Plato, for example, favoured the dialogue form. So his political philosophy in *The Republic* has a range of characters, each of whom presents and argues for a particular viewpoint. Other philosophers gradually unpack the implications of their particular theory in a more linear fashion.

There was a phase in Anglo-American philosophy – starting early in the twentieth century – when some thinkers claimed that the sole task of philosophy was to clarify the meaning of words. They assumed that, once the linguistic problems were sorted out, all else would follow. Today that view is giving way to a broader perspective. Philosophy is indeed about language, and it is essential to understand the language you use. However, it is also important to rise above language in order to explore the basic ideas and concepts it expresses, and then to move on to examine features about the world which would not have come to light without that process of serious thinking and analysis.

Of course, philosophers do not always agree on how to do philosophy, or what is of value. The late A. J. Ayer, an Oxford philosopher best known for his work on 'logical positivism' (see page 101), interviewed about his work in a 1980 interview, commented in his usual direct way on the work of various other philosophers, describing the German philosopher Heidegger's idea about 'the Nothing' as 'sheer rubbish' and saying that people might sometimes be impressed because they like to be mystified. In Chapter 2, we shall be looking briefly at the work of Heidegger. You may feel inclined, after reading that, to agree with Ayer, or you might feel that Heidegger is describing something of greater importance than Ayer's analytic approach. The essential thing to realize at this stage is that philosophers do not all agree on the topics about which to philosophize, the way to set about doing so, or the conclusions reached. Philosophy is not monolithic. There is no body of established and unquestioned work; it is an ongoing activity and one that often raises more questions than it answers.

Ayer's comment on Heidegger also reflects a division that held for much of the twentieth century between 'analytic' philosophy, practised mainly in English-speaking universities, and 'continental' philosophy from mainland Europe. The former was obsessed with language, precision argument and definition of terms; the latter was more literary and focused on broader questions of life's meaning and experience. Today, that division is less significant. Analytic philosophy is regarded by some as largely defunct (although it still represents a substantial core of academic work), replaced by a broader approach which includes the issues and thinkers of the continental tradition.

Philosophers have also disagreed about the extent to which their work can make a difference to the world in any practical sense. In the middle years of the twentieth century, when linguistic philosophy dominated discussion of ethics, it was assumed that philosophers would not argue about what was right or wrong but only about what it might *mean* to say that something was right or wrong. Theirs was language about language, sometimes called 'second order' language. It was only later, from about the 1970s, that philosophers became more engaged with practical issues, particularly in medical ethics, the ethics of war and peace, sexual ethics, environmental ethics and so on.

The range of views on the practical impact of philosophy may be illustrated by comments from two hugely influential thinkers. The nineteenth-century, political and social philosopher Karl Marx, said:

The philosophers have only interpreted the world, in various ways. The point, however, is to change it.

(*Theses on Feuerbach*, 1845)

Contrast this with arguably the most influential twentieth-century thinker, Ludwig Wittgenstein, who was quite happy to proclaim that:

Philosophy leaves everything as it is.

For most thinkers, the truth lies somewhere between the two.

Remember this: Eastern approaches

Philosophy is not limited to any one culture or continent. The philosophy introduced in this book, and taught in departments of philosophy in most universities in Europe and North America, is Western philosophy – but that is only one part of a much larger tradition.

Eastern philosophy is generally taken to include the major religious and philosophical systems of India (the various traditions collectively known as Hinduism, along with Buddhist and Jain philosophy) and the Far East, including Confucian and Taoist thought and the later developments of Buddhism.

It is commonly said that the big difference between Eastern and Western philosophy is that the former is religious, and is concerned with salvation as much as with knowledge, whereas the latter is secular, seen by many as almost an alternative to religion. That is not entirely true. In the West, the Christian, Jewish and Muslim religions have had a profound influence on philosophical thought, and the philosophy of religion continues to be an important aspect of philosophy. In the East, although philosophy is seen as a matter of practical and spiritual importance, the process of reasoning can be examined in itself, quite apart from any religious connotations. It may also distort Eastern thought to try to draw a distinction between religion and philosophy: Buddhism, for example, sees the path to overcoming suffering in terms of understanding the fundamental truths of life. It is not a matter of religious doctrines on the one hand and secular thought on the other – this is a Western distinction that is not really relevant to Eastern thought.

As there is little enough scope within this book to introduce the main areas of Western thought, no attempt has been made to explore Eastern philosophy. In this series there is a book called *Eastern Philosophy*, by the same author.

Definite answers and progress?

When studying the natural sciences, you can generally trace a progression of ideas and a gradual expansion of knowledge. By contrast, in reading philosophy, you will find that, although you can see who influenced who, progress can sometimes appear to be circular rather than linear, so that the questions explored by the ancient Greeks are still very much debated today. Philosophy is always suggesting new ways of looking at questions, new ways of expressing ideas, and new views about the purpose and function of philosophy itself, but those new ideas may not necessarily be an improvement on older ones. Each generation explores similar questions, but does so in a new context.

It is not possible to live in Western Europe, or North America, without having your language and ideas influenced by generations of thinkers. To be aware of that heritage enhances your appreciation of your own culture. Even though it may not always be easy to spot, there is always going to be progress of some kind in philosophy, because we benefit from this developing history of ideas. But just as a modern painter may admire but not seek to copy the work of the old masters, so philosophers continue to follow the tradition set by their predecessors, but seek to explore familiar issues anew.

Hence, for those who crave a definitive answer to every question, philosophy is likely to prove a source of constant frustration. But for those who constantly question themselves, and are prepared to examine and modify their own views where necessary, it is a source of fascination and a means of sharpening the critical faculties.

Philosophy today – like the froth on the crest of a wave – is carried forward by the whole movement of thought that stretches back at least 2,500 years, and far further if you include Eastern thought. What this book seeks to do (while acknowledging its severe limitations in terms of coverage and depth) is to point to the reality of the wave, and the general direction of the water within it. A society without philosophy would be cut off from its own roots; it would have to start from scratch, time and time again, to sort out its values and its self-understanding. With philosophy, that process is shown in its historical and logical perspectives. With philosophy, you start at an advantage, for you look at each problem with the benefit of knowing something of the accumulated wisdom of some of the best thinkers in Western culture.

Philosophy as therapy

In this book, we shall be exploring a broad range of philosophical arguments that continue to shape our view of the world today. By doing that, and by appreciating the skill of good philosophical argument, we achieve greater clarity in our thinking and precision in presenting our own ideas. That, in itself, is a substantial benefit.

Some, however, take philosophy a step further and use it as a therapeutic tool. You do not have to be clinically depressed or schizophrenic to have your judgement clouded or your view of life warped by emotional confusion or uncertainty. To some extent, we all suffer from failure to see things clearly and appreciate their value – that's a problem inherent in the human condition. We may despair of life, or become cynical about any attempt to improve it. We may feel that we have not lived up to our own ideals, or those of others; we may strive to make sense and make changes.

Since the 1980s there has developed a form of therapy generally called Clinical Philosophy (or philosophical counselling), which seeks to use the skills of philosophy to reshape the way people understand their lives or deal with social issues. The theory behind such practice is an extension of the aim of philosophy in general, namely to clarify a person's views and belief systems, or to give them new ways of looking at issues they face, with a view to helping them to achieve a measure of personal insight. This approach was popularized by Dr Lou Marinoff, in his many publications, including *Plato Not Prozac! Applying Eternal Wisdom to Everyday Problems*.

This present book does not set out to offer therapy, but the fundamental principle behind it is the same: we can all benefit from the attempt to clarify our thoughts and reflect on the values and principles that shape our lives.

Worth the hemlock?

One of the most remarkable moments in the history of Western philosophy was the death of Socrates in 399 BCE. The event was recorded by Plato, whose respect for his teacher was such that he set out most of his philosophy in the form of dialogues in which Socrates plays the central role. Charged with impiety, Socrates was condemned to death on the grounds that his questioning and teaching was corrupting the young (with whom he appears to have been popular for challenging conventional beliefs and ideas). Plato presents Socrates as declining to propose an acceptable alternative punishment, and being prepared to accept death (by drinking a cup of hemlock). For Plato, reason and the freedom of the individual to live in accordance with it, took priority over the social and political order. Socrates would not compromise his freedom to pursue the truth, even if it appeared subversive and a danger to the state. Indeed, as Plato was later to expound in *The Republic*, justice and the institutions of state should be based on reason, and rulers should be philosophers, willing and able to apply reason with disinterested objectivity.

For Socrates, the task of the philosopher was not peripheral to life, but central. To stop questioning and challenging accepted concepts was unthinkable; Socrates chose to accept death rather than leave Athens. He is presented as calm, rational and a man of absolute integrity.

Philosophy can be a frustrating discipline. Sometimes it appears dry and remote from life. Sometimes it takes the role of linguistic handmaid, clarifying the terms used by other disciplines without appearing to offer anything of substance to the sum of human knowledge. Sometimes philosophers insist on setting down their thoughts in a style that obscures rather than clarifies. From time to time, one may be tempted to ask, 'Is it worth it? Why not settle for established thoughts and values, however superficial? Why make life difficult by this constant questioning?' or, in the case of Socrates, 'Is it worth the hemlock?'

That I leave the reader to judge.

Why 'Philosophy for Life'?

The earlier editions of this book – entitled *Teach Yourself: Philosophy* and *Understand Philosophy* – aimed to provide an overview of philosophy as a subject and to introduce some of the great thinkers, as well as encouraging the practice of critical thinking about a wide range of issues.

This book, *Philosophy for Life*, continues that approach but seeks to add a new dimension. It will argue that philosophy matters because it makes a difference, both to the individual thinker and to society. So we shall start each chapter by asking 'Why?' and will regularly step back and ask about the relevance of the ideas under discussion.

For convenience, it is usual to divide up philosophy into its different branches – the Theory of Knowledge, the Philosophy of Mind, Ethics, Political Philosophy, Philosophy of Religion and so on – so the book is structured in the same way. However, the different branches of philosophy interpenetrate; you can start from any one question and find yourself drawn outwards to consider many others. Start with 'the self', and you find that matters of metaphysics or religion are drawn into your thinking.

Philosophy for Life therefore seeks to offer a broad introduction to the main branches of Western philosophy and its key arguments, not just for those who want to go on to study the subject in an academic context, but for everyone. However, reading other people's thoughts is no substitute for thinking. If this book attempts to offer 'pegs' upon which to hang a reasoned argument, it is merely a way of assisting those who are new to philosophy to present their case without having to re-invent the philosophical wheel!

One final point: Many philosophical arguments are presented simply in terms of their logic rather than set within a historical context, and that has been particularly true of Anglo-American analytic philosophy. However, it is my personal conviction that philosophical arguments are best seen against their historical background. There really is no point in examining the arguments of a thirteenth-century monk as though his context did not shape his thoughts, nor to submit his works to rational scrutiny as though they were merely logical puzzles waiting for some clever resolution. Wisdom and insight always emerge from a context – personal, social, cultural and historical – and only when set in their original context can they show their relevance (or otherwise) to our own situation. So much of what appears in this book is the historical context of philosophy, examining where it has come from, so that you may assess where you might want to take it.

Warning

This is a book *about* philosophy, rather than a book *of* philosophy. If it were the latter, it would take a subject and present arguments and 'thought experiments' in order to come to a conclusion or at least clarify a set of options. But the task of this book is rather different. It aims to introduce philosophy by giving an outline of the range of topics covered and the kinds of arguments that have been presented. It is a survey; more a 'history of thought' than a work of philosophy although, hopefully, the reader may pick up a fair bit of philosophy along the way.

1

The What and How of Knowing

In this chapter you will:

▶ *Explore how some philosophers have sought to explore the most basic and general feature of existence*

▶ *Examine whether knowledge starts with thought or with experience*

▶ *Consider whether your own approach should be sceptical or pragmatic*

Why?

How exactly do we know what to believe? Is anything certain? Should I trust my senses or my rationality? Why do intelligent people differ in their beliefs? Making sense of life requires skill and clarity in thinking and balanced judgement in reflecting on what we already know. Asking how we understand the world is a good starting point for philosophy. But be warned: in a confusing world, philosophy does not always offer certainties and often raises more questions than it answers.

There are two basic questions which have been asked throughout the history of philosophy and which affect the way in which many different topics are considered:

▶ What can we know?

This question is about the basic features of existence; not the sort of information that science gives about particular things, but the questions that lie beneath all such enquiry: questions about the fundamental nature of space, time or causality; about whether concepts like 'justice' or 'love' have any external, objective reality; about the structure of the world as we experience it. In the collected works of Aristotle, such questions were dealt with after his material on physics and were therefore called **metaphysics**. But as soon as we start considering metaphysics, yet another question arises:

▶ How can we know it?

Is there anything of which we can be absolutely certain? Do we depend entirely on our senses, or can we discover basic truths simply by thinking? How can we justify or prove the truth of what we claim? All such questions are considered under **epistemology** – the theory of knowledge.

Metaphysics is the oldest and most fundamental branch of philosophy, but not always the most popular. However, it is important to start with these basic questions, as they introduce us to some of the great philosophers of the past.

As a starting point, to illustrate why metaphysical questions might be interesting, we could ask 'Which is more real, the whole or the parts of which it is comprised?' – the question may sound abstract to the point of being irrelevant. However, unpack it and we arrive at issues that are of importance both morally and politically. The basic problem here concerns **reductionism**, the attempt to reduce complex entities or general concepts to the parts of which they are made, or even to deny their existence. Consider these questions:

▶ How does a painting relate to the individual pigments or threads of canvas of which is it made?

▶ How does music relate to vibrations in the air?

▶ How does a person relate to the individual cells in his or her body?

▶ How does a nation relate to the citizens from which it is made up?

A 'reductionist' approach to metaphysics takes the 'nothing but' view, for example that music is 'nothing but' vibrations in the air.

Key idea for life

When, on Christmas Day, the British and German soldiers facing one another in the First World War came out of their trenches, played football together and shared cigarettes, they ceased to be merely representatives of nations and acted as individuals. Later, they returned to their trenches and continued to kill one another. There are many practical and moral issues here, but also a metaphysical one. Which is more real – a nation or the individuals who make it up? Should we act as a group of loosely connected individuals, framing political decisions on the basis of what we want as individuals, or should we give primacy to the 'nation' or the 'class', even if individuals have to suffer as a result?

That is a matter for ethics, but we can go further and ask, 'Do nations actually exist? Is there any such thing as society, or are there just people and families?' Does 'justice' exist over and above individual actions that we might choose to call 'just'? These are fundamental and rather abstract questions, but they have important practical and moral consequences. People have been jailed in the name of 'freedom', killed in the name of 'honour' or given their lives in the quest for 'justice'; so, it is always worth thinking about the status of such abstract ideas.

If you believe that what is ultimately real is matter – the solid, external world that we experience through our senses – then you are probably going to call yourself a **materialist** or a **naturalist**. A full-blown naturalist tends to see philosophy as a relic of the past, to be replaced by the various branches of science – replacing metaphysical speculation with solid facts and data.

On the other hand, if you hold that the basic reality is mental – that the world of your experience is in fact the sum of all the sensations and perceptions that have registered in your mind – you may call yourself an **idealist**. Although idealism sounds improbable, consider this: How can you tell whether, at this moment, you are experiencing the external, physical world rather than dreaming it? If you just consider the experience you are having, it's not quite as simple as common sense would suggest. We shall examine this approach again in examining the philosophy of mind.

Knowledge and justification: are you certain?

Within epistemology (the theory of knowledge) there is a fundamental issue about whether our knowledge originates in, and is therefore dependent upon, the data we receive through our senses, or whether (because we know that all such sense data is fallible) the only true certainties are those that come from our own minds – from the way in which we think and organize our experience; from the principles of reason and logic.

The following are two key terms:

▶ **empiricism** – all knowledge starts with the senses

▶ **rationalism** – all knowledge starts with the mind.

However, the issue of experience and the way the mind categorizes it is far from straightforward.

Whenever I experience something, that experience involves two things:

▶ The sensations of sight, sound, taste, touch or smell, all of which seem to me to be coming from outside myself, and therefore to be giving me information about the world.

▶ My own sense organs. If I am partially deaf, I may be mistaken in what I hear. If I am colour-blind, I will not be able to distinguish certain patterns, or appreciate the subtleties of a multi-coloured fabric. If I am asleep, all sorts of things may go on around me of which I am quite unaware.

Imagine that I am taken to a police station and questioned about something that is alleged to have happened in the recent past. I give my account of what I have heard or seen. If it sounds credible, or agrees with the evidence of others, I am likely to be believed. On the other hand, the police may ask, 'Are you sure about that? Is it possible that you were mistaken?' The implication is that, even if I am trying to be accurate and honest, the senses may be mistaken, and there may be two quite different ways of interpreting an experience.

When philosophers ask, 'What can be known for certain?' or 'Are the senses a reliable source of knowledge?', they are trying to sort out this element of uncertainty, so as to achieve statements that are known to be true.

Basically, as we saw above, there are two ways of approaching this problem, corresponding to the two elements in every experience.

Empiricists are those who start with the sensations of an experience, and say that all of our knowledge of the world is based on sensation.

Rationalists are those who claim that the basis of knowledge is the set of ideas we have – the mental element that sorts out and interprets experience. Rationalists consider the mind to be primary, and the actual data of experience to be secondary.

However, before we look at these approaches in more detail, let us be clear about one category of things that we can know for certain. If I say that 2 + 2 = 4, there is no doubt about the truth of that statement. Mathematics and logic work from agreed definitions. In general terms I can say that: If A = B + C, and if B and C are contained in, or implied by, the definition of A, then that statement will always be true. Understand the words in the statement and you understand its truth.

DESCARTES (1596–1650)

René Descartes placed one question centre-stage: 'Of what can I be certain?' He used the method of systematic doubt, by which he would only accept what he could see clearly and distinctly to be true. He knew that his senses could be deceived, therefore he would not trust them, nor could he always trust his own logic. He realized that he might even be dreaming what he took to be a waking reality. His approach is one that will be examined below, in the section on scepticism. Yet the one thing Descartes could not doubt was his own existence. If he doubted, he was there to doubt; therefore he must exist. The famous phrase which expresses this is 'cogito ergo sum' ('I think, therefore I am'). His argument is set out in his *Discourse on Method* (Section 4), 1637:

But then, immediately, as I strove to think of everything as false, I realized that, in the very act of thinking everything false, I was aware of myself as something real; and observing that the truth: I think, therefore I am, was so firm and so assured that the most extravagant arguments of the sceptics were incapable of shaking it, I concluded that I might have no scruple in taking it as the first principle of philosophy for which I was looking.

(Penguin Classics (trans. A. Wollaston), 1960)

Descartes could doubt even his own body but, while doubting, he could not deny himself as a thinking being. All else was open to the challenge that he could be mistaken.

In many ways, Descartes' argument represents the starting point of modern philosophy (modern, that is, as compared to that of the ancient Greeks and of the mediaeval world), not because later thinkers have been in agreement with him but because, challenged by scepticism, they have followed his quest to find the basis of certainty and knowledge. In other words, Descartes set the theory of knowledge at the heart of the philosophical agenda.

Key idea for life

Do we always need to be that sceptical about what we experience? After all, we live with the assumption that the world is what we perceive it to be. Might it not be better to take a pragmatic view and not challenge what works perfectly well most of the time? We shall need to consider both pragmatism and scepticism a little later.

RUSSELL (1872–1970)

Bertrand Russell's early philosophy was as hugely influential as his later writings were popular. He contributed to mathematics and logic, and introduced analytic philosophy, an approach that dominated the Anglo-American philosophical scene for half a century.

Moving on from Descartes' systematic doubt, a useful next step is to look at Russell's analysis of experience in his book *The Problems of Philosophy* (1912). He examines the table at which he sits to write. He observes that its appearance changes in different light and from different positions, and comes to the conclusion that our sense perceptions (the actual experiences of colour, shape and texture) are not the same thing as the table itself (otherwise we would have to say that the table becomes black once the light is turned out, or that it gets smaller when we walk away from it), but that we have to *infer* the table from those perceptions.

He therefore distinguishes sense data from the 'physical object' that gives rise to them.

He refers to Bishop Berkeley (see page 31), who argued that there is nothing given in our perception of something that proves it exists even when nobody is perceiving it. In order to maintain continuity when things are not being observed, Berkeley used the idea that they were being observed by God. In other words, what we call matter (the external physical world) is only known to exist in dependence upon minds that perceive it.

Having commented on Descartes' systematic doubt, Russell points out that common sense suggests there are ongoing objects which certainly do continue to exist when not being observed. He gives the example of a cloth thrown over a table. Once that is done, the table cannot be observed, but it is implied by the shape of the cloth, apparently suspended in mid air. He also considers the situation where a number of people look at the same table. Unless there were some underlying reality, there seems to be little reason why everyone should see exactly the same thing.

Russell takes the idea of a cat, which becomes equally hungry whether it is being observed or not. If it did not exist except when being observed, this would not make sense. Indeed, he points out that the cat's hunger is something that one cannot observe directly, and therefore (in terms of sense data) it does not exist.

All this leads him to accept the idea, given in an instinctive belief that he has no reason to reject, that there is indeed an external world which gives rise to our sense experience.

The external world: appearance and reality

As we have already seen, metaphysics examines what lies behind, or is implied by, our experience of the world. It explores general ideas such as 'goodness' or 'honesty' or 'beauty' and tries to say what role they play in our understanding of reality. Without metaphysics, the world may appear to be just a jumble of experiences without overall coherence.

The debate about knowledge of external reality predates Descartes, even if he is a convenient starting point because of his radical doubt. The ancient Greeks were concerned to explore both the nature of experience and the words we use to describe it.

PRE-SOCRATIC PHILOSOPHERS

The philosophers Plato (427–347 BCE) and Aristotle (384–322 BCE) are the most important of the Greek thinkers for the subsequent history of Western philosophy, and they set much of the agenda for those who followed. Plato took his inspiration from Socrates (470–399 BCE), whose ideas are known primarily through his appearance in Plato's dialogues. However, before Socrates there were a number of philosophers who were concerned with metaphysics from what would later become a 'scientific' standpoint. They sought the principles that lay behind all natural phenomena.

The pre-Socratics include Thales and Anaximander from the sixth century BCE, along with the philosopher and mathematician Pythagoras, and Parmenides from the following century. Although there is no scope here to discuss them individually, they are covered in most histories of Western philosophy, and are well worth studying. Of particular interest are the views of the 'atomists', Leucippus and Demoncritus, who (anticipating modern physics) thought of all material objects as made up of atoms, operating according to fixed laws; they also recognized that many secondary qualities (colour, etc.) were dependent upon the perceiver, rather than qualities inherent in what was perceived.

There was also a fascination with the problems of permanence and change. Heraclitus (early sixth century BCE) claimed that one could not step into the same river twice, on the grounds that the water that made it up was constantly changing. Can the river be considered a permanent entity if fresh water is always flowing down it?

Key idea for life

This was a radical question to ask in the sixth century BCE, and one that is interestingly parallel to the metaphysics being developed by the Buddha in northern India at about the same time. It reflects a profound existential question: How can I find meaning and purpose in a world where everything changes, knowing that I and everything that I hold dear will one day cease to exist?

With the benefit of 2,500 years of philosophical hindsight, the earliest thinkers may seem to have primitive ideas of cosmology and physics. What is remarkable, however, is that they should have set out to give an overall explanation of the world in the first place: to make it a 'cosmos', a unified, rationally understood world. There had been, and continued to be, myths and images through which the world could be explored and given meaning, but these pre-Socratic philosophers set out to examine the nature of the world in a more systematic way, and to use their reason to formulate general principles about its fundamental structure and composition. While their contemporaries were thinking in terms of fate or the influence of the gods to explain things, they pressed ahead with what was later to develop into philosophy and science.

PLATO (427–347 BCE)

It has been said that the whole of Western philosophy is a set of footnotes to Plato, and there is a great deal of truth in that, as Plato covered a wide range of issues, and raised questions that have been debated ever since.

In *The Republic*, Plato uses an analogy to illustrate his view of human experience and his theory of knowledge. Some prisoners sit in a row near the back of a cave, chained so that they cannot turn to face its mouth. Behind them is a fire, in front of which are paraded various objects. The fire casts shadows of these objects on to the wall at the back of the cave, and this is all the prisoners can see. Then a prisoner is freed so that he can turn round and see the fire and the objects that cast the shadows. His first impression is that the objects are not as 'real' as those images he has been accustomed to seeing. Then, however, he is forcibly dragged up to the mouth of the cave and into the sunlight and he gradually adjusts to the light of the sun. The experience of daylight and perceiving the sun is painful, and requires considerable adjustment. Only then does it become clear to the prisoner that his former perceptions were only shadows, not reality. This, for Plato, corresponds to the journey from seeing particular things, to seeing the eternal realities of which the particulars are mere shadow-like copies.

In Plato's dialogues, Socrates debates the meaning of words as a means of getting to understand the reality to which they point. So, for example, he argues that 'Justice' is not just a word that is used to bracket certain events and situations together. Justice actually exists, as a reality over and above any of the individual things that are said to be just. Indeed, the individual things can be said to be 'just' only because we already have knowledge of 'Justice' itself and can see that they share in its reality.

These general realities he calls 'Forms'. If we did not have knowledge of such Forms we would have no ability to put anything into a category. The Form of something is its essential feature, the thing that makes it what it is.

Case study

If I do not know the essence of 'dogginess', I will not be able to tell whether the animal before me is a dog or a camel. Is it possible that I am looking at a tall dog with a hump, a long neck and bad breath? Equally, could that dachshund on a lead be a hump-less, short-necked, particularly squat camel?

Description requires general terms, and general terms require an understanding of essences. Only with a prior appreciation of 'dogginess' or 'camelity' – if that is the correct term – can I hope to distinguish between them.

The ultimate Form for Plato (and the goal of the philosophical quest) is the Form of the Good. An understanding of 'the good' enables all else to be valued; it is the equivalent of the sun that the escaped prisoner sees as he leaves the cave. So, in both the doctrine of the Forms and the analogy of the cave, Plato is describing the same process that concerns modern philosophers: the way in which we can relate our present experiences to reality itself. What Plato is saying is that our ordinary experience is no more than shadows, and that reality itself lies beyond them. We can have certain knowledge of the Forms, because they are known by reason, whereas our awareness of individual things in the world can yield no more than 'true belief', since it is always provisional and changing.

But how do we come by knowledge of the Forms? In Plato's dialogues, the protagonist (generally Socrates) challenges someone to explain the meaning of a particular concept and, by introducing examples by which to test out the explanation, refines the concept. This implies that true knowledge can be developed by the use of reason alone. But how is that possible, if all experience is of particulars? Plato believed that we must have had direct knowledge of the Forms in the eternal realm, before our birth into this world, but that such knowledge is then cluttered by the changing experiences of the everyday world (as we sit in our cave, watching shadows). For Plato, we do not gather knowledge, we remember it.

ARISTOTLE (384–322 BCE)

In the great legacy of Greek thought, Aristotle offers an interesting contrast to Plato. Whereas Plato explored the world of the 'Forms', known only to the intellect – a perfect world, free from the limitations of the particular things we experience – Aristotle's philosophy is based on what is known through experience. He categorized the sciences (physics, psychology and economics all come from Aristotle) and gave us many of the terms and concepts that have dominated science and philosophy (including energy, substance, essence and category).

In rejecting Plato's Forms, Aristotle nevertheless acknowledged that people need to consider 'sorts' of things, rather than each particular thing individually (try describing something without using general terms to indicate the kind of thing it is), but he believed that the Forms (to use Plato's term) were immanent in the particulars. In other words, I may look at a variety of things that are red, and say that what they have in common is redness. The quality 'redness' is actually part of my experience of those things. But what would it mean to have absolute redness; a redness that was not a red something or other? In Aristotle's philosophy, we do not go outside the world of experience in order to know the meaning of universal concepts; we simply apply them within experience. This aimed to overcome a basic problem with Plato's Forms, illustrated by the example below.

Case study

I believe that this particular creature in front of me is a man.

Why? Because I have knowledge of the Form of man.

But, given that all particulars are different, how do I know that this one belongs to the category 'man'? (It could be a robot, an ape, a pre-hominoid.)

Answer: There must be a concept of 'man' over and above the Form and the particular, to which I refer when I claim that the one is a particular example of the other.

But how do I know that **that** is in the right category? Only by having yet another concept of 'man' to which I can refer – and so on *ad infinitum*! (Which means that I can never know for sure that this is a man!)

This is generally known as the 'third-man argument', and was recognized as a problem by Plato himself. By denying that the Form is separate from the particulars, but simply a way of describing the particular sort of thing that these particulars are, Aristotle reckoned that he had avoided this problem.

For Plato, knowledge had been limited to the world of Forms, whereas the world known to the senses could yield, at best, only true belief. Eternal truths were detached from particular things. By contrast, having Forms immanent within particulars, Aristotle claims that we can have true knowledge of the world of the senses.

There are many other important elements in Aristotle's metaphysics. One of them, his idea of causality, is of particular interest because it has implications both for metaphysics and the philosophy of religion.

Aristotle argued that everything had four causes:

▶ **Material** – the matter from which the thing is made.

▶ **Formal** – the kind of thing that something is (i.e. the issue described in the box above).

▶ **Efficient** – the agent that brings something about (the sense in which modern science would speak of a cause).

▶ **Final** – the goal or purpose for which a thing is the way it is, and to which it is moving. This introduces the concept of the telos, or 'end'. If the world is rational, everything has its part to play, its purpose.

This had a considerable impact on the later philosophy of religion (see Chapter 7) and also on the 'natural law' approach to ethics (see Chapter 8). It is also important because it acknowledges that the reality of a particular thing is not just a matter of its present substance and form, but is related to agents in the past that have produced it and goals in the future towards which it moves.

Key idea for life

When science asks 'Why?' it looks for an 'efficient' cause or causes. When religious or moral thinkers ask 'Why?', they are asking about the 'final' cause or purpose. Both are important questions, but they are very different.

Every metaphysical system has to take account of the fact that we experience individual things, but also (every time we use concepts and language) we think in terms of universals. Which of these should take priority?

This dilemma is illustrated by two major systems, those of Spinoza and Leibniz. Both are examples of rationalism (that one can come to a knowledge of reality by means of pure reason) and both follow the tradition established by Descartes of trying to move from first principles to construct an overall view of the world.

SPINOZA (1632–77)

Baruch Spinoza was born to Jewish parents in Amsterdam, and was brought up in the Orthodox Jewish community, but expelled from it at the age of 24 for his heterodox views. Thereafter he earned his living grinding lenses, which allowed him freedom to develop his ideas and to write. He was later offered a professorship, but declined it in order to maintain his freedom to explore philosophy in his own way.

For Spinoza (and for Leibniz) the reality of the world, as known to reason, is very different from the appearance of the world as known to us through experience. Spinoza, a radical Jewish thinker, argued that God was the only absolute substance. His argument may be summarized as:

- If God is infinite, he must co-exist with everything.

- God must therefore be the only thing whose explanation lies within itself (all limited things can be caused by something external but God can't, because there is nothing external to God).

- God is therefore the whole of the natural order.

- Although individual things may appear to be separate, they are, in reality, parts of a larger whole, which is God.

- The one true thing is therefore the world as a whole.

Key idea for life

Spinoza considered that everything existed as part of a greater whole, and that the mental and the material were two different aspects of the same fundamental reality. His view was the opposite of Descartes'. Rather than being a thinking self, separate from the physical world, you are part of a universal whole. How might that perspective influence your view of religion, of other people, and of the environment?

LEIBNIZ (1646–1716)

Born in Leipzig, the son of a professor of moral philosophy, Gottfried Wilhelm Leibniz was a brilliant philosopher, mathematician (he developed calculus independently of Newton) and logician.

Leibniz takes a view about particulars and wholes that is exactly the opposite of Spinoza. For Leibniz (following Descartes) the world is divided between mental things and physical or material things, and the essential difference between them is that physical things exist in space, but mental things do not. Leibniz saw that any material thing can be divided into its constituent parts, and these can be sub-divided again and again. Ultimately, the world must therefore consist of an infinite number of these parts, which cannot be divided any more. But if they are indivisible, they cannot occupy space (if they did, they could be divided), so they cannot be physical. Therefore (because things are either physical or mental) they must be mental in nature. He called them monads.

Remember this

In modern usage, 'mental' is taken to refer to the process of human thought, and as such it is difficult to see how Leibniz's monads can be so described. But, following Descartes, everything was designated either material or mental, so Leibniz did not have much of a choice. Perhaps, in modern terms, it might be better to describe his monads as having a quality of pure energy or pure activity.

How do these monads come together to form complex entities? Leibniz took the view that the monads – because they were not physical – could not influence one another directly. Rather, the world was arranged with a *pre-established harmony*, so that all the separate monads, each following its own course, actually managed to combine to give rise to the world that we know, with its complex bodies.

Key idea for life

How is it that everything works together to produce our interconnected and interdependent world? Is there some plan, set out by a designer God? Is it a natural outworking of the laws of physics? Is it, at the biological level, all down to natural selection? Can it be all of these? And how then do we understand ourselves within this world? These questions are about as fundamental as you can get. Answers we give to them will influence not just how we think, but how we *feel* about ourselves.

Some of the basic questions for metaphysics, raised by the philosophers we have considered so far in this chapter:

▶ Which is more real – the whole or the parts of which the whole is comprised?

▶ Are there such things as justice and beauty (or any universal idea) or are there simply individual things that we choose to describe as just or beautiful?

▶ How do you get beyond the things that appear to the senses? Is there a reality that lies beneath them and, if so, can we ever get to understand it?

> **Key idea for life:** Don't despair at this stage!
>
> Metaphysics is the most abstract of all the branches of philosophy, but stick with it, because it is relevant. Today, rather than asking about what exists, philosophers are more likely to ask about the *structure* of existence. A reductionist might say that my thoughts are *nothing more than* the action of neurons in my brain. But today, a philosopher is more likely to talk about how thoughts are 'grounded in' neurons, or about what is 'foundational', in the hope of finding a level of reality that is not mind-dependent.
>
> Get to grips with what you consider to be foundational, and you have a valuable tool for interpreting questions about science, the mind or even political or ethical issues. So stay with it, and the reason why these questions are important will become apparent.

Starting with experience

In the quest for knowledge, there are two contrasting approaches: one (rationalism) starts with the mind; the other (empiricism) starts with experience. The essential thing to grasp as we look at empiricism is that sense data (which make up the content of our experience) are not simply 'things' out there in the world. They depend upon our own faculties – the *way* in which we experience as well as *what* we experience.

The rationalism/empiricism debate can be seen by contrasting Descartes' views (as briefly outlined above) with those of John Locke, George Berkeley and David Hume, who are key figures in the development of empiricism.

LOCKE (1632–1704)

John Locke is known both for his empiricism, analysing sense experience and the way in which we learn, and for his political philosophy. In his *Essay Concerning Human Understanding* (1689), he was on the same quest as Descartes: the desire to know what the mind can comprehend and what it cannot. But his conclusions were radically different. He claimed that there are no such things as innate ideas, and that all that we know comes to us from experience, and from reflecting upon experience. Hence we are born *tabula rasa* – as a blank sheet.

Locke held that there are primary qualities (solidity, extension, motion, number) and secondary qualities (colour, sound, taste, etc.). The former inhere in bodies (i.e. they are independent of our perceiving them); the latter depend upon the act of perception (i.e. being able to see, hear, etc.).

He also held that we really can know of the existence of bodies through our senses. The sense data we receive cannot be subjective, because we do not control them. (This is similar to the position outlined by Russell as he looks at his table – because others see it as well, he concludes that the table itself cannot depend upon his own sensations of it.)

Locke accepted that substance itself was unknowable; all he could know was what came to him through his senses. In this he anticipated to some extent the more general conclusions of Kant (see page 35), who made the radical distinction between things as they are in themselves (noumena) and things as we perceive them to be (phenomena).

Remember this

The crucial difference between Locke and Kant is that, while Kant thought that space, time and causality were contributed by the perceiving mind, Locke thought that space and time existed as realities in the external world, waiting for us to experience them. How much of all that we know is down to the way in which we think and see?

BERKELEY (1685–1753)

Bishop George Berkeley was a fascinating character. He wrote his philosophy while in his twenties, later became a bishop, and took an interest in higher education in the American Colonies (where he lived for some time), leaving his library of books to Yale University.

Berkeley argued for 'idealism', which is the theory that everything that exists is known to us directly through our perceptions and that there is no other, material world separate from what we perceive. This sounds an unlikely view to hold about the world, as it appears to deny what is most obvious, namely physical existence, but it follows from the way in which we perceive things. An idealist might argue as follows:

▶ All we actually know of the world are sensations (colour, sound, taste, touch, the relative positions of things that we perceive). We cannot know the world by any other means. For us, these sensations are what we mean by 'the world'.

▶ All these sensations are 'ideas': they are mental phenomena. (The colour red does not exist independent of the mind perceiving something of that colour.)

▶ Things are therefore collections of these ideas; they exist by being perceived.

The obvious problem for Berkeley was showing how something can exist while not being perceived.

Case study

I am aware of a tree in front of me. I see the trunk, branches and leaves with their different colours. I may reach forward and touch the bark. The tree, for me, is the collection of all these sensations. In order to test out idealism, I shut my eyes, put my hands by my side, and attempt to cut off all sensations of the tree. Convinced that the tree no longer exists, I step forward. The tree immediately reappears in the form of an acute pain in the nose and forehead!

But what does it mean to say that the tree exists in the moment between shutting my eyes and hitting the trunk?

It is possible to say that an object continues to exist only if it is being perceived by someone else; but what if nobody perceives it? Berkeley's answer to this (or his way of dodging the problem, if you prefer) is that the tree continues to exist because it is being perceived by God.

In thinking about Berkeley's theory, it is worth reflecting on where sensations are located. Because they take place as a result of brain and sensory activity, Berkeley says that they are mental – in effect, that they are taking place 'in' the mind. But just because a sensation varies with different conditions, as colours change with different lighting, does that imply that the whole of what we mean by colour is subjective?

Even if Berkeley's view sounds improbable, it is actually close to common sense. If material bodies are separate from the sensations we have of them, they are largely unknowable and detached from us. For me, an apple is something that I can see, touch, weigh in my hand, and munch on; it has a particular taste and I can savour its juices. That is *exactly* what an apple is. I do not doubt its existence, for it is what I experience it to be.

Berkeley also held that there are no abstract general ideas. If you think of a triangle, you are thinking of a particular triangle. It shares its qualities with other triangles, but there is no concept of triangle that does not spring from some particular triangle. What we think of as a 'universal' is just a set of qualities abstracted from particulars.

Remember this

Few things are new in philosophy. This issue can be traced back to the different views of Plato and Aristotle. If you believe that universals are 'real', then you are likely to be called a '**realist**' and will tend to agree with Plato, but if you think that universals are only the 'names' we give to groups of individuals, you are a '**nominalist**' and will tend to agree with Aristotle. The key question for life is this: Is 'truth' or 'beauty' any less real if it is just a name we give to a range of particular things? Do we need to believe in absolutes 'out there' to which we aspire?

HUME (1711–76)

David Hume was a popular and radical philosopher and man of letters who lived in Edinburgh and contributed to the eighteenth-century Scottish Enlightenment. In his day, he was better known – and more widely read – as a historian than as a philosopher, having produced a six-volume history of England.

In taking an empiricist approach – that all knowledge is derived from sense experience – Hume made the important distinction between what we have called 'analytic' and 'synthetic' statements. In other words, between:

▶ Those statements that show the relationship between ideas. These are known to be true *a priori* (before experience) because their denial involved contradiction, e.g. the propositions of maths and logic. They offer certainty, but not information about the world.

and

▶ Those that describe matters of fact. These can only be known *a posteriori* (after experience). They are not certain, but depend on empirical evidence.

This leads to what is known as Hume's Fork. In this, you may ask of a statement:

▶ Does it contain matters of fact? If so, relate them to experience.

▶ Does it give the relationships between ideas?

If neither, then it is meaningless.

Key idea for life

This suggests that moral, religious or value statements are meaningless, because they do not simply depend on facts, nor on pure logic. We shall examine this later, because it was a view taken up by the logical positivists in the twentieth century. But notice how this strictly empiricist approach limits the function of language to one of *picturing* the world as it is, rather than *shaping* it as we wish it to be. However, on a personal level, the most significant statements are those that *do* something rather than simply *describe* something.

Hume's argument concerning evidence runs like this:

▶ I see something happen several times.

▶ I therefore expect it to happen again.

- I get into the mental habit of expecting it to happen.

- I may be tempted to project this mental habit out on to the external world in the form of a 'law' of physics.

So, for example, 'A causes B' could be taken to mean 'B has always been seen to follow A'. It might be tempting to say 'Therefore, B will always follow A', but this would imply that nature is uniform, and you can never have enough evidence for such an absolute statement.

To the statement 'Every event must have a cause' Hume would say:

- It can't be justified by logic, because its denial does not involve self-contradiction.

- It can't be proved from experience, because we cannot witness every event.

What, then, are we to do? Hume says that we can accept the idea of causality because it is a habit of the imagination, based on past observation. This may seem obvious, but an important distinction has been made between claiming that something *must be* the case, and saying that, in practice, we have always *found it to be* the case.

In section 10 of *An Enquiry Concerning Human Understanding* (1758), in which Hume is considering miracles, he sets out his position about evidence:

A wise man ... proportions his belief to the evidence. In such conclusions as are founded on an infallible experience, he expects the event with the last degree of assurance, and regards his past experience as a full proof of the future existence of that event. In other cases, he proceeds with more caution: He weighs the opposite experiments: He considers which side is supported by the greater number of experiments: to that side he inclines, with doubt and hesitation; and when at last he fixes his judgement, the evidence exceeds not what we properly call probability.

Hume's approach is also valuable in assessing the question of whether or not the external world exists, and whether we could prove it to exist. He says that it cannot be *proved*, but gives two features of experience that lead to the idea being accepted – constancy and coherence. I see that objects remain in the same place over a period of time, and I assume that they remain there even when not observed. Also, I may see someone at different times in different places, and I infer from this that they are moving about. In other words, the assumption that the world is predictable enables me to fill in the gaps of my own experience. However, the key thing for Hume is that this is something we *assume*, not something that can be *proved*.

KANT (1724–1804)

Immanuel Kant is one of the most influential figures in the development of Western philosophy. His entire life was spent in Königsberg in East Prussia, where he was a professor at the university. This in itself is remarkable since, prior to the twentieth century, most philosophers were not professional academics.

In many ways, Kant's philosophy can be seen as an attempt to take seriously the claims of the empiricists (e.g. Hume) that everything depends upon experience and is open to doubt, but to do so in the context of Newtonian physics and the rise of science. Science seeks to formulate laws that predict with certainty, and causality is an essential feature of Newtonian science. We just *know* that everything will be found to have a cause, even before we experience it. So how can you reconcile an empiricist view of knowledge with common sense and the findings of science?

Kant sought to achieve this through what we generally call his 'Copernican Revolution'. Just as Copernicus totally changed our perception of the world by showing that the Earth revolves round the Sun and not vice versa, so Kant argued that the world of our experience is shaped by our own means of perceiving and understanding it, making the important distinction between what we perceive with our senses (which he called **phenomena**) and the world of things as they are in themselves (which he called **noumena**).

Kant argued that certain features of experience, including space, time and causality, were not in themselves features of the external world, but were imposed on experience by the mind. This was a revolutionary way of looking at the theory of knowledge and at metaphysics. Take the example of time. When I see a sequence of things, I say that time is passing and that one thing follows another. But where is that time? Is it something that exists 'out there' to be seen? Is time there to be discovered? Kant argued that time was one of the ways in which the mind organizes its experiences; it is part of our mental apparatus.

Key idea for life

'But what happened before the "Big Bang"?' is an example of the mind trying to impose the category of time on something to which scientists try to tell us it cannot be applied. However much I accept the idea of space and time coming from that 'singularity', my mind rebels and demands yet more space and time before and beyond it. I am given a description of the universe, and ask 'But what lies outside it?' If I am told that nothing lies outside it, I become confused, for my mind automatically tries to imagine an expanse of nothingness stretching outward from what is known.

The same is true for causality. We assume that everything has a cause, even when we have no evidence for one. We assume that this is the way the world works; Kant would say that it is the way *the mind* works.

The implication of this is that there is nothing 'out there' that can be independent of our perception: not only qualities like colour and texture, but also space, time and causality, depend upon the way in which human beings perceive things.

'Realism' is a term frequently used in discussions of appearance and reality. It stands for the view that science is able to give us a true representation of the world 'out there', including entities that are unobservable. There are different forms of realism: 'naïve realism' is generally used for the view that what we perceive is what is actually there; 'representative realism' takes one step back from this, but says that we can form correct representations of what exists. This is particularly important for the philosophy of science.

Intuitive knowledge

Intuitive knowledge creates particular problems for those who base their knowledge of the world on sense experience. For example, I may feel, listening to a piece of music or looking at a painting, that it 'says something' about life – something that is far beyond any analysis of the particular notes being played or the particles of pigment on canvas.

An alcoholic drink can have the same effect – the opening up of intuitive faculties, and a conviction that suddenly the whole world makes sense, that there is something of universal importance that one wants to say. But somehow, once sober again, it is difficult to put into words.

A. J. Ayer, interviewed in *The Observer* in 1980, was asked whether, when listening to music, there might be something other than what is scientifically verifiable; whether, for example, there could be a sense of ecstasy, and of something that was not fully explained. He replied:

> I don't particularly want to reduce aesthetic experiences to anything expressible in purely physical terms, but I don't think it's more mysterious than any other statement you might make about yourself. Clearly there is a problem about communicating feelings of any kind, since one has to take the other person's word for it. I can't, as it were, get inside your head and measure your ecstasy, but the statement that you feel ecstatic doesn't seem to me to create any particular problem. I know roughly what kind of feeling you're describing, what causes it, how it leads you to behave, when you are susceptible to it, how it fits in with the general pattern of your behaviour. Is the fact that you feel ecstatic more mysterious than that you feel bored, or any other sort of feeling?
>
> (*The Observer*, 24 February 1980, p. 35)

Notice what Ayer does here. The questioner has implied that there could be an intuition of something beyond scientific analysis. Ayer reduces this to the actual feeling – ecstasy – which is itself similar to other feelings, such as boredom. But the question is not ecstasy as 'feeling' but ecstasy as 'knowledge' – and it is just this that Ayer does not accept.

It seems to me that a suitable analogy for the process of reducing intuitive knowledge to empirical evidence is that of taking a car engine to pieces in order to discover the joy of motoring. It's fine as an academic exercise, but you can't drive the car while it's in a dismantled state, and it certainly does not get you any closer to the experience of the road!

Key idea for life

Many things are intuited before they are understood – whether it be Einstein's intuition of relativity, or a mathematician who described a particular mathematical argument as 'elegant'. Intuition is the driving force of creative thinking; analysis and assessment generally come later.

Intuition has become important in recent philosophy because of its use of **thought experiments**. Both in popular philosophy (for example Julian Baggini's *The Pig that Wants to be Eaten*, 2010), and as a method of teasing out issues in extended discussions (as, for example, in Derek Parfit's *Reasons and Persons*), arguments often depend on our intuitive response to practical questions: 'Who would I be if I had a brain transplant?' and 'Should you cannibalize one healthy hospital visitor to provide transplant organs for five desperately sick patients?' are examples of thought experiments. The idea is that such an experiment can highlight and clarify philosophical issues by rationalizing from our intuitive responses to practical situations.

The problem with thought experiments is that, just like scientific ones, they reduce the complexities of actual life to a simple relationship between a limited number of variables. In such situations, we may indeed have a clear intuition about what we should do, but that may not reflect how things are, or what we might do, in the real world.

Scepticism

The term 'sceptic' is generally used of a person who claims that we cannot know anything for certain, and that one view is likely to be as valid as any other. People tend to be sceptical about particular things – the validity of scientific claims, for example, or politics or morals.

It may be helpful, however, to make a distinction between scepticism as a conclusion and sceptical questioning as a process. Philosophers need to question and challenge all claims to knowledge, so – as a process – being sceptical about a claim is both valid and important for philosophy. However, there are some sceptical conclusions – for example, that the world may not exist at all, but may all be a dream – that are an interesting challenge, because common sense tells you they are wrong, but the arguments for them may be difficult to refute.

Descartes was particularly concerned about scepticism, and wanted to counter it by finding something that he could not doubt. In order to achieve this, he set about using the very process that proved so threatening: sceptical doubt. This is how he sets about his task in Section 4 of his *Discourse on Method* (1637):

> I had noticed long ago ... that in matters of morality and custom, it is often necessary to follow opinions one knows to be highly doubtful, just as if there were no doubts attaching to them at all. Now, however, that I intended to make the search for truth my only business, I thought it necessary to do exactly the opposite, and to regard as absolutely false anything which gave rise in my mind to the slightest doubt, with the object of finding out, once this had been done, whether anything remained which I could take as indubitable.
>
> (Penguin Classics (trans. A. Wollaston), 1960)

Therefore, recognizing that his senses sometimes deceived him, he decided to assume that they always did so. Equally, he recognized that people could be mistaken in their reasoning, so logic and mathematics could not be accepted as indubitable. He even went on to assume that the world as he encountered it was perhaps no more than a dream.

He concluded that the only thing he could not doubt was his existence as a thinking being, for the very act of doubting required him to think. Hence his famous starting point for knowledge: 'I think, therefore I am'.

Having reached that point, he then tried to build up an account of what he could actually know – and it is this process, along with his one point of certainty, that the true sceptic will not accept. Scepticism is significant within the philosophy of religion (where the ability to know religious truths may be challenged by those who emphasize the role of faith) and the philosophy of science (where realism is challenged by a variety of equally valid ways of describing the same phenomenon), as well as within the theory of knowledge.

Key idea for life: Positive scepticism

Scepticism is sometimes viewed as a first step towards cynicism, but that is unfair. A positive use of sceptical method is a useful reality check, especially valuable if you are tempted to be swayed, by skilful rhetoric or emotional appeal, into accepting a post-truth claim that really needs to be backed up by reason and evidence if it is to be taken seriously. Philosophy encourages a healthy measure of scepticism.

The genealogy of ideas

In examining an idea, argument or claim, it is often useful to consider where is has come from. Thinkers such as Friedrich Nietzsche in the nineteenth century and Michel Foucault in the twentieth, have explored the genealogy of ideas – in other words, they have sought to show where ideas have originated and how they have developed, putting them in an historical and social context.

Some appreciation of the history of ideas is valuable in order to see the context of a particular concept or argument, but the danger in relying too much on the genealogy of an idea is that it may be dismissed simply because we do not approve of its origins, or the reputation of the person who has put it forward. *Ideas need to be examined and criticized on their own terms, quite apart from their origins.*

The proof of the pudding ...

When examining matters of epistemology, you may be tempted to take a common-sense view: that a theory would seem to be right because it is the generally accepted and practical way of looking at things. We may be justified in accepting a theory if it is useful and solves problems. The tradition of philosophy that follows this line of reasoning is **pragmatism**. Developed in the USA, it is associated particularly with C. S. Peirce (1839–1914), William James (1842–1910) and John Dewey (1859–1952). In the simplest of terms, pragmatism says:

▶ We act; we are not just spectators. The 'facts' about the world are shaped by our concerns, and what we hope to do.

▶ Beliefs should accord with known facts. But what should you do if the evidence is balanced between two theories? Accept the theory that gives the *richer consequences*; in other words, the one that will be *of the greater practical use.*

Dewey emphasized the fact that we are not detached observers, but that we need to survive in the world, and that thinking is *a problem-solving activity* related to that need. Science is a dynamic process of gaining knowledge, enabling us to get some mastery over our environment.

A basic test to be applied to all statements is that of *coherence*. At any one time, we have a number of ways of seeing the world and working within it. A new theory, if it is to be accepted, needs to be compatible with existing accepted theories. Of course, this cannot be an absolute criterion of truth, or truth would be decided by committee and science would make little progress, but it is an important factor to be taken into account.

One of the most controversial figures in recent American philosophy was Richard Rorty (1931–2007). In *Philosophy and the Mirror of Nature* (1979), he challenged the empiricists' notion that we understand things because our minds 'represent' them as ideas, or that 'truth' is what corresponds to reality; in other words that the mind 'mirrors' nature. Instead, he argued for a form of pragmatism where language is judged by its ability to solve problems. He had always been concerned with politics and for fair representation in democracy, and wanted philosophy to take a broad approach to social issues, criticizing what he saw as the narrow professionalism of academic philosophy in the USA. His move away from pure philosophy to a broader concern with the humanities is seen as one of the key moments in the decline of the analytic tradition and its emphasis on precision in language. For Rorty, no one particular form of language could claim to be inherently better than any other, all being judged by their effectiveness. He argued that truth cannot exist 'out there' independent of the human mind, simply because truth is a feature of thought and propositions. There is reality out there, of course, but as soon as we try to understand or describe it, we do so using – and therefore become limited by – human reason and language. His position (which he called 'ironism') was that one should continue to question and doubt one's own language, and not try to claim that it alone could reveal reality or encapsulate truth. Hence all truths are contingent rather than absolute. On the political front, he feared that participation in the democratic process was in decline and saw engagement with democracy as promoted by his pragmatic approach.

The philosophy of education

The philosophy of education is concerned both with the nature and purpose of education, and with the content of what is taught. As such it relates to many other areas of philosophy – the theory of knowledge, language, ethics, religious and political philosophy. As a specialist area of philosophy, however, it is generally taught within departments of education rather than in those of philosophy.

There are a number of key questions with which the philosophy of education is concerned:

▶ What is education for?

▶ By what process do we learn?

▶ What should determine the content of education?

In *The Republic*, Plato considers the nature of the state and the qualities of those who are to rule it, but he couches his argument in terms of the sort of education that will be necessary in order to produce leaders fit to rule. For Plato, education is not an end in itself, but a tool of social engineering – turning out the sort of people the state is going to need. However, that is not the whole truth, for Plato wants his rulers to be philosophers capable of seeing reality itself, rather than the passing shadows of sense experience.

Key idea for life

Should education be seen as having value in itself, or is it justified in terms of the need to train people for their roles in society? Should education be dependent upon selection on the basis of ability? Should it be equally available for all? Your answer to those questions will influence your views about funding for university departments, or the allocation of grants for research, or the place of independent or selective schools.

The process by which people learn is influenced by the general philosophical approach to knowledge of the world. Thus a philosopher such as John Locke, who sees all knowledge as based on sense experience, wants education to encourage experimentation and a rejection of the uncritical acceptance of tradition. A key feature of his theory of knowledge is that we start with minds like blank sheets of paper (*tabula rasa*) and acquire knowledge though experience. By contrast, Plato held that we have innate knowledge of the 'Forms', which we recognize as soon as we encounter them.

John Dewey thought that knowledge is best achieved through practical problem-solving, an approach that is generally termed 'instrumentalism'. This view has been enormously influential in terms of both educational theory and practice. Today, it is generally recognized that learning is most effective when it is based on problem-solving methods, and that the process of checking and testing gives a clearer knowledge of the subject than the simple learning of facts.

With the pragmatists' contribution to education, we have an interesting example of philosophy recognizing the significance of one sphere of life (the success of the scientific method), developing from it a general theory of meaning (that the truth of a statement is shown by the practical implications that follow from it), and then applying it to another sphere of life (education) with overwhelming success. Throughout the world, primary school children learn through doing, examining and testing out, and this is largely due to the influence of pragmatism.

There are many other areas of education with which philosophy is concerned. For example, when it comes to the content of what is taught, there is debate about the appropriateness of religious or political education and the danger that education might descend into indoctrination. Central to many of these issues is the matter of personal autonomy. The essential difference between education and indoctrination is that the former seeks to empower and give autonomy to the individual learner, whereas the latter imposes an already formulated set of ideas.

Creative and personal knowing

Knowing is a creative activity, and always involves an element of interpretation. We know nothing with absolute certainty, except things that are true by definition, logic or mathematics. On the other hand – as we saw Russell doing as he contemplated his desk – we can gradually build up a degree of reasonable certainty, and even Descartes, famed for his systematic doubt, saw no reason to believe that the created order should deceive us, and was therefore willing to accept as true those things he perceived clearly to be so. Perhaps, after all, there is scope for common sense in philosophy!

The American pragmatists recognized that human beings do not simply contemplate the world but are – at least on a temporary basis – part of it, and engaged in the business of living. So part of our understanding of reality should include the way in which we engage with it.

Consider the practical and emotional implications of Plato's theory of the Forms. It is possible for a Platonic approach to lead to a view that the present world, as encountered by the senses, is inferior, partial and lacking in inherent value, and hence for us to look beyond what is present to another, ideal world. Justice, love, beauty, truth – if these are encountered at all in the present world, they are but pale reflections of their abstract, ideal counterparts. The religious implications of this (and indeed, the influence of Plato on the development of the Christian religion) is considerable. Reality, from this perspective, is located outside the present known world, not within it. By contrast, a materialist may insist that everything is of value in itself and needs no external or ultimate justification.

A personal postscript

A fundamental problem within much Western philosophy has been caused by the view that 'self' and 'world' are separate things, with the one trying to find out if the other is actually there. In my opinion, this is mistaken. In reality, what we call 'self' is a temporary and changing part of what we call 'world'. There are not two separate realities, only one, and we are part of it.

Equally, experience is not an object (sense data do not 'exist'); it is the term we use for the relationship that all sentient beings have with the rest of the world. It is both physical and mental;

it is sharing not gathering; it is plastic not fixed. If we fail to experience the world around us we are likely to die, for we are part of the world and depend upon the rest of it for our very existence.

Philosophers can be rated according to how well they account for the fundamental unity and interconnected nature of everything. On this basis, Plato, Descartes and Kant do rather badly; their worlds are fundamentally dualist. Reality, for them, is always beyond what we experience. Aristotle, Spinoza and the Pragmatists do better. For them, there is one world, and we need to engage with it and make sense of it.

Thinking about how we know what is true is an essential first step in philosophy, a clearing away of confusion. It finds expression in science and in the quest to understand the human mind and how it relates to the body. But there is another aspect of philosophy: the personal quest to make sense of life, not just in terms of what exists, but what it means for our own happiness and how we should understand ourselves and respond to our world. This finds expression in religion, ethics and politics, but also in the often unspoken motive for much of what we do – the quest for personal integrity and happiness, to which we now turn.

2

Existentialism, Integrity and Happiness

In this chapter you will:

► *Examine key features of existentialist philosophy*

► *Consider some philosophical issues in feminism*

► *See how philosophy may seek to promote happiness*

► *Explore the relevance of altruism and compassion for life*

Why?

Existentialism is a philosophy about radical freedom and the quest for integrity, encouraging you to take control of and responsibility for your life. It is part of a general movement in philosophy to explore happiness and well-being. Although a recent phenomenon in the West, this practical application of philosophy has always been a common feature of Eastern thought, and shaped the key insights of the Buddha. In this chapter, we shall explore whether or not philosophy can improve and enhance your own life and that of the society within which you live.

Philosophy is not just about finding what is true in a detached and analytic way, it also addresses the personal questions of life – about meaning, happiness, integrity and the way in which we work alongside other people. That has always been true of the best philosophy, but has been brought to the fore during the last century through existentialism and other philosophies that have sought to understand and promote human happiness.

To appreciate the significance of this, we need to be aware that, through the middle decades of the twentieth century, there developed a broad division, relating both to the way of doing philosophy and the sort of subjects covered, with most philosophers being described as belonging either to the 'analytic' or the 'continental' tradition of philosophy.

Analytic philosophy is a tradition that flourished particularly in the USA and Britain. It is especially concerned with the meaning of statements and the way in which their truth can be verified, and with using philosophy as an analytic tool to examine and show the presuppositions of our language and thought. Well-known philosophers in this school include Quine, Putnam, Searle, Rawls, Hampshire and Strawson. It also includes many philosophers already mentioned, including Russell and Ayer.

Continental philosophy is a term used to describe a range of philosophers from mainland Europe. In a tradition that goes back to the European Enlightenment and particularly the work of Kant, and includes thinkers such as Hegel, Nietzsche, Husserl, Heidegger, de Beauvoir and Sartre, it has avoided the narrowness of the analytic tradition and has explored the broad issues of how people understand and engage with life. 'Continental' philosophy often reflects an intellectual approach to the creative arts in general, rather than the more narrowly defined tasks of the analytic school. Sartre, for example, explored his ideas through novels, short stories and plays. Michel Foucault, a controversial French philosopher, was interested in the history and 'archaeology' of ideas and how they are shaped by society. It is within this 'Continental' school that we meet the terms **structuralism**, **postmodernism** and **hermeneutics** (the study of interpretation), and enter a philosophical world that is often both colourful and controversial.

Today, the distinction between the two ways of doing philosophy is less pronounced and philosophers of the Continental tradition are widely studied in all philosophy departments – with some, like Nietzsche, Heidegger and Sartre being hugely popular. It is also important to recognize that the Continental approach to philosophy, as it developed in the twentieth century, looked back and responded to the work of Nietzsche, Hegel, Kant, Rousseau and other great thinkers, back to Descartes – thinkers that have always been there in the core of philosophical study.

Key idea for life

Continental philosophy has always been free to explore aspects of life that were beyond the concerns of philosophers of the Analytic tradition. They were able to ask not just 'What does this *mean*?' but 'What does this mean *for me*?' Particularly through existentialism, the key question became 'What makes life worthwhile?' and philosophers such as Nietzsche and Foucault saw philosophy as a tool with which to affirm and transform yourself.

Key idea for life: Phenomenology

In order to appreciate the context within which existentialism was to develop, we need to take a very brief look at a theory and approach known as phenomenology.

Edmund Husserl (1859–1938), the founder of phenomenology, was a Jewish-German philosopher, who taught at the University of Freiburg. Like Descartes, he wanted to find the basis of knowledge, making philosophy a 'rigorous science' that was founded on necessary truths independent of all presuppositions. His most important work was *Logical Investigations* (published in two volumes in 1900 and 1901). In this he declared that, for certainty, we had to start with our own conscious awareness. What is it that we actually experience? Husserl suggested that every mental act is directed towards an 'intentional object': what the mind is thinking about, *whether or not that object actually exists*.

Here are a couple of examples:

* I want to eat a cake. I need a physical cake if I am going to eat, but thinking about a cake requires only an 'intentional object' – indeed, I am especially likely to think about a cake when there is no actual cake to be had!
* If I reflect on feeling depressed, depression is an 'intentional object' of my thought, although there is no external object corresponding to it. Someone may say 'depression is nothing, it doesn't exist', but for me, at that moment, it is real.

Husserl takes the subject matter of philosophy to be these 'objects of consciousness' and seeks to strip individual objects of all that makes them particular, seeking the pure essence – what they share with other objects of the same sort. These fundamental 'essences', he argues, are known by intuition. As soon as we think about something, it takes on meaning for us because of the various essences by which we understand it. I have a consciousness of 'tree' as a pure essence, and as soon as I see (or think about) an actual tree, that essence is there to give it meaning for me. More sophisticated, the artist will play with unusual shades of red, testing out the 'horizon', the limits of the essence 'red'. Is it red, or is it really magenta? Add a touch more blue to the paint: now how do we see it?

Husserl argued that consciousness required three things:

1 A self (which he called the 'transcendental ego')
2 A mental act
3 An object of that mental act

Objects become objects of consciousness only when they have been given meaning and significance. An object is only understood (only really 'seen') once the mind has gone to work on it and given it meaning in terms of its pure essences. Everything is therefore dependent on the 'transcendental ego' for its meaning and significance. Once we encounter the world, we start to give it meaning; we start to interpret it in terms of pure essences. In other words, we start to deal with it in terms of its 'objects of consciousness'.

In this way, phenomenology allowed questions of meaning and value, and the whole range of emotions and other experiences, to become a valid subject matter of philosophy.

Existentialism

Existentialism is the name given to the branch of philosophy concerned with the meaning of human existence – its aims, its significance and overall purpose – and the freedom and creative response to life made by individuals.

It has its roots in the nineteenth century, with thinkers such as Kierkegaard (particularly in his emphasis that truth is subjectivity) and Nietzsche (in presenting the challenge to affirm oneself in a world without meaning or purpose), but the following are key figures for understanding the development of existentialism in the twentieth century:

▶ Martin Heidegger (1889–1976) was a German philosopher whose *Being and Time* (1927) is a key work in exploring what it means to experience yourself as a human being, thrown into a particular situation in life, being free to choose what to do, but always aware that life is transient. He resisted being called an existentialist, although his work provided many of the insights that made existentialism possible.

▶ Jean-Paul Sartre (1905–80) was a French philosopher, novelist and playwright. His most important work of philosophy is *Being and Nothingness* (1943), and his lecture and short book *Existentialism is a Humanism* (1946), launched existentialism as a philosophical craze in post-war Paris. Probably his best-known quote is from the end of his play *No Exit* (1945): 'Hell is other people.'

▶ Simone de Beauvoir (1908–86), Sartre's long-term partner, who also wrote both philosophy and fiction, is regarded as an inspirational force for the feminist movement. She is most famous for declaring the (utterly existential) conviction that 'One is not born, but becomes a woman', which launched the whole idea that what it means to be a woman is socially determined and chosen, rather than innate.

▶ Maurice Merleau-Ponty (1908–61), in his influential *Phenomenology of Perception* (1945), emphasized that 'being-in-the-world' is the starting point for our self-understanding, and it arises prior to the division between subject and object. As with Heidegger, we always find ourselves immersed in a world. The key idea here is that we should not think of the world as 'out there', separate from us, so that we can examine it in a detached way: we are in it and should understand ourselves as *participants* rather than *observers*.

This last point is a central feature of existentialism. It works on the basis of the self as involved, as engaged with the world. We seek to understand things because we have to deal with them, live among them, find the meaning and significance of our own life among them.

An example:

Case study

You pick up a hammer and start hammering a nail. You use it automatically; your mind is engaged with the activity of hammering. Heidegger sees this as a 'ready-to-hand' way of dealing with things: not as an observer, but as an engaged individual.

Existentialism emphasized that our engagement with life is always from a particular point of view. This raises the general philosophical question about whether every view carries with it the values and understanding of the person who has it. The alternative (often sought by science, and by empirical philosophy) is a 'view from nowhere': a view that does not take a personal viewpoint into account. But is that possible?

For Heidegger, we are 'thrown' into the world, and our main experience of *Dasein* ('being there' – his general term for human existence) is 'concern', in the sense that some of the objects we encounter in the world are going to be more important for us than others, and so we become involved with them. Sartre was to describe this particular situation in which we find ourselves as our 'facticity'; we are ourselves in a particular situation, but we are radically free to decide what we are to make of it.

Heidegger argued that *we are what we take ourselves to be*; we do not have a fixed human nature. To live in an authentic way, you have to take each situation as it comes and show your true nature through what you do.

If, as a philosopher, you imagine that you can get an intellectual bird's-eye view, detached from the everyday reality of life, then you are likely to misunderstand what life is about. You are where you are, in your own situation with all its limited particularity; this is your perspective, and your understanding of time, or your world, or the significance of the choices you make, depend upon that unique perspective. It is not absolute, nor is it perfect, but it is *yours* to affirm and live by.

Key idea for life

If you've never felt a general anxiety about the radical contingency of life, and the threat of meaninglessness, then existentialism is probably not for you. The sad alternative is to try to escape from the anxiety of being true to yourself by conforming to what others expect of you, taking on masks that fit your social roles. Part of the attraction of existentialism was that it encouraged people to dare to throw off such social masks and to take charge of their lives.

For Sartre, each of us is radically free. A person need not (and should not) be defined by his or her duties, responsibilities or social background; to pretend otherwise is to fall into 'bad faith' and to lose one's personal integrity. Sartre's own example of this is of a waiter who perfects waiting at table such that he is utterly absorbed in carrying out that role, his every gesture and action prescribed. The alternative of personal freedom, recognizing that nothing in the world is fixed as we might expect it to be, can be threatening; it produces disorientation and possibly even (as in his novel of that title) nausea.

As philosophical background to this idea, Sartre described three kinds of being:

1 **Being-in-itself.** This is the being of non-human objects, things just exist as they are.

2 **Being-for-itself.** At the level of consciousness or self-awareness, a being is aware of the world around it, of other things that are not itself. If we are self-aware, we cannot be reduced to a thing-in-itself. For example, I may work as a postman, but I am not fully described as 'postman' (as a thing-in-itself) because, as a human being, I am always more than any such description. If people treat me simply as 'postman', they dehumanize me: they take from me the distinctive thing that makes me a person.

3 **Being-for-others.** As human beings, we form relationships and express our human nature through them. Relating to others, and aware of our own freedom, we are able to live in an 'authentic' way: we are being fully ourselves.

Key idea for life

If I act out a role, I do not engage the whole of myself. To be authentic and to express my own integrity, I need to act in a way that reflects my self-awareness and the awareness of my own freedom. This is who I am; this is what I choose to do; this is the real me, and I will not dodge responsibility for being myself.

'Bad faith' is saying 'I couldn't help it!' Authenticity is achieved by admitting your freedom and choice, so that our authentic self is something we consciously set about constructing.

Existentialism is a challenging philosophy. It is equally challenging to live alongside an existentialist! The ego is placed centre-stage, and that may prove to be self-destructive, as we shall see when we explore an alternative approach – altruism.

Existentialism can be summed up in Sartre's claim that 'existence precedes essence'. I do not have a fixed essence and then try to live it out in the world; rather, I give meaning to my life in the course of living it. By my present choices, I can shape my future, taking responsibility for what I become.

There is, however, a certain ambiguity in existentialist thought, one that is reflected in Simone de Beauvoir's book *The Ethics of Ambiguity*. In it, she recognizes that one's own freedom depends to some extent on other people; we are shaped (defined almost) by our relationships. So there is always going to be a balance between absolute freedom and the constraints imposed by our particular situation and the relationships in which we are involved. She argued that no existence can be fulfilled if it is limited to itself – or, to put it in John Donne's words, 'no man is an island'. Our relationships with others provide the opportunity for us to discover who we are.

Key idea for life

Although nuanced by de Beauvoir, existentialism remains largely an individualistic philosophy in a world of relationships. Sartre hated the way in which other people impose restraints on our freedom and appear to judge us ('hell is other people'), but perhaps our authenticity is also a matter of being true to the relationships and circumstances within which we find ourselves. Rejecting them all in the name of individual freedom may appear to be somewhat adolescent. Would you want to risk being married to a wholehearted existentialist? Perhaps, but only if you follow Nietzsche's advice to live dangerously!

Existentialism gave philosophical underpinnings to a view of life that rejected social conformity, promoting self-expression and freedom. Taken up by literature and art, it became a cultural phenomenon, centred on the smoke-filled cafes of Paris in the 1940s and 1950s.

Notice how utterly different this kind of philosophy is from most of what we discussed in the first chapter. Traditional metaphysics and epistemology was all about assessing evidence, careful reasoning and formulating general principles to enable us to understand reality. Here we are in the more ambiguous, threatening and challenging world of human individuals affirming themselves in the face of the ambiguities and absurdity of existence. This is not so much 'philosophy for life' as a 'philosophy *of* life.'

A feminist perspective

It may not have escaped the notice of many readers that almost all the philosophers mentioned so far in this book have been male. The agenda, both philosophically and politically, appears to have been set by men, and the rational and legal approaches to many issues seem particularly appropriate to a male intellectual environment and one that may tend to ignore the distinctive contribution of women.

A feminist perspective may therefore highlight any gender bias in the discussion of personal identity and integrity, and also in the moral and political concepts of justice, fairness and rights, pointing out those areas where men have sought to exclude or marginalize women, and seeking to rebalance the issues by adding a distinctively feminine approach.

A key work in the campaign on behalf of women was Mary Wollstonecraft's *A Vindication of the Rights of Women* (1792), in which she argued for equality on the grounds of intellect. This did not imply that there should be no distinction between men and women, however, and she was quite happy to see women and men play very different roles within society. In fact, she saw women as primarily contributing from within the home.

In the nineteenth century, a key issue for the feminist perspective on British political life was the campaign for women to receive the vote. This was not an issue presented only by women, for it received the support of John Stuart Mill, the utilitarian philosopher. Behind it lay that the Enlightenment perspective on the value of democracy and the autonomy of the individual – insisting that gender equality was implicit within it, masked only by a social conservatism that was entirely to the benefit of men.

Feminism has generally sought to present a historical critique of the social injustices suffered by women, suggesting that gender bias is not simply a matter of individual prejudice, but is inherent in social and political institutions. On a broader front it has also initiated discussion on the relationship between the sexes, the distinctive role of women, and the ethical implications of gender. In her book *The Second Sex* (1949), Simone de Beauvoir opened up a serious consideration of the myths and roles that women were expected to play within society, as mothers, wives, lovers and so on.

Key idea for life

De Beauvoir's key complaint is that, in a society shaped by men, women are seen as 'relative beings', existing only in relationship to men – hence they are the 'second' sex. The key question in any quest for integrity and happiness is whether or not we, as individuals, are prepared to accept the gender and other constructions that society places upon us. Can we resist 'becoming' a man or a woman?

Among the many thinkers contributing to the feminist perspective are Judith Butler (b.1956) who in *Gender Trouble* (1990, new edition 2006) introduced the idea that gender is something that is created by behaviour, by the habitual ways in which women speak and act, and Luce Irigaray (b.1930), who attacked the idea of women being seen in a male-dominated society as a commodity with an exchange value – as mother, virgin or prostitute.

However, a gender-balanced perspective is also achieved by women who contribute to philosophy generally, quite apart from addressing distinctively feminist issues. Thus, for example, Martha Nussbaum (b.1947) writes on ethics and political philosophy, so that her contribution to philosophy in general goes far beyond her specific book on *Sex and Social Justice* (2000). Those wanting a general overview of the feminist perspective, including its contribution to the different branches of philosophy (ethics, political philosophy, philosophy of science, metaphysics etc.), might look at *The Cambridge Companion to Feminism in Philosophy* (CUP, 2008) edited by Miranda Fricker and Jennifer Hornsby.

Particularly in its early days, feminism sought *equality* between men and women, pointing out the way in which society has been dominated by men. This was seen, for example, in the campaign for women to have the vote on the same terms as men. But equality was not to become an end in itself. Feminist thinkers go far beyond simple equality, to insist that women should be able to define their own values and goals, rather than having them imposed by men. This, of course, follows from our consideration of existentialism – it is a matter of taking responsibility for one's own freedom and choices, refusing to be limited by the expectations of society.

More recently, feminist thinking has focused on issues of transexuality, and particularly trans-women. If being a woman is a social construct, then what do you say of someone who now identifies as a woman, but who was born male and for many years was treated as a male, and therefore appeared to accept a male gender identification? It is also recognized that not all women have the same sort of social experience – it varies, for example, in terms of race, social class or the dominant religion of the culture within which one is brought up.

The quest for happiness

Aristotle argued that the good life is a matter of happiness (*eudaimonia* – a Greek term for living well), and that its primacy was shown by the simple fact that people did many things in order to achieve (or try to achieve) happiness, but that nobody would think of being happy in order to achieve anything else.

But how do we achieve happiness, and what does it involve? Material goods? A sense of purpose? Integrity (or authenticity – to use existentialist-speak)? Supportive relationships? Perhaps it requires all of these things. But how do we set about achieving it? These questions have been taken up in recent years by sociologists, psychologists and even economists, in an attempt to frame what is needed for the good life in society and for personal satisfaction and psychological health. It has a long history in both Eastern and Western philosophy upon which, in this and the two following sections, we can touch only very briefly.

In ancient Greece, the quest for happiness was taken up by the Stoics, who believed that one could only achieve it by living the moral life, orientating yourself in line with the fundamental design of the universe. One should remain indifferent to one's fate, engaged with the world but with an element of detachment, being free by being master of oneself and one's desires. In particular, Epictetus insisted that we should distinguish between things that depend on us (such as our own emotions and wishes) and those that don't (fate, circumstances and other people), with the advice that we can always do something about the former and that there is no point in fretting about the latter. Stoicism is a matter of living in a thoughtful and balanced way – with a kind of cool superiority over those caught up in the frantic passions of life. Stoics believed that the universe was controlled by reason and therefore sought the good life by applying reason and balance to their lives.

From the same period, a rather different approach was taken by Epicurus (341–270 BCE) and his followers. They saw the world as entirely material and indifferent to us, and therefore sought happiness in terms of cultivating pleasure, not in the sense of accumulating goods or experiences, but of living modestly and savouring the enjoyment of ordinary things. Their key idea was to achieve inner tranquillity: freedom from anxiety and fear.

Key idea for life

Both Stoic and Epicurean approaches are found today, in cognitive therapy, and in the development of 'mindfulness' as a spiritual tool. Reading those ancient philosophers suggests that, in its human basics, life has not changed that much over the last two thousand years; anxiety, status, peer pressure and fear of failure were as real then as they are now, and some of their advice may still prove valuable.

As the Stoics and Epicureans acknowledged, the quest for happiness has always come up against a fundamental problem: human life is fragile and limited. Whatever we hope for or work towards, we know that we are vulnerable to the normal contingencies of life, including the prospect of being incapacitated by illness, and that eventually – whether by some sudden trauma, or illness or eventually old age – we will die. So, if we are to find life worthwhile and meaningful, any retreat into simple hedonism in order to seek happiness is likely to prove futile and certainly short-lived. To be effective, the quest for happiness must come to terms with human fragility. So, for example, Epicurus himself found a simple remedy for fear of your own death, namely that you won't be around to experience it!

IS LIFE ABSURD?

One approach to happiness is to establish a direction in life and stick to it, creating your own satisfaction by doing so. Nietzsche said that the secret of his happiness was 'a straight line, a goal' and he presented humankind with the challenge of creating its own values and direction, rather than trying to find them already given in the world. He sought the heroic virtues of trying to maximize one's own potential – working towards the next stage in human development, the 'superman' (*übermensch*). Life may be meaningless, but it is our task to give it meaning by an act of will. But what happens when that meaning comes into conflict with life as it is with all its limitations?

The French novelist and philosopher Albert Camus (1913–60) suggested that life was inherently absurd, in that we have hopes, plans and know what we want, but life will inevitably frustrate us. In his novel *The Myth of Sisyphus*, he uses the ancient story of Sisyphus pushing a rock up a steep hill, only to see it roll back down, at which point he simply goes back and starts rolling it up again. Faced with the idea of struggling for a success that is never achieved, in a world that is meaningless, he concludes that 'We must imagine Sisyphus as being happy.' Camus considered that we should apply that approach to the drudgery of daily commuting to an office or factory.

Key idea for life

Some people may set and pursue goals, assuming that happiness will follow from their success; others struggle with heroic tasks that seem never-ending. In each case, the existential impetus is likely to come up against the facts of life and death. A key question here is whether happiness can indeed survive heroic failure, and whether a life may be judged successful by having made the attempt, even if it is just a matter of surviving the crushing boredom of a routine.

PRACTICAL SUGGESTIONS?

One of the most down-to-earth philosophers concerned with human welfare and happiness was Jeremy Bentham, best known for his theory of utilitarian ethics (see page 234). His 'hedonic calculus' sought to find a formula by which he could fairly allocate benefits, and considered all human life to be ruled by the twin forces of pain and pleasure. For some philosophers, politicians and economists today, the problem of happiness is primarily one of understanding what people want, what is likely to be for their long-term benefit, and how society and morality can be shaped in order to deliver the desired goods. Particularly under the influence of free-market capitalism, there is the largely unquestioned assumption that an increase in goods and services implies an increase in happiness and satisfaction. However, that is demonstrably not the case. Once life gets beyond the satisfaction of basic needs for security, food and shelter, people look for far more in their quest for happiness.

The French philosopher Emile Chartier (using the pen name Alain), writing on happiness in 1925, suggested that it is to be found primarily in action – 'gardening, cooking, writing, painting, playing football' – finding a kind of poetry in action. That reflects the happiness of being totally absorbed in an activity, giving yourself to it and losing yourself in it. 'Practical philosophy' provides many recommendations for finding happiness: coming to terms with yourself, recognizing ways in which you are lucky, creating opportunities for celebration, becoming reconciled with your past and your limitations, sharing with others and listening to them, and finding a sense of direction in life. Most advise that happiness is an inner disposition to be cultivated. Chartier noted that this was not always achieved by thinking, but that reflecting on life, its meaning and its direction, can contribute to an overall sense of self. So developing the skills of philosophy may have a part to play in the quest for happiness.

Bertrand Russell (1872–1970), the distinguished British philosopher whose colourful personal life reflected one rather basic aspect of the quest for happiness, tackles the issue head-on in his book *The Conquest of Happiness* (1930). He looks at the causes of unhappiness, including the practical ones in terms of social deprivation, poverty and illness, and also at the sense of powerlessness if these things are beyond your control. He is also very aware of the way in which people seek the approval of others, and comes to the Stoic conclusion that it is better not to be dependent for one's happiness on what others think. He also criticizes (in a way that parallels the aim of some Buddhist meditation techniques) the tendency to concentrate on our plans for the future rather than appreciating the present moment.

He regards self-absorption as an obstacle to happiness, and gives it three labels – the 'sinner', the 'narcissist' and the 'megalomaniac'. The first is preoccupied with his or her own guilt and failure, seeking an impossible perfectionism; the narcissist relates everything to the self, obsessed with his or her own status and plans; and the megalomaniac is simply driven by the lust for power. The main thrust of his argument is that happiness comes from turning outwards to appreciate other people and activities in the world, and escaping from the tyranny of the self.

Russell offers plenty to reflect on in our quest for happiness, but his key point – that we need to overcome an obsession with self and look outwards – reflects a feature of life through which people claim to find happiness and personal satisfaction, as well as benefiting the world as a whole, by following a policy of *altruism*.

Altruism

Altruism is the selfless concern for the welfare of others. It is a well-documented feature of human life – whether in small acts of kindness shown to strangers, or in the more dramatic actions of those who die, or risk losing their lives, in the attempt to help those in urgent distress or danger. While warring factions fight and destroy lives and property, an army of medics care for the wounded, and civilians caught up in the conflict risk their lives to help one another.

So far in this chapter, we have been looking at self-fulfilment and what it means to flourish. An important element in this, however, and one that might go against the most obvious meaning of human flourishment, is the willingness of people to help others. So what should we make of the phenomenon of altruism? Is it natural? Is it secretly selfish? And what does it say about our ethics, religion, politics and what it means to be human?

To some thinkers, self-interest takes priority. Thomas Hobbes (see below page 258) saw the natural human condition as one in which each person is in a constant state of war against all others. Adam Smith's economic theory in *The Wealth of Nations* emphasizes competition, and some interpretations of Darwin's theory of natural selection might suggest that selfishness is in some way fundamental to human life. Friedrich Nietzsche went further and considered altruism to be the mark of a 'slave morality' as opposed to the 'master-morality' of those who strive to develop themselves to the limit.

In the spheres of politics and economics, it is commonly assumed that we all strive for happiness, and do so, if necessary, at the expense of others. Capitalism and evolution together present life as essentially competitive, and in a competitive environment there will be winners and losers. Nobody wants to be a loser; all want to succeed. However, a society based on competitive selfishness is unlikely to enable everyone to flourish, and suggesting that we are naturally selfish fails to explain the phenomenon of altruism.

Altruism impacts on a number of different areas of philosophy. Political philosophy may need to take it into account when deciding both human's essential or natural state (see, for example, the difference between Thomas Hobbes and Jean-Jaques Rousseau) and what sort of society could be both desirable and possible. In the philosophy of mind, we could examine the function of altruism in shaping the nature of the person. In ethics, most particularly, we need to examine why one would seek to do what is right, and why one should, for example, seek the greatest good for the greatest number. Indeed, both the 'moral sense' view of ethics, that we have a natural desire to help those in distress or need, put forward by Hutcheson and Hume and utilitarianism depend on the willingness of individuals to engage in acts of kindness towards others, setting aside any absolute claim to personal gain in doing so. In general we speak of an altruistic *disposition*, in other words, the tendency of a person to opt to go to the aid of other people when circumstances demand it.

If people can be genuinely altruistic, however, their behaviour appears to go against the assumptions of the two dominant social, economic and political movements of modern times – neo-liberal, free-market capitalism and socialism. Both theories are based on an impersonal view of the individual, such that people's individual welfare can and is set aside in the interests of capitalist market forces or a monolithic and ideologically driven socialist theory, where people become mere pawns in the conflict between classes. It is therefore important, in considering what we mean by the 'good life' and the 'good society', to recognize the harm that selfishness can produce and the importance of developing a philosophy within which altruism can play a part. In his huge and influential book *Altruism* (Atlantic Books, 2013, translated into English, 2015), Matthieu Ricard, who is both a philosopher and a scientist, presents the challenge this way:

> Selfishness is at the heart of most of the problems we face today: the growing gap between rich and poor, the attitude of 'everybody for himself', which is only increasing, and indifference about the generations to come.

To take one obvious example, free-market capitalism tends to favour giving individuals and companies maximum freedom to profit from their work, and to negotiate terms and conditions for employment and trade. It is argued that, by encouraging people to generate wealth, they will then spend that wealth on goods and services which will subsequently benefit those who are less fortunate – sometimes called the 'trickle-down effect'. However, as has become apparent in recent years, exactly the opposite happens. Those who own capital or whose status is directly linked to capital values (as, for example, the CEOs of major companies, who are paid in line with company performance and often by way of shares and other bonus payments), tend to get wealthier exactly as the wages paid to those who produce goods are forced down on a supply-and-demand basis. This is exacerbated by the globalized market, where goods may be produced in countries where labour is cheapest, but profits are channelled through regimes of lowest tax.

Key idea for life

To make these observations is not to argue for a particular partisan point of view, but simply to point out that the assumption of competition, with self-interest as its driving force, is deeply ingrained in modern society, but that this view of human relations (in which individuals are seen primarily as producers or consumers) conflicts with the more generous, and 'altruistic' attitude displayed by individuals towards one another.

So, in assessing our personal, ethical and political views, we may want to consider which is the more fundamental aspect of human nature, the competitive or the altruistic? Which is likely to be the more productive in terms of satisfaction and happiness?

It is also worth reflecting that the media generally get a better story out of conflict than out of peaceful co-operation – hence the bias in favour of a negative evaluation of human behaviour. We tend to fear the worst of people, reinforced by every example of selfish or bad behaviour; yet, statistically, the opposite is the case. So, for example, the vast majority of people who deal with young people are not paedophiles, but work to the best of their ability solely for the benefit of those for whom they have responsibility. However, they do not make the news, and so our view is coloured by the minority who abuse their position. If human beings were only motivated by selfishness, we should *anticipate and assume* that all those working with young people are in it for their own selfish reasons. But we don't. We are horrified, because we assume and hope that people *can be* genuinely selfless and caring, and that those who deal with the young *should be*.

Some philosophers, notably Ayn Rand (see page 271), argue that individualism and the prioritizing of selfish concerns are natural, and regard the suggestion that people can and should act from altruistic motives as an unfair demand for them to make a sacrifice. However, the fundamental question is whether, in the long run, altruism is a sacrifice, or whether it is of benefit – both to those who are the recipients of altruistic actions and those who perform them.

Those who argue for universal self-interest have an additional question to address: How, if we are essentially selfish, do you explain the fact of altruism? One possibility is to argue that helping others produces a sense of personal satisfaction, or avoids guilt. If that is so, then being unselfish is essentially selfish; we help others in order to benefit ourselves in the long term, or to improve our self-esteem, or simply to feel good by doing so. As an argument, however, this fails. Take the simple example of risking one's own life to save a drowning child. If you jump in and try to save the child, you are accused of doing so simply to appease your own super-ego, or to make yourself a hero, or to win recognition for your bravery. In other words, jumping in is selfish. On the other hand, if you walk on and leave the child to drown, that too is selfish. Hence, the argument would say that you are selfish no matter what you do.

But if all possible choices are selfish, then selfishness becomes meaningless; it is just a term for being human, because nothing you can choose to do would enable you to escape the claim that you are acting selfishly. Selfishness of this sort – following Hobbes, or Freud – is simply a chosen way of interpreting life; it cannot be based on facts and observations. If you ask, 'What would it take for an action to be done from unselfish motives?' and the answer is that it is impossible, then you know that the word 'selfish' has become meaningless.

Another possibility is that altruism is an extension of group selection in evolution. In other words, when it comes to groups and kinship ties, an individual may sacrifice himself or herself to the benefit of the larger kinship group – thus ensuring a better survival of the combined gene stock. Or, as we find in colonies of ants, individuals understand themselves, and are prepared to sacrifice themselves, for the sake of the group. This might be taken to explain the phenomenon of those who volunteer to fight in times of war. However, although admitting that a gene may achieve its own selfish goals by fostering a limited form of altruism, Richard Dawkins adds that:

> Much as we might wish to believe otherwise, universal love and the welfare of the species as a whole are concepts that simply do not make evolutionary sense.
>
> (*The Selfish Gene*, OUP, 1990. p3)

The implication of this is simply that evolutionary theory *cannot explain altruism*. It does not follow that altruism does not or should not exist. Matthieu Ricard (in *Altruism*) presents an evidence-based account of altruism. He also argues that, for the benefit of society as a whole, and indeed of the survival of our species in its environment, altruism is not only possible but essential.

Given that we all seek happiness, the fundamental question about altruism is whether, as a matter of fact, people are (or claim to be, or appear to be) happier as a result of co-operating selflessly with others, or of pursuing their own self-interest? The answer to that question, either as a result of social investigation or personal reflection, is likely to impact on a whole range of ethical, political and religious questions, as well as influencing the personal quest for satisfaction in life.

Key idea for life

Studies in the neuroplasticity of the human brain show that we can, by training, influence our habitual patterns of thought and our emotional responses. Hence philosophy has the potential to be not simply an intellectual diversion, but a tool that we can develop and put to use at a personal level.

3

The Philosophy of Science

In this chapter you will:

- ► *Examine the historical development of science in relation to philosophy*
- ► *Consider the way in which scientific theories are derived from observations and experiments*
- ► *Explore the issues about how science makes progress*

Why?

Science has a positive impact on all our lives; through technology we benefit from healthcare, transport, communication and much else. But its success may lead us to accept a simplistic form of 'scientism', the view that science alone can offer answers to all life's problems. It is intellectually healthier to examine scientific method in order to understand exactly what science is, or is not, able to show. How can we tell genuine science from bogus? How does science make progress? What about conflicting scientific claims? Science is not a set of ready-made answers, but a method of investigation – it offers a range of tools for understanding the world. However, it is up to us to decide how those tools should be used.

The philosophy of science examines the methods used by science, the ways in which hypotheses and laws are formulated from evidence, and the grounds on which scientific claims about the world may be justified.

We often tend to assume that science offers a straightforward and incontrovertible way of getting information about the world – and indeed, by and large, that is true. But even science throws up difficult questions. Karl Popper, a major twentieth-century figure in the philosophy of science, criticized both Marx and Freud on the basis that they would not allow new evidence to falsify their theories, whereas Popper insisted that genuine science must always remain open to having its theories overturned if new evidence contradicts them. It is, however, far from clear just how willing (or appropriate) it is for science to drop useful theories at the first appearance of conflicting data. Hence there are issues about scientific method for philosophy to address.

Philosophy and science are not in principle opposed to one another, but are in many ways parallel operations, for both seek to understand the nature of the world and its structures. Whereas the individual sciences do so by gathering data from within their particular spheres and formulating general theories for understanding them, philosophy tends to concern itself with the process of formulating those theories, and establishing how they relate together to give an overall view of the world.

A major part of philosophy is the process of examining the language people use and the criteria of truth that they accept. Therefore, while the individual sciences use 'first order language' (speaking directly about physical, chemical or biological observations), philosophy tends to concentrate on 'second order language' (examining what it means to speak about those things) and considers whether claims that are made within the sciences are logically justified by the evidence on which they appear to be based.

Key idea for life

Today, scientists specialize, because it is quite impossible for anyone to have detailed knowledge of the current state of research in each of the various branches of science. It is even more difficult for a philosopher to get a view of the current workings of science 'as a whole'. Hence the main task of philosophy is to examine *the logic of scientific claims*, and to probe *the limits of what can be said*. This is important, if we are to avoid deferring thoughtlessly to anyone who claims that something is shown 'by science'.

Scientists, mathematicians and philosophers work in separate disciplines, even if they are interested in and may benefit from the work of the others, but it was not always so. Physics was originally known as 'natural philosophy', and some of the greatest names in philosophy were also involved with mathematics and science. Aristotle examined and codified the various sciences within his overall scheme of philosophy. Descartes, Leibniz, Pascal and Russell were all mathematicians as well as philosophers. Indeed, Russell and Whitehead argued in *Principia Mathematica* (1910–13) that mathematics was a development of deductive logic. Bacon, Locke and others were influenced by the rise of modern scientific method, and were concerned to give it a sound philosophical basis. Kant wrote *A General Natural History and Theory of the Heavens* in 1755 in which he explored the possible origins of the solar system.

Some philosophical movements (e.g. logical positivism, in the early years of the twentieth century – see page 101) were influenced by science and the scientific method of establishing evidence. Many of the philosophers that we considered in the chapter on the theory of knowledge can therefore reappear in considering science, largely because scientific knowledge and its methods are such an important part of our general appreciation of what we know and how we know it.

A historical overview

Within Western thought, there have been two major shifts in the view of the world, and these have had an important influence on the way in which philosophy and science have related to one another. We may therefore divide Western philosophy of science into three general periods: early Greek and Mediaeval thought; the Newtonian world-view; and twentieth-century developments (although recognizing that such a division represents a simplification of a more complex process of change).

EARLY GREEK AND MEDIAEVAL THOUGHT

In 529 CE the Emperor Justinian banned the teaching of philosophy in order to further the interests of Christianity. Plato had already had a considerable influence upon the development of Christian doctrines, and elements of his thought – particularly the contrast between the ideal world of the Forms and the limited world of everyday experience – continued within theology. The works of Aristotle were preserved first in Byzantium and then by the Arabic scholars, being rediscovered in the thirteenth century, when the first translations were made from Arabic into Latin.

In the thirteenth century, with thinkers like Thomas Aquinas (1225–74), Duns Scotus (1266–1308) and William of Ockham (c. 1285–1349), Greek thought began to be explored again in a systematic way. From that time, philosophy became very much a development of, or reaction to, the work of the Greeks.

Aristotle set out the different branches of science, and divided up living things into their various species and genera – a process of classification that became a major feature of science. He had a theory of knowledge based on sensations which depended on repetition:

sensations repeat themselves ———→ *leading to perception*

perceptions repeat themselves ———→ *leading to experience*

experiences repeat themselves ———→ *leading to knowledge*

Thus, for Aristotle, knowledge develops out of our structured and repeated perception of evidence that comes to us from our senses – an important feature in the development of science.

He also established ideas of space, time and causality, including the idea of the Prime Mover (which became the basis of the cosmological argument for the existence of God – see page 198). He set out the four 'causes' (see page 25), thus distinguishing between matter itself, the form it took on, the agent of change and the final purpose or goal for which it was designed. He considered a thing's power to be its potential. Everything had a potential and a resting place: fire rises up naturally, whereas heavy objects fall. Changes, for Aristotle, are not related to general forces like gravity (which belong to the later Newtonian scheme), but to the fact that individual things, by their very nature, have a goal.

Let us look at a few examples of the influence of Plato and Aristotle.

For Plato, the unseen 'Forms' were more real than the individual things that could be known through the senses. This way of thinking (backed by religion) suggested that human reason and its concepts of perfection were paramount, and that observation and experience were secondary.

Cosmology and astronomy give examples of this trend: Copernicus (1473–1543) and later Galileo (1564–1642) were to offer a view of the universe in which the Earth revolved around the Sun, rather than vice versa. Their view was opposed by those whose idea of the universe came from Ptolemy, in which the Earth was surrounded by glassy spheres – perfect shapes, conveying the Sun, Moon, planets in perfect circular motion. Their work was challenged (and Galileo condemned) not because their observations were found to be at fault, but because they had trusted their observations, rather than following tradition.

These astronomers were struggling against a background of religious authority that gave Greek notions of perfection priority over observations and experimental evidence. In other words, the earlier mediaeval system of thought was deductive (it deduced what should be observed to happen from its pre-conceived ideas), in contrast to the later inductive method of developing a theory from observations.

Along with the tendency to look for theory and perfection rather than accept the results of observation, there was another, stemming from Aristotle. Following his idea of the final cause, everything was thought to be designed for a particular purpose. If something falls to the ground, it seeks its natural purpose and place in doing so. So, in a religious context, it was possible to say that something happened because it was God's will for it, or because it was designed for that purpose.

Key idea for life

From this perspective, there was less interest in looking for a scientific principle or law to explain events in terms of 'efficient' causation. Everything had its place and purpose, given by God and fixed. Does that give us a sense of security and direction in life, or a feeling of being trapped within an intentional scheme from which we can never escape?

THE NEWTONIAN WORLD-VIEW

The rise of modern science would not have been possible without the renewed sense of the value of human reason and the ability to challenge established ideas and religious dogma that developed as a result of the Renaissance and the Reformation. But what was equally influential was the way in which information was gathered and sorted, and theories formed on the basis of it. Central to this process was the method of induction, and this was set out very clearly (and in a way that continues to be relevant) by Francis Bacon.

Bacon (1561–1626) rejected Aristotle's idea of final causes, and insisted that knowledge should be based on a process of induction, which, as we shall see later, is the systematic method of coming to general conclusions on the basis of evidence about individual instances that have been observed. He warned about 'idols' that tend to lead a person astray:

▶ The desire to accept that which confirms what we already believe.

▶ Distortions resulting from our habitual ways of thinking.

▶ Muddles that come through our use of language (e.g. using the same word for different things, and then assuming that they must be one and the same).

▶ Believing things out of allegiance to a particular school of thought.

Bacon also pointed out that, in gathering evidence, one should not just look for examples that confirm a particular theory, but one should actively seek out and accept the force of contrary examples. After centuries of using evidence to confirm established views, this was revolutionary.

Key idea for life

It was only with Descartes (see page 18) that philosophy attempted consciously to start again from first principles, setting aside authority in favour of reason, and this coincided with the development of 'modern' science. Much of what we take to be a 'modern' view of life has its origins in the seventeenth century. But beware of any simplistic view that sees the 'modern' or 'enlightenment' views of the seventeenth and eighteenth centuries as in utter contrast with a previous world of crude superstition and supernatural explanations. Many earlier thinkers – Aristotle, Aquinas, Copernicus, Bacon – showed careful reasoning and assessment of evidence, while superstition continues into the twenty-first century.

The general view of the world that came about as a result of the rise of science is usually linked with the name of Isaac Newton (1642–1727). In the Newtonian world-view, observation and experiment yield knowledge of the laws that govern the world.

In it, space and time were fixed, forming a framework within which everything takes place. Objects were seen to move and be moved through the operation of physical laws of motion, so that everything was seen as a machine, the workings of which could become known through careful observation. Interlocking forces kept matter in motion, and everything was predictable.

Put crudely, the world was largely seen as a collection of particles of matter in motion, hitting one another, like billiard balls on a table, and behaving in a predictable way. It was thought that science would eventually give an unchallengeable explanation for everything, and that it would form the basis for technology that would give humankind control over the environment, and the ability to do things as yet unimagined. Science became cumulative – gradually expanding into previously unknown areas; building upon the secure foundations of established physical laws.

Newton was a religious believer; he thought that the laws by which the universe operated had been established by God. But his god was an external creator who, once the universe had been set in motion, could retire, leaving it to continue to function according to its fixed laws. This view freed science from the need to take God into account: it could simply examine the laws of nature, and base its theories on observation rather than religious dogma.

With the coming of the Newtonian world-view, the function of philosophy changed. Rather than initiating theories about cosmology, the task of philosophy was to examine and comment on the methods and results of scientific method, establishing its limits. Kant, for example, argued that space, time and causality – the very bases of Newtonian science – were not to be found 'out there' in the world of independent objects, but were contributed by the mind. People saw things as being in space and time because that was the way their minds processed the information given through the senses.

Hume pointed out that scientific laws were not true universal statements, but only summaries of what had been experienced so far. The method used by science – gathering data and drawing general conclusions from them – yielded higher and higher degrees of probability, but could never achieve absolute certainty.

Key idea for life

Genuine science remains open to the possibility of contrary evidence – something utterly unexpected, requiring us to reconsider and perhaps modify our theories. All scientific theories are therefore provisional and limited. Beware the danger of dogmatic scientism; however convincing a theory may appear today, it will eventually be challenged and may need to be adjusted or replaced.

But not all philosophers supported Newton's fixed mechanical universe. Bishop Berkeley criticized Newton's idea that space and time are fixed. For Berkeley, everything (including matter and extension) is a matter of sensation, of human experience. Thus everything is relative to the person who experiences it, and there is no logical way to move from the relativity of our experience to some external absolute. In his own way, Berkeley anticipates the arrival of the third era for science and philosophy.

TWENTIETH-CENTURY DEVELOPMENTS

For most thinkers prior to the twentieth century, it was inconceivable that space and time were not fixed: a necessary framework within which everything else could take place. Einstein's theories of relativity were to change all that. The first, in 1905, was the theory of *Special Relativity*, best known in the form of the equation $E = mc^2$. This showed that mass and energy are equivalent, and that (as energy was equal to mass multiplied by the speed of light squared) a very small amount of matter could be converted into a very large amount of energy. This, of course, is now best known for its rather drastic practical consequences in the development of nuclear weapons.

Einstein published the second theory, *General Relativity*, in 1916. It made the revolutionary claim that time, space, matter and energy are all related to one another. For example, space and time can be compressed by a strong gravitational field. There are no fixed points. The way in which things relate to one another depends upon the point from which they are being observed, so that, as you look out through space you are also looking back through time.

Modern physics and cosmology offer a view of space and time that contrasts with that of Newton. The reason that Newton's physics worked on the basis of fixed space and time was that he considered only a very small section of the universe, and within that section, his laws do indeed hold true. However, as our view of the universe has enlarged, so space and time are seen as linked in a single, four-dimensional space–time continuum. In such a world, there is no fixed point from which to observe anything, for observer and observed are both in a process of change.

Key idea for life

Although anticipated by earlier thinkers (including Heraclitus and the Buddha) this represents, along with evolution, probably the greatest single shift in perspective in the history of thought, and the paradigms of relativity and evolution may easily permeate our thinking in all spheres of life. Reality is defined by perspective and common-sense views are overthrown. Absolutism may be seen as reflecting an old-fashioned, designed universe with fixed physical realities and (often) moral norms. However, relativity should be treated with caution; just because it works in one sphere of life does not necessarily make it a valid or useful paradigm for all.

Alongside relativity came quantum mechanics, which raised questions about whether events at the sub-atomic level could be predicted, and what it means to say that one thing causes another. Quantum mechanics is notoriously difficult to understand. A general view of it is that it works, even if we don't understand it as a theory. The older certainties of Newtonian physics might still apply, but only within very limited parameters. Once you stray into the microscopic area of the sub-atomic, or the macroscopic world of cosmic structures, the situation is quite different.

A similar revolution took place within the understanding of living things. Through the discovery of DNA, the world of biology is linked to that of chemistry and of physics, because the instructions within the DNA molecule are able to determine the form of the living being.

These raised a basic philosophical question: What do we mean by scientific 'truth' in such a strange, flexible and relativistic world?

Through the twentieth century, therefore, philosophy engaged with a scientific view of the world that had changed enormously from the mechanical and predictable world of Newton. In particular, science started to offer a variety of ways of picturing the world, and cosmology – which had been dominated first by religious belief and Aristotle, and then by astronomy – was now very much in the hands of mathematicians. It became clear that the world as a whole was not something that could be observed; its structures could only be explored by calculation.

During much of the first half of the twentieth century, philosophy (at least in the United States and Britain) became dominated by the quest for meaning and the analysis of language. It no longer saw its role as providing an overview of the universe – it left that to the individual scientific disciplines. Rather, it adopted a supportive role, checking on the methods used by science, the logic by which results were produced from observations, and the way in which theories could be confirmed or discredited.

In broad outline, this historical survey would suggest that:

▶ Up to the sixteenth century, Greek concepts, backed by religious authority, determined the general view of the world. Evidence was required to fit the overall scheme, so philosophy was seen as *shaping the content* of scientific investigation.

▶ In the period characterized by Newtonian physics, philosophy mainly offered *a critique of scientific method*, based particularly on the principles of induction.

▶ Since the twentieth century, radical movements within science (particularly in theoretical physics) have made the conceptual basis of science more flexible, counter-intuitive and far removed from common sense. During the first half of the twentieth century, Analytic philosophy tended to concentrate on *the analysis of concepts*; inspired by the apparent clarity of an earlier generation of scientific theories, philosophers also offered a *critique of the criteria by which science should be validated and the way in which it makes progress.*

Remember this

In 2010, Stephen Hawking (in *The Grand Design: new answers to the ultimate questions of life*, Bantam Press) suggested that philosophy was 'dead', that philosophers were out of touch with developments in science, and therefore that Philosophy of Science was a waste of time.

Whatever the merits of his claim, it highlights the importance of distinguishing between philosophy as a mental activity (examining evidence, sorting arguments and so on) and philosophy as a body of knowledge or academic discipline. Scientists may claim that the philosophy of science is irrelevant but, in their case, they are simply… doing philosophy!

From evidence to theory: scientific method

In terms of the philosophy of science, the most important approach to gathering and analysing information was the 'inductive method'. This was championed by Francis Bacon, and then by Thomas Hobbes (1588–1679), and became the basis of the Newtonian world of science. In its practical approach to sifting and evaluating evidence, it is also reflected in the empiricism of Hume (see page 32). Indeed, it was the inductive method that distinguished 'modern' science from what had gone before, and brought in the first of the two major shifts in worldview.

THE INDUCTIVE METHOD
This method is based on two things:

▶ A trust that knowledge can be gained by gathering evidence and conducting experiments; i.e. it is based on facts that can be checked, or experiments that can be repeated.

▶ A willingness to set aside preconceived views about the likely outcome of an experiment, or the validity of evidence presented.

With the inductive method, science was claiming to be based on objectively considered evidence, in contrast to traditional religion and metaphysics, which were considered to be based on doctrines backed by authority rather than reason.

In practice, the method works in this way:

1 Observe and gather data (evidence; information), seeking to eliminate, as far as possible, all irrelevant factors.

2 Analyse your data, and draw conclusions from them in the form of hypotheses.

3 Devise experiments to test out those hypotheses; i.e. if this hypothesis is correct, then certain experimental results should be anticipated.

4 Modify your hypothesis, if necessary, in the light of the results of your experiments.

5 From the experiments, the data and the hypotheses, argue for a theory.

6 Once you have a theory, you can predict other things on the basis of it, by which the theory can later be verified or falsified.

This process of induction, by which a theory is arrived at by the analysis and testing out of observed data, can yield at most *only a high degree of probability*. There is always the chance that an additional piece of information will show that the original hypothesis is wrong, or that it applies only within a limited field. The hypothesis, and the scientific theory that comes from it, is therefore open to modification.

Theories that are tested out in this way lead to the framing of scientific laws. Now it is important to establish exactly what is meant by 'law' in this context. In common parlance, 'law' is taken to be something that is imposed, a rule that is to be obeyed. But it would be wrong to assume that a scientific law can dictate how things behave. The law simply describes that behaviour, it does not control it. If something behaves differently, it is simply that either:

▶ There is an unknown factor that has influenced this particular situation and therefore modified what was expected. Or

▶ The law of nature is inadequately framed, and needs to be modified in order to take this new situation into account.

Key idea for life

To point out that all theories based on the inductive method are open to the possibility of modification is a *positive*, rather than a negative, comment. Often termed the 'black swan' issue, a willingness to take in new possibilities, think in new ways and set aside previous assumptions are essential for intellectual growth. To cling to an already disproved theory, just because it offers comfort, is an understandable human weakness, but is seldom a wise long-term policy in any area of life, scientific or personal.

FALSIFICATION

It may sound illogical, but science makes progress when a theory is falsified, rather than when it is confirmed, for it is only by rejecting and modifying a theory, to account for new evidence, that something better is put in its place. This view was argued by Karl Popper (1902–94), an Austrian philosopher from Vienna, who moved to New Zealand in 1937 and then to London in 1945, where he became Professor of Logic and Scientific Method at the London School of Economics. He was a socialist, and made significant contributions to political philosophy as well as the philosophy of science.

In his book *The Logic of Scientific Discovery* (1934, translated in 1959) Popper makes the crucial point that science seeks theories that are logically self-consistent, and that can be falsified. He points out that a scientific law goes *beyond* what can be experienced. We can never prove it to be absolutely true; all we can do is try to prove it to be false, and accept it on a provisional basis until such time as it is falsified.

This leads Popper to say that a scientific theory *cannot* be compatible with all the logically possible evidence. If a theory claims that it can *never* be falsified, then it is not scientific. On this basis, he challenged the ideas of both Marx and Freud.

In practice, of course, a theory is not automatically discarded as soon as one possible piece of contrary evidence is produced. What happens is that the scientist tries to reproduce that bit of contrary evidence, to show that it is part of a significant pattern which the theory has not been able to account for. Science also seeks out alternative theories that can include all the positive evidence that has been found for the original one, but also includes the new conflicting evidence.

Case study

In Newtonian physics, light travels in a straight line. (This was confirmed over the centuries, and was therefore corroborated as a theory.) But modern astronomy has shown that, when near to a very powerful gravitational field, light bends.

This does not mean that the Newtonian view was entirely wrong, simply that light does indeed travel in a straight line when in a uniform gravitational field. The older theory is now included within one that can take into account these exceptional circumstances.

Where you have a choice of theories, Popper held that you should accept the one that is not only *better corroborated*, but also *more testable* and entailing *more true statements* than the others. And, in addition, that you should do this even if you know that the theory is false. Because we cannot have absolute certainty, we have to go for the most *useful* way of understanding the world that we have to hand, even if its limitations have already been revealed. In other words, Popper argues that science should take a pragmatic approach to truth.

NEW EVIDENCE?

A theory should not necessarily be ignored just because present evidence fails to be conclusive, as we do not know what might come to light in the future. A theory may survive when it adapts to new situations that yield new evidence.

A particularly appropriate example of this may be Charles Darwin's theory of natural selection. Darwin published *The Origin of Species* in 1859. He observed that within a species there were slight variations, most of which gave no particular benefit to the individual who displayed them. Sometimes, however, a beneficial variation gave that individual an advantage and, in a world of limited resources of food and habitat, the advantaged individual was more likely to survive to adulthood and breed. Hence, the beneficial variations would be passed on to a proportionately larger number of the next generation, and so on. Thus a competitive natural environment was doing exactly what a breeder of domestic animals would do in selecting and breeding individuals who showed particular qualities.

He presented natural selection as a process that he considered to be the best explanation for the variety of species that he had observed and catalogued.

Darwin thus claimed to have discovered the mechanism by which species evolve, and also an explanation of those features of each species that seem most appropriate to its own survival. In effect, natural selection explained how nature could design itself, rendering obsolete the idea that the appearance of design necessitated the existence of a designer God. Its implications were far beyond his areas of research. If species are not fixed, then everything is subject to change. To accept such an idea (with all its scientific, social, emotional and religious implications) on the basis of limited evidence was to take a great risk.

Key idea for life

The theory of natural selection illustrates how a strictly inductive method of scientific argument, gathering and interpreting evidence, can then take an imaginative leap in order to grasp a more general theory. A new insight that can reorganize and make sense of all existing data is a mark of intellectual genius.

However, the debates that followed the publication of Darwin's theory were not simply about his perceived challenge to religious ideas, but about his interpretation of evidence. In particular, there did not seem to be adequate fossil evidence for a gradual evolution of species. In other words, the fossil evidence lacked sufficient 'halfway' stages that might illustrate the change from what appeared to be one fixed species to another.

Today, we have evidence to support the theory of natural selection that was unavailable to Darwin. So, for example, in a book entitled *The Beak of the Finch* (1994), Jonathan Weiner describes a 20-year study of finches on one of the Galapagos Islands, showing, for example, that in times of drought only those finches with the longest beaks could succeed in getting the toughest seeds, and therefore survived to breed. At the same time, DNA studies of blood from various finches corresponded to their physical abilities and characteristics.

New evidence for survival of those best able to adapt to their changing environment is seen all the time in terms of medicine and agriculture. As soon as a pesticide appears to have brought a particular pest under control, a new strain is found that is resistant to it. Equally, in medicine, new strains of disease are appearing that are resistant to the available antibiotics. What is happening is that those examples of a pest or a disease that survive the onslaught of a pesticide or treatment breed. The next generation is therefore resistant. These examples show the flexibility of nature: the present disease has been 'designed', not by some original designer but in response to existing treatments. We see an evolution of diseases over a space of a few years, mirroring the longer-term evolution of species over millennia.

More generally, we now know that random genetic mutations are the cause of the tiny variations that form the basis of natural selection. Genetics therefore provides a whole new level of evidence. Analysis of the genetic make-up of each species is able to show how closely those species are related and may trace them back to common genetic ancestors.

There is no way that Darwin could have considered his theory from the standpoint of genetic mutation, or from the way in which viruses adapt and take on new forms, but such new areas of evidence may be used to corroborate a previously held theory, particularly where (as was the case with Darwin) the problem was not so much that his theory had been falsified as that there was a perceived lack of positive evidence.

Experiments and objectivity

Karl Popper argued that science is not subjective, in the sense of being the product of a single human mind, but neither is it literally objective (i.e. a scientific law is not an external 'fact', but a way of stating the relationship between facts as they appear to us). Rather, science transcends the ideas of particular individuals, as does art, literature or maths. So how do the theories we devise, based on evidence and experiment, relate to what is 'out there' in the world?

The process of induction is based on the idea that it is possible to get evidence that does not depend upon the person who observes it. Indeed, from Francis Bacon onwards the theory has been that a scientist sets aside all personal preferences in assessing data. But can we observe nature without influencing it by our act of observing it, and how much of what we think of as evidence is contributed by our own minds?

The sensations that we have are not simply copies of external reality, they are the product of the way in which we have encountered that reality: colour is the result of a combination of light, surface texture and the operation of our eyes; space is perceived as a result of our brain linking one thing to another; time is a matter of remembering that some experiences have already taken place. Our experiences (and any theories based on them) are not independent facts, but the product of our ways of looking and thinking. As Kant argued, when we observe something, our mind has a contribution to make to that experience.

Case study

I look out of the window of a stationary train at the train at the next platform. Suddenly, what I see starts to move. But is my train moving forward, or is the other train pulling away? Unless I feel a jolt, it will be a moment before I can decide between the two. But if, at that moment, someone else says 'Ah, we're off', his or her interpretation will reinforce my own.

In the same way, scientific evidence, repeated in various experiments, gives a trans-personal element of truth, even if the object being studied, and the way in which it is described, ultimately depend upon individual human perceptions.

Right, wrong or what?

The Newtonian world was at least predictable. A law of nature could be regarded as a fixed piece of information about how the world worked. That has now gone. We find that science can offer several equally valid but different ways of viewing the same phenomenon. Light can be understood in terms of particles or in terms of wave motions. They are two utterly different ways of understanding the same thing, but the fact that one is right does not mean that the other is wrong. There are no absolutes in space or time. Quantum theory is seen to work (results can be predicted on the basis of it) but without people understanding exactly why.

As laws and theories become established within the scientific community, they are used as a basis for further research, and are termed 'paradigms'. Occasionally there is a paradigm shift, which entails the revision of much of science. In terms of cosmology, the move from an Aristotelian (Ptolemaic) to a Newtonian world-view, and then the further move from that to the view of Einstein, represents two shifts of paradigm.

Science offers a set of reasoned views about how the world has been seen to work up to the present. Taken together, the laws of science that are understood at any one time provide a structure within which scientists work; a structure that guides and, influences, but does not dictate how scientific research will progress. With hindsight, we can see philosophers and scientists boldly proclaiming the finality of their particular vision of the world just as the scientific community is about to go through a 'paradigm shift', as a result of which everything is going to be re-assessed.

Case study

In 1899, Haeckel published *The Riddle of the Universe*. He argued that everything, including thought, was the product of the material world and was controlled by its laws. Freedom was an illusion and religion a superstition. He was proposing scientific materialism, popularizing Darwin's theory of evolution, and sweeping away all earlier philosophy that did not fit his material and scientific outlook. For Haeckel, science had discovered just about everything there was to discover; there would be no more surprises.

What would he have made of relativity, quantum theory, genetics or computing?

T.S. Kuhn, in his book *The Structure of Scientific Revolutions* (1962), described these paradigms as the basic *Gestalt* (or world-view) within which science at any one time interprets the evidence it has available. It is the paradigm that largely dictates scientific progress, and observations are not free from the influence of the paradigm either.

What makes Kuhn's theory particularly controversial is that he claims that there are no *independent* data by which to decide between competing paradigms (because all data are presented either in terms of one paradigm or the other) and therefore there is no strictly logical reason to change a paradigm. This implies relativism in science, which seemed to threaten the logical basis of the development of scientific theories, as expounded by Karl Popper.

The general implication of the work of Kuhn and others is that, if a theory works well (in other words, if it gives good predictive results), then it becomes a *possible* explanation: we cannot say that it is *the definitive or only one*.

Imre Lakatos (1922–74) argued that science is generally carried out within research programmes, and is essentially a problem-solving activity. There are core theories within a research programme (without which the whole programme would fail) and a 'protective belt' of theories that are more open to modification, while continuing with the overall programme. Core theories are not simply abandoned at the first piece of contrary evidence. At any one time, there will be many research programmes on the go, and they are gradually modified in a way that is rather more subtle than a straight 'falsificationist' view might suggest.

But beyond that, there are other criteria for assessing theories. 'Instrumentalism' is the term used for the evaluation of a theory on the basis of whether or not it actually works in making valuable predictions. Hence a theory may be useful, even if we are unable to say whether or not it is right.

If one scientific theory continues to be regarded as 'right' (however provisional it may be), does this imply that alternative theories must be 'wrong' or what? This is a question for the philosophy of science: Can we say that something is 'right' in a world of optional viewpoints?

There are two views on what scientific theories can show – realist and anti-realist – corresponding to whether or not science can describe reality itself, or only our perceptions of reality, and therefore whether scientific claims can ever be definitively right or wrong, or simply a useful way of seeing things, eventually to be replaced.

An anti-realist approach is suggested by two things:

▶ Most theories are underdetermined by available evidence. In other words, such evidence as we have is generally open to more than one interpretation.

▶ However much they seemed correct at the time, all past theories have eventually proved to be inadequate and have therefore been replaced. On that basis, it is likely that our present theories, however convincing they may appear to us now, will eventually be shown to be wrong or at least inadequate.

It can therefore be argued that as all observations are 'theory laden' (everything is interpreted in terms of the theory that I already hold) there can be no straightforward or 'objective' evidence to decide between competing theories. This can lead to a form of anarchy, in which any theory is seen as being as good as any other – a view often associated with Paul Feyerabend (1924–92), who pointed out (in his controversial book *Against Method*, 1975) that theories may be chosen for social, aesthetic or cultural reasons. His argument was that there was no single method for doing science, and that philosophers should look at what science was actually doing and how it was developing, rather than trying to impose a narrow interpretation of the scientific method. But if he was critical of some philosophers, he also demanded of scientists that they should constantly review and evaluate their theories and methods – in other words, that they should do a bit more philosophy!

Remember this: Ockham's Razor

William of Ockham (1285–1349), a logician who commented on Aristotle, is best known for his argument that one should not multiply entities unnecessarily. In other words, given a number of possible explanations, one should incline towards the simplest. This is generally known as *Ockham's Razor*. It is a useful principle for assessing scientific theories.

The social sciences

Humankind is clearly a valid object of study for science. When Darwin published *The Origin of Species*, much of the controversy that followed was generated because his theory of natural selection applied to humankind as well as all other species, and that was seen as particularly threatening to the special place accorded to the human species in most traditional religious and philosophical thinking. In more recent debates, Richard Dawkins (in *The Selfish Gene* and elsewhere) examines the relationship between human behaviour and life at the genetic level, where genes are inherently 'selfish', in that their task is simply to promote survival and to reproduce successfully. It is also possible to show that human behaviour can be examined alongside, and in the same way as that of other species, as Edward Wilson did in his controversial book *Sociobiology*.

There are, however, particular problems when science examines humankind. First of all, there continues to be a widespread view that science is basically determinist. In other words, setting aside the subtleties and developments that we have already examined in this book, it sees science as giving a single, fixed and empirically based explanation of every phenomenon. On the other hand, the experience of being human – the subjective side of what science examines objectively – is of freedom, complexity, mixed motives and so on. In spite of philosophers like Kant, who were quite able to see us as being phenomenally determined (as seen by others) but noumenally free (as experienced in ourselves), many people find it difficult to accept any scientific attempt to 'explain' human life at either a social or individual level.

On the other side of the argument, two disciplines in particular – sociology and psychology – have sometimes had their methodologies and findings challenged by the mainstream physical sciences. We shall therefore look at each of these briefly, to see what special issues they raise for the philosophy of science.

SOCIOLOGY

The scientific method relies on measurable data. Today, we are accustomed to statistical information about humankind, from life expectancy and income to our shopping preferences and voting intentions. However, it was only in the nineteenth century that information began to be gathered and presented in the form of statistics. Before that, philosophers made observations about humankind in general, but were unable to move from those observations to produce scientifically based theories about society.

Most widely known of the early sociologists is Emile Durkheim (1858–1917). He analysed regularities in society and formed theories to explain them. Although each individual was aware of a measure of freedom over his or her actions, the assumption upon which Durkheim worked was that there were social forces at work, as real as physical forces, which influenced behaviour. These forces put pressure on individuals to conform, and the number of individuals influenced would then show up in statistics.

Key idea for life

Statistics inform but may also 'nudge'. If I read that most people of my age are overweight, drink too much, exercise too little and that their health is likely to suffer as a result, I may sense that I am being nudged to change my lifestyle. Alternatively, I may relax and realize that I am behaving just like everyone else. Statistics in themselves do not prescribe a course of action; they simply inform.

On the political side, Karl Marx (1818–83), as a result of researching social and political patterns in societies over history, formulated his theory (dialectical materialism) that social activity is based on people's material needs and the means of producing and distributing them. He saw evidence for a pattern within society, in which classes oppose one another, and thus drive forward a process of social and political change.

Karl Popper (see page 82) questioned whether Marxist theory should be considered to be genuine science, on the grounds that Marx appears to interpret evidence in the light of an overall theory, whereas Popper sees genuine science as always open to the possibility that a theory will be falsified and replaced.

Nevertheless, it is clear that sociology and political science are valid disciplines, operating using methods which are not that far removed from the physical sciences. They are based on the interpretation of data, gathered using the normal checks to obtain objectivity. One major difference between these disciplines and, say, physics is the scope for conducting experiments. Because human beings are involved, it is perfectly valid to collect data about their behaviour, but it is not considered ethical to subject them to intrusive testing that may cause them harm. Hence (in spite of the present interest in reality shows on television) it would not be acceptable to send a bunch of people into an extreme environment to measure who died first and from what!

PSYCHOLOGY

Sigmund Freud (1856–1939) was a hospital doctor with a particular interest in neuro-pathology, who subsequently set himself up as a private practitioner for the treatment of nervous conditions, particularly hysteria. As is well known, he developed the method known as psychoanalysis in which, through dream analysis and free association, patients were encouraged to become aware of those experiences buried in their unconscious which were having a harmful effect on their conscious behaviour. So, for example, examining those who had compulsive washing routines, he sought the origin of the compulsion in buried childhood experience of uncleanness. Psychoanalysis worked on the assumption that, once the origin of a problem was discovered and articulated, it would lose its power, and the patient would be cured.

Psychoanalysis depends on the analytic skills of the practitioner. What the patient says is analysed and given significance, and that analysis is done in the light of the overall theory and approach of the analyst. Notice here the old problem for the philosophy of science – which comes first, the data or the interpreting theory? Popper criticized Freud as much as Marx, on the grounds that their work did not have the scientific discipline that allowed their theories to be open to falsification.

Other branches of psychology are more in line with traditional scientific method. Behaviourism, for example, set up animal experiments, and thus produced data that could be analysed in much the same way as in the physical sciences. However (as we shall see in Chapter 5), there are issues about the validity and scope of behaviourism as a way to understand human behaviour. By being more traditionally scientific in its method, it limited what it could examine. Measuring the ability of a rat in a box to learn how to press a lever in order to get food is hardly likely to explain the sort of compulsive neuroses that interested Freud!

Cognitive science is a major area of research today, and we shall examine it again in Chapter 5. For now we only need to note the basic fact that the study of humankind, whether in sociology, psychology or cognitive science, presents a special set of problems for the application of traditional scientific methods.

What counts as science?

At one time, an activity could be called 'scientific' if it followed the inductive method. On these grounds, the work of Marx could be called scientific, in that he based his theories on accounts of political changes in the societies he studied. Similarly, behavioural psychology can claim to be scientific on the basis of the methods used: observing and recording the responses of people and animals to particular stimuli, for example.

Science is generally defined by method rather than by subject. So, for example, Astronomy is regarded as a science, but Astrology is not. This is because the former is based on observable facts, while the latter is based on a mythological scheme.

So how should we distinguish between science and what Popper called 'pseudo-science'? Distinguishing features of science include the consistent attempt at the disinterested gathering of information and the willingness to accept revisions of one's theories. Popper criticized both Marx and Freud, not because he considered they failed to observe and gather evidence, but because of what he saw as their willingness to interpret new evidence in the light of their theories, rather than to allow that evidence to challenge or modify those theories. But what happens in science if one's conclusions are radically different from those of other scientists? This leads us to ask about the nature of authority within the scientific community.

SCIENCE AND AUTHORITY

With the rise of science in the seventeenth and eighteenth centuries, it was widely believed that the days of superstition and authority were over; everything was to be considered rationally. But has that always been the case with science?

Once a theory, or a method of working, has become established, the scientific world tends to treat it as the norm and to be rather suspicious of any attempt to follow a radically different approach. When Darwin introduced the idea of natural selection, or Einstein the theory of relativity, the radical changes in scientific outlook that they implied were seen by some as a threat to the steady accumulation of knowledge along the previously accepted ways of seeing the world. Although both were accepted, there was a pause for consideration.

Scientists may be considered to be 'heretics' within the world of scientific orthodoxy, if their views are radically different from those of the majority of their peers.

As it is possible that there will be different but equally valid theories to account for phenomena, there will always be an element of debate within scientific circles. But are there limits to the range of views that can be accommodated within the scientific community?

Case study

The chemist Linus Pauling claimed that vitamin C was a panacea that could not only cure colds, but could help resist cancer and prevent heart disease. In spite of the recognition of his work on molecular structures, for which he had received a Nobel Prize, his views on this were generally dismissed by the scientific community, although they became popular with the general public.

New scientific work is presented to the international scientific community by being published, generally in one of the established 'peer reviewed' journals. In order to be accepted for publication, of course, it must be plausible as a piece of work, at least to those who are reviewing it. Once published, the theory may be evaluated by other scientists. The original experiments are repeated elsewhere to see whether the same results can be obtained. Sometimes the results of attempting this are ambiguous; sometimes the attempt to repeat the experiment fails completely, and the validity and reliability of the original results are then called into question.

Case study

In 1989, two chemists, Martin Fleischmann and Stanley Pons, claimed to have achieved a breakthrough in the quest for cold nuclear fusion, offering the possibility of creating unlimited supplies of energy. But nuclear fusion, the process that powers the sun, normally only happens at extreme temperatures generated in particle accelerators, and even then the amount of energy generated by fusion is only a fraction of the amount taken to generate those extreme conditions. If it were found that cold nuclear fusion were possible using seawater, as Fleischmann and Pons suggested, it would revolutionize the production of energy.

This was received with a degree of scepticism, and although their experiments were studied and repeated many times by other scientists, they failed to give any positive confirmation. Is that the end of the story? Not exactly. By the end of 2016, research into the possible use of nuclear fusion to generate energy was being carried out in the USA, Russia, the EU, Japan and elsewhere. True, the methods were far from creating the 'cold' nuclear fusion envisaged by Fleishmann and Pons (because they involved the creation of plasma at extreme temperatures in tokamac reactors) but the research area is considered of extreme importance, as offering a potential for limitless supplies of carbon-free energy. But alongside all this, there continues to be interest in understanding low-energy nuclear reactions – in effect, a legacy of the 'cold fusion' idea. So, if it seems potentially valuable, a line of research, even if dismissed in its present form, may be revived in the future.

Scientists have to earn a living. Some are employed by universities and are therefore, in theory, free to explore their theories without external influence – other than the requirement that they show real advance in research in order to continue to attract funding. On the other hand, the funding for such research often comes from the commercial world, and is not, therefore, necessarily totally disinterested. Many other scientists work within commercial organizations.

Commercial funding looks for new products and ideas for developing those things in which it has a vested interest, and even state funding favours those projects that promise economic benefit. Philosophers like Bacon and Hume insisted that the quest for knowledge should be a disinterested one. Indeed, the fact that a scientist stands to gain a great deal from a particular conclusion to his or her research might indicate that the results should be treated with some caution. We have already seen that there are really no facts that are free of interpretation and this flexibility, coupled with a personal motive, makes the tendency to incline towards the most favourable conclusion a real threat to impartiality. To acknowledge that, however, is not to take a cynical view of science itself, but merely to recognize that science takes place within a social context and a nexus of values that are not provided by science itself.

Overall, whether something counts as genuine science depends on whether its methods and results are in line with other scientific views and also whether it is accepted as science by the rest of the scientific community.

Science and philosophy

What can be said about the world, and what cannot? In *Tractatus* (see page 102), Wittgenstein takes the view that the function of language is one of picturing the world, and the book opens with the bold statement, 'The world is everything that is the case' (*Tractatus* 1), and he equates what can be said with what science can show, 'The totality of true propositions is the whole of natural science' (*Tractatus* 4.11). The book ends, however, with the admission that, when it comes to the mystical (the intuitive sense of the world as a whole), language fails and we must remain silent. It cannot be expressed literally.

Wittgenstein points to other things that cannot be described – the subject self (it sees a world, but is not part of that world) and even death (we do not live to experience death). Wittgenstein is thus setting limits to what can be said and, by implication, limits to science.

His thought might prompt us to ask:

▶ Is not modern cosmology a bit 'mystical'? Does it not seek to find images (including that of the 'big bang') by which to express events so unlike anything experienced on Earth, that literal language is of little use?

▶ Does science not sometimes require imaginative leaps beyond evidence, in the formation of new paradigms, within which detailed work and calculation can subsequently find its place?

▶ What is the place of intuition within the scientific process? Like an eye, which sees everything other than itself, intuition may underpin much of the scientific endeavour without itself featuring directly.

Science offers a very rich and exciting view of the world. Whether you start by considering the idea that matter is a collection of nuclear forces, rather than something solid and tangible, or whether you start with the idea that the universe is expanding outwards from the space–time singularity, creating its own space and time as it does so, modern science seems to contradict our common-sense notions. Yet, in doing so, it performs the valuable function of shaking us out of our ordinary assumptions and reminding us that the world is not as simple as it may at first sight appear. In this, science acts rather like philosophy: challenging our assumptions and examining the basis of what we can say about reality.

Philosophy cannot determine what information is available to science: it cannot provide data. At most, it can examine the use of data and the logical processes by which such information becomes the basis of scientific theories.

Most importantly, philosophy can remind scientists that facts always contain an element of interpretation. Facts are the product of a thinking mind encountering external evidence, and they therefore contain both that evidence and the mental framework by means of which it has been apprehended, and through which it is articulated.

To some scientists, philosophers have a tendency to meddle in matters that are strictly scientific, and there are historical precedents for that view. But science itself, as a method of gaining knowledge, develops and uses philosophy, sifting the relevance of evidence and showing the logic of the conclusions it derives from such evidence. Its arguments should therefore be open to philosophical scrutiny.

4

Language and Communication

In this chapter you will:

- ► *Learn about how different forms of language function*
- ► *Consider how language may be assessed and its claims verified*
- ► *Look at formal logic and the limitations of rational discourse*
- ► *Explore issues with structuralism and the media*

Why?

We all use language, and the more careful and precise our use of it, the greater clarity we have in explaining ourselves and assessing the value and cogency of what others say. Not all language is factual – we may enjoy reading fiction or poetry, may cheer on a team or whisper endearments into a lover's ear. Is that strictly true or false? Should it/could it be justified in terms of facts? What does language actually *do*? 'With this ring I thee wed' is a classic example of language that makes something happen. So does saying it make it true? None of us wants to be called illogical, but language is more than logic and description. When a politician says 'Take back control!', what does that actually mean? Beware of the power of the slogan.

Language is the vehicle through which the ideas and concepts of philosophy are transmitted. It might be tempting therefore to assume that language has a necessary but secondary role, communicating what is already known. But that would be mistaken, for philosophical issues arise *within,* and often *as a result of* our language. A basic question in philosophy is, 'What do we mean by…?' which asks for more than a definition; it seeks to relate the thing we are interested in to the rest of our ideas and language. *The language we use colours the way in which we think and experience the world, so it is unwise to philosophize without being aware of the role played by language.*

We need to be aware of three quite different things:

▶ **Philosophy of language** (looks at what language is, how it works, whether statements are meaningful and how they may be verified)

▶ **Linguistic philosophy** (is a way of doing philosophy through the analysis of problematic statements)

▶ **Logic** (examines the structure of arguments to see whether their conclusions can be shown to follow from their premises)

Language and certainty

A key question for the study of language is **'verification'**. How can you show that a statement is true?

Do you set out bits of evidence that correspond to each of the words used? (An empiricist might encourage you to do that. A reductionist might say that your statement was nonsense unless you could do it!) This assumes that language has a picturing or pointing function.

Is a statement 'true' if its logic is sound? If so, does its truth also depend on some sort of external evidence?

Probably the greatest influence in shaping modern life is science, and its obvious success tempted some philosophers to see the scientific method and scientific language as a paradigm for the way in which all knowledge could be gained and expressed.

At the beginning of the twentieth century, it was assumed that all science is based on observation, with each claim it makes being backed up with reference to data of some sort. The language used by science was therefore justified with reference to external objects; it 'pictured' them. A statement was therefore judged to be true if it corresponded to what has been observed, false if it did not so correspond. But could that test be applied to all language?

LOGICAL POSITIVISM

Ludwig Wittgenstein (1889–1951), an Austrian who did most of his philosophy in Cambridge and studied under Bertrand Russell, was deeply impressed by the work done in mathematics and logic by Gottlob Frege (1848–1925), Russell and A. N. Whitehead, with whom Russell had written *Principia Mathematica*, a major work attempting to establish the logical foundations of mathematics. These thinkers had argued that logic and mathematics were objective, not subjective; that is, they described features of the external world, rather than simply showing ways in which the mind worked.

Wittgenstein suggested that philosophical problems would be solved if the language people used corresponded to the phenomenal world, both in terms of logic and the evidence for what was being said. In the opening statement of his hugely influential book *Tractatus* (1921), he identifies the world with the sum of true propositions: 'The world is everything that is the case', but he has to acknowledge that there are therefore certain things of which one cannot speak. One of these is the subject self: 'The subject does not belong to the world; rather it is a limit of the world.' Another is the mystical sense of the world as a whole. Whatever cannot be shown to correspond to some observable reality cannot be meaningfully spoken about.

His ideas were taken up by the Vienna Circle, a group of philosophers who met in that city during the 1920s and 1930s. The approach they took is generally known as **logical positivism**. Broadly, it claims that:

▶ Analytic propositions tell us nothing about the world. They are true by definition, and therefore tautologies. They include the statements of logic and mathematics.

▶ Synthetic propositions depend on evidence. Therefore, there can be no necessary synthetic propositions.

▶ Metaphysics and theology are literally 'meaningless' – because such statements are neither matters of logic (and therefore true by definition – *a priori*) nor are they provable by empirical evidence.

Moritz Schlick, one of the Vienna Circle, argued that 'the meaning of a statement is its method of verification'. This became known as the 'verification principle'.

Logical positivism was promoted by the British philosopher A. J. Ayer (1910–89) in an important book entitled *Language, Truth and Logic* (1936). In that book, he asks: 'What can philosophy do?' His answer is that it certainly cannot tell us the nature of reality as such – in other words, it cannot provide us with metaphysics. If we want to know about reality, we have to rely upon the evidence of our senses.

He therefore argued that philosophy cannot actually give new information about anything, but has the task of analysis and clarification. It looks at the words people use and analyses them, showing their logical implications. By doing so, philosophy clarifies otherwise muddled thought. Presenting the key features of logical positivism, learned when he joined discussions of the Vienna Circle as a young graduate, Ayer's dismissal of religious and moral language as 'meaningless' was particularly controversial.

Of course, there are other kinds of meaning, but Ayer is concerned with statements that claim to have 'factual meaning'. In other words, if experience is not relevant to the truth or falsity of a statement, then that statement cannot claim to have factual meaning, whatever else it may claim by way of meaning or significance for the person making it.

Ayer distinguished between two forms of the verification principle:

1 A proposition is said to be verifiable and have meaning if and only if its truth may be established in experience. This is the *strong* form of the verification principle, as originally proposed by Moritz Schlick: meaning and verification are identical.

   An example of the strong form:

   'There are three people in the next room.'

   Meaning: If you go into the next room, you will see three people there.

2 A proposition is said to be verifiable if it is possible for experience to render it probable, or if some possible sense experience would be relevant to determining whether it was true or false. This *weaker* version was the one Ayer himself favoured. Clearly, it is not always possible to get factual evidence – about the past, for example, or about events predicted to happen in inaccessible places. Where evidence is simply not available, it was thought important at least to be able to specify what sort of evidence would count for or against the factual truth of such a statement.

An example of the weaker form:

'Within the universe there are other planets supporting life.'

Meaning: If you were able to examine every planet in the universe, you would find others with life on them. Although we have not been able to detect signs of carbon-based life like our own as yet, such a discovery could show that the statement is true. The statement is therefore factually 'meaningful'.

Statements are meaningless if there is nothing that would count for or against them being true. On this basis, much of what passes for religious language, or aesthetics, or morality, would be categorized as 'meaningless', because none of these things can be specified in terms of concrete facts that can be checked by observation. However, just because your statement is meaningful, does not mean that it is factually true. Evidence may be mistaken and is subject to interpretation.

There is a criticism of the verification principle that sounds plausible, but is actually based on a false notion of what it claims to do. It asks: How do we verify the statement: 'The meaning of a statement is its method of verification'? Is it synthetic? If so, what is the evidence for it? What evidence could count against it? Or is it analytic? If so, then the word 'meaning' is logically the same as 'method of verification' and the theory doesn't say anything at all.

But the verification principle itself never claimed to be a *factual* proposition, rather it set out a *policy* for evaluating propositions that claimed to be factual, and that is a very different matter. After all, at a road junction a sign may tell you to turn right, but the sign itself does not turn to the right! *An instruction is not the same thing as a statement of fact.*

The key thing about logical positivism was that it represented a particularly strong form of empiricism and a particularly narrow form of language. The service it rendered philosophy was that, by arguing that a wide range of propositions was 'meaningless', it forced philosophers to think again about the way in which we use language. Whereas the logical positivists had concentrated on a simple 'picturing' view of language, it was soon realized that language can be meaningful in terms of many other functions (for example: expressing feelings, giving commands, stating preferences). In this way, by reacting against the logical positivists, it became widely recognized that a more sophisticated view of the function of language needed to be developed.

That said, the verification principle is a valuable check, to make sure that statements about personal preferences or commands do not parade themselves as though they were straightforward empirical statements of fact.

Few today would want to take on the bold claims of meaning and certainty of the logical positivists or Ayer, because philosophy has in general recognized the far more flexible nature of language, but they came from a period when science and mathematics were generally thought to provide suitable images of clarity and precision, and therefore became models of an approach to which ordinary language was pressed to conform. Towards the end of his life (see the interview extract on page 37), Ayer admitted that his thought had moved on since the time of writing *Language, Truth and Logic*, but that book remains an important touchstone for a particular view of language and approach to philosophy.

Key idea for life

Language is complex: an average line of poetry, a joke, a command, a piece of moral advice or the whispered endearments of lovers can quickly dispel any simple theory of verification. We need to move on from 'Is it true?' to the broader issue of 'What, if anything, does it mean?'

Language and perception

Statements can be true by definition (analytic statements) or with reference to evidence (synthetic statements). For those based on experience, we need to think about how we use general words in order to describe particular things.

Imagine a situation in which there are no general words. How would you describe a tree without the word 'tree', or without the words 'green', 'tall' or 'thick' and so on? Each of these words, unlike a proper name, has a meaning which can be applied to a whole variety of individual things – indeed, learning a language is about learning the whole range of general terms that we can put together in order to describe particular things.

However, do these general terms refer to things that exist, or are they simply 'names'? Does 'goodness' exist, or is it just a name for certain kinds of things of which I approve? We saw this reflected in differences between Plato and Aristotle, and in the realists/nominalists debate.

In looking at logical positivism, we saw a philosophy that was based on the 'picturing' function of language. Statements had meaning only if they reflected evidence (or potential evidence) from the world of the senses. But how far can we trust our perception? And is perception the same thing as sense data?

Case study: It's all a matter of interpretation

There are a number of examples of drawings that can be interpreted in a number of different ways. Here is a simple example:

Do you see the profiles of two people facing one another, or do you see an elegant chalice?

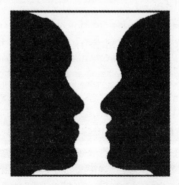

Try switching your perception from one to the other – notice the mental effort involved.

Is there any difference between the one and the other perception – difference, that is, in what is actually being seen?

Such visual games illustrate the ambiguity of all experience. As you make the mental effort to shift from one interpretation of what you see to the other, you are discovering the reality of 'experience as' – that all experience requires an element of interpretation.

Key idea for life

It takes effort to shift one's general view of reality. Hence, most people are content to settle into their habitual ways of seeing things. The greatest enemy of creative thinking is inertia.

Here is the dilemma facing any empirical method of verification for language:

▷ All experience involves 'experiencing as'.

▷ Two people may therefore interpret the same data differently.

▷ How then do you decide between them or verify the truth of what they say?

What we need to recognize at this point is that even descriptive language is seldom simple or transparent. Add intuition, emotion, existential angst and the general confusions of human life, and the resulting language is very complex indeed.

Linguistic philosophy

While the logical positivists were analysing statements in terms of their verification through sense experience, other philosophers – notably, G. E. Moore (1873–1958) and J. L. Austin (1911–60) – were investigating the ordinary use of words and Wittgenstein was changing his mind.

In his later work (published after his death as *Philosophical Investigations*), Wittgenstein developed a broader view of how language worked, accepting that it could take on different functions, of which the description of phenomena was only one. He recognized that the expression of values and emotions, the giving of orders and making of requests were all valid uses of language. His keynote idea was that language was a 'form of life' and that, to understand it, it had to be observed in use.

He described the different uses of language as 'language games'. Just as a game, such as chess, can only be appreciated once the rules for moving the various pieces are understood, so language can only be understood within its context; words have meaning that is related to their function in the 'game'. This is not to trivialize language (it is not a 'game' in that sense), but to recognize that language is a tool for doing something – a tool that is based on rules that are understood by those who use it for a particular purpose.

Case study (taken from Wittgenstein)

When a builder calls to his assistant 'bricks' or 'beams', he is not *describing* those things, but is calling for the assistant to bring him more of them. The assistant understands this and obeys; the words serve their purpose within the 'language game' associated with building a house.

By the 1950s the shift (sometimes referred to as the 'linguistic turn') in the function of philosophy with regard to language was complete. The change was influenced by Wittgenstein's later philosophy and by Austin's 'ordinary language' philosophy, but also due to the impact of a single essay, published in 1951 by a major thinker in the analytic tradition, Willard Van Orman Quine (1908–2000), entitled 'The Two Dogmas of Empiricism'. In it, he argued that statements could not simply be reduced to tautologies or bits of factual information, but that their meaning could only be fully understood in a wider, more holistic, context.

Between them, Wittgenstein, Austin and Quine installed language at the heart of the philosophical quest in the English-speaking world. Philosophy was to be concerned exclusively with language and the clarification of concepts, and Austin's 'ordinary language' approach explored the internal logic and implications of statements and dissected the meaning of words in amazing detail.

This approach, known as 'linguistic philosophy', worked on the assumption that philosophical problems arose because of the ambiguities and confusions of normal speech. Once that speech could be analysed and its confusions exposed, new insights and clarity would emerge and its problems would be solved (or rather dissolved). So philosophy was given a role rather like that of an indigestion tablet: something necessary in order to purify the system and enable comfort and efficiency to return. *Philosophy, according to that view, would help every other subject by clearing away linguistic confusions.*

Linguistic philosophy had a significant influence on the philosophy of mind (in asking what we mean when we use words like 'mind' or 'person') and ethics (seeing moral statements as recommending a course of action, for example). It is *a way of doing philosophy*, and it is *not* the same as the philosophy of language, which asks questions about how language develops, what it does, how it relates to the things it describes or brings about, and how it is learned.

Key idea for life

As a student, I found linguistic philosophy clever but frustrating. It seemed all to do with the subtleties of meaning and nothing to do with life. Over the last 50 years that has largely changed, with philosophy engaging directly with substantive issues in ethics, politics and personal identity, rather than simply analysing the language used. However, clarity of language is a necessary feature of clarity of thought, so it should not be neglected.

Formal logic

Logic is the branch of philosophy that examines the process of reasoning. When you start with a set of premises and reach a conclusion from them, the process of doing so is called *deductive logic*. An argument is *valid* if it is impossible for the conclusions to be false if the premises are true. An argument can be valid even if the premises are false (and therefore the conclusion is false); just because you are mistaken, it does not mean that your reasoning is not logical. An argument where the premises are true and the logic is valid is *sound*.

Deductive logic differs from the 'inductive' method of reasoning used by science. The inductive method starts with evidence and concludes that (on the balance of probability) this or that is to be expected in the future. A conclusion reached by that method is always open to be revised if there is new evidence. Deductive logic is not about evidence; it is the formal and abstract way of looking at the structure of an argument.

Logic has a long history. In Plato's dialogues, we find Socrates debating with various people. He invites them to put forward propositions and then analyses their implications and the arguments they have used. His argument often takes the form of, 'If B follows from A, and B is clearly wrong, then A must also have been wrong.'

But the main influence on logic for 2,000 years was Aristotle. He set down the basic features of deductive logic, in particular the **syllogism**, in which major and minor premises lead to a conclusion.

The most quoted piece of logic ever, has to be the syllogism:

> All men are mortal.
> Socrates is a man.
> Therefore Socrates is mortal.

This can be expressed as:

All As are B.

C is an A.

Therefore C is B.

From the basic syllogism, we can go on to explore the forms of *inference* – in other words, what can validly follow from what.

Logic is often able to highlight common errors. One of these is known as the *argumentum ad ignorantiam*, which is to argue for something on the grounds that there is no evidence *against* it, whereas to establish that something is the case, one needs to show evidence *for* it. Another is an argument *ad hominem*, where you try to undermine an argument by attacking the character or trustworthiness of the person making it.

Key idea for life

There may be no evidence that someone did not commit a particular crime, but that cannot be offered as proof that he or she did commit it. If this basic feature of logic were overlooked, the justice system would be in deep trouble. Notice that an *argumentum ad ignorantiam* may sometimes be slipped into a popular discussion of the paranormal: there is no evidence to show that extra-terrestrials were not the cause of some phenomenon, therefore, in the absence of any other explanation, we can take it that they were!

Logic can become very complex, with parts of an argument depending on others: 'if not this, then that, but if that then something else ...'. Clearly, it would be cumbersome to write out all the elements of each argument in order to examine the logic involved.

To overcome this problem, formal logic uses an artificial form of language. This language uses sets of letters, A, B, C and so on to stand for the various component premises and conclusions, and also a set of signs to act as connectives. These signs stand for such logical steps as 'and', 'or', 'it is not the case that', 'if ... then' and 'if and only if'.

This use of artificial language is particularly associated with the German philosopher and mathematician Gottlob Frege (1848–1925).

Case study

The connective 'if ... then' is shown by an arrow pointing to the right. The conclusion (therefore) is shown as a semi-colon.

Take this argument:

I have missed the train. If I miss the train I arrive late at work. Therefore I shall arrive late at work.

We can formalize this by using the letter 'A' for 'I have missed the train' and 'B' for 'I will arrive late at work'. Rewritten, the argument becomes:

A (A → B); B

An important feature of logic is that it breaks down each sentence into its component parts and makes clear the relationship between them. So formal logic helps to clarify exactly what is and what is not valid. Arguments set out in this way become very complex indeed, and there are a large number of unfamiliar signs used for the various connectives. If you pick up a copy of Russell and Whitehead's famous *Principia Mathematica* or browse through *The Journal of Symbolic Logic*, you will see page after page of what looks like advanced mathematics or complex scientific formulae. For the uninitiated, it is extremely difficult to follow!

MATHEMATICS

Much work on logic has been done by mathematicians, and that is not surprising because mathematics, like logic, works on premises and rules. Two philosophers already mentioned, Frege and Russell, independently came to the conclusion that the rules of mathematics could be shown to be elementary logic, and that it should therefore be possible to *prove* the basis of mathematics. In their work, developed by Russell in *Principia Mathematica* (published in three parts, 1910–13), mathematics becomes an extension of logic, and in theory (although not in practice, because it would take far too long to set down) all mathematical arguments could be derived from and expressed in logical form.

A classic example of an analytic statement is $2 + 2 = 4$. One does not have to check numerous examples to come to the conclusion that their sum will always be 4 and never 5. This is true in general of mathematics; it is a matter of logical deduction and certainty. But does that mean that mathematics is true only in the mind? Is it not the case that two things, added to another two things in the external world, will always make four? If this is so, then things in the 'real' world can be understood through mathematics and logic; *it has to do with actual relationships, not simply with mental operations.*

Perhaps, like so many other issues, this can be traced back to Plato. He held that numbers, or geometrical shapes such as triangles or squares, were all perfect; you don't get 'almost square' or a 'nearly 2' in mathematics. However, in the real world, nothing is quite that perfect. Plato therefore held that mathematics is about objects known through the mind rather than the senses, objects which (like his 'Forms') belong to a world different from the one we experience. Hence, mathematics could be known *a priori*, with a certainty impossible with things in this world.

Predictably, Aristotle countered this with the claim that mathematical concepts are abstractions and generalizations, based on things experienced. The debate between the Platonic and Aristotelian views has been very influential in the history of mathematics, as in so many other areas of philosophy.

The philosophy of mathematics is a major area of study, beyond the scope of this book. All we need to note here is the close relationship between mathematics and logic. Debate continues into whether arithmetic can validly be reduced to 'set theory' and whether mathematics as a whole can fully be reduced to logic and, if so, what value there is in making such a reduction.

Structuralism and the media

Logic and mathematics represent the most precise and certain form of thought and language, but meaning is not always clear-cut. Sometimes the meaning of a book or an article depends as much on the reader as the author. When I read something, my understanding of it is linked to how I have understood those words when I've previously read or spoken them, and the book itself has a context – I am reading it for a purpose, and within a culture. When I read a text, I'm not simply plugging myself into the brain of the author, but taking up this piece of writing and understanding it on its own terms. In a real sense, all that the author has done is just reorganize and re-present ideas that are already in circulation. If that were not so, I couldn't understand the text anyway. This led Roland Barthes (1915–80) to speak of the 'death of the author'.

This approach, called **structuralism,** suggests that you can only understand something once you relate it to the wider structures within which it operates. Things are defined primarily in terms of their relationships with others. So, for example:

▶ To understand a word, consider its meaning in terms of other words related to it and the language as a whole.

▶ To understand a political statement, look at the politician, how he or she is to stay in power, what the media expect, what effect he or she needs to make with this statement.

▶ A 'soundbite' or a newspaper headline can only really be understood in terms of the significance of the paper or the broadcast within which it is set.

Existentialism (see page 51), which was hugely popular after the Second World War, focused on the individual, creative self, especially in its freedom and choices in its engagement with the world. Structuralism (and particularly its later development, known as post-structuralism) was a reaction against the importance given to that 'self' – structures and relationships now take priority.

Key idea for life

There's a kind of arrogance about the existentialist, shaping himself or herself and using the world as an opportunity within which to do it. By contrast, a structuralist recognizes that to be a human, and to communicate, requires the humility of recognizing that most of what we do is provided from outside ourselves. We are a very small part of a large linguistic and intellectual whole, and we can only find our meaning within it.

Jacques Lacan (1900–80) argued that we do not first become fully formed individuals and then start to express our individuality through language, but we become individuals (we develop our personalities, if you like) through the use of language. And that language, with its ideas and its grammar, predates us. We don't make it up as we go along; we inherit it.

Lacan was primarily a psychoanalyst, and it is interesting to reflect that in psychoanalysis it is through a free flow of ideas that thoughts and feelings buried in the unconscious may appear. The flow of language is not controlled by the ego. Indeed, it is in order to heal and change the ego that the analysis is taking place. The subject emerges through language. For Lacan, it would seem that, if there were no speech, there would be no subject. He goes further, to claim that, without language, there would be no metaphysical entities at all. God, for example, is a function of the 'Other' in language, not something that exists outside language.

Two features of a structuralist/post-structuralist approach:

1 There is no transcendent self that has some pure idea that it wants to convey, and that is later, imperfectly translated into a medium of communication – spoken, written or visual. Rather, the meaning is just exactly what is spoken or written. It is to be understood in terms of the structures of communication, not with reference to some outside author. A story does not *have* a meaning; a story *is* its meaning.

2 To understand a piece of writing, one should carry out a process of **deconstruction**, laying bare the presuppositions of the text, and comparing what an author claims to be saying with the actual form and structure of language used.

Deconstruction has been developed particularly by Jacques Derrida (1930–2004) as the attempt to deal with the end of metaphysics. For Derrida, there is no external or fixed meaning to a text, nor is there a subject that exists *prior* to language and prior to particular experiences. *You cannot get outside or beyond the structure.*

Derrida is concerned with 'actuality', with being in touch with present events. Yet the information we receive through the media is never neutral, but is the product of the structures by which the media operate. This has practical consequences:

Hegel was right to tell the philosophers of his time to read the newspapers. Today the same duty requires us to find out how news is made, and by whom: the daily papers, the weeklies, and the TV news as well. We need to insist on looking at them from the other end: that of the press agencies as well as that of the tele-prompter. And we should never forget what this entails: whenever a journalist or a politician appears to be speaking to us directly, in our homes, and looking us straight in the eye, he or she is actually reading, from a screen, at the dictation of a 'prompter', and reading a text which was produced elsewhere, on a different occasion, possibly by other people, or by a whole network of nameless writers and editors.

(From 'The deconstruction of actuality', an interview with Derrida published in *Radical Philosophy*, Autumn 1994)

Derrida warns against 'neo-idealism': the idea that nothing really happens, that all is an illusion just because it is set within a structure by the media. Rather, he wants to emphasize that deconstruction is about *getting down to an event*, to a 'singularity', to what is irreducible and particular in an individual happening.

News comes to us through the media; it is the product of a process by which information is sorted and expressed in particular ways, often for a particular purpose. Real events are unique; reports of them put them into categories and start to colour our interpretation of them.

Key idea for life

Structuralism makes explicit what any critical reader or viewer knows – that we need to see through what is said and ask *why* it is said and *in whose interest* it is published or broadcast. Communication cannot be innocent of the complex web of political, financial, cultural and personal influences within which it is set.

But where does this all end? If we move away from a simple descriptive meaning and allow concepts to be understood as part of a language game, and then we move away from the creative author and see every communication as part of an overall structure of thought, where next for language?

One destination along such a trajectory is to be found in the work of Michel Foucault (1926–84), a controversial and radical French intellectual. In the course of his studies of insanity, prisons, punishment and sexuality, he carried out what he called an '*archaeology*' of knowledge. He dug down, layer by layer, through the historical and cultural changes in attitudes to, for example, sexuality – showing how language is always related to a context and to the power relations that influence thought. He also exposed the '*genealogy*' by which meaning changed and developed over time. His view – broadly described as post-structuralist, although he himself rejected almost every attempt to categorize it – is one that thrives on uncertainty and relativism, and in some ways is the very opposite of what traditional philosophy has tried to achieve. He explores his subjects with an almost mischievous freedom, deliberately flouting convention.

Remember this: Living dangerously!

Foucault was a hugely impressive intellectual and political activist, whose personal and sexual life veered between the almost monastic and the wildly unconventional. Deliberately taking risks, against the advice of his friends, he has the sad distinction of being the first philosopher to have died of AIDS. Yet that does not in any way detract from the value of his philosophy. He accepted Nietzsche's advice to 'live dangerously'. Never assume that philosophy requires a life of narrow introversion.

THE IMPACT OF MEDIA ON PHILOSOPHY

Plato complained about the Sophists, who used rhetoric in order to win arguments for their own advantage, rather than in the dispassionate search for truth. That complaint is equally valid today. We admire those who speak well and persuasively, but are aware that the quality of their rhetoric may influence our willingness to be persuaded by what they say. It is all too easy for style and presentation to make palatable content that otherwise would have been rejected.

The variety of media today enables philosophical ideas to be communicated globally at a speed unimaginable only a couple of generations ago. Philosophers tweet, blog and podcast; they present their latest thinking on their own websites and appear as guest contributors on others. Debates happen spontaneously as different people respond on social media to the same event or publication. Philosophers appear on radio and television, with the expectation that they will be able to give a reasoned view on whatever topic is being discussed.

This brings with it at least one advantage and one danger:

▶ The advantage is that the relevance of a clearly thought through philosophical position is immediately obvious. Philosophers – whether professional or amateur – can sometimes cut through emotional, linguistic and rhetorical confusions to provide clarity. By this means, philosophy can contribute to current debate in an unprecedented way.

▶ The danger is that, in order to provide the expected soundbite or instant comment, a thinker may have to leave aside the more subtle nuances of his or her argument, an easily understood but potentially superficial perspective on a complex issue. That may be inevitable in the circumstances, but other media may then take that simplified argument and further reduce it in order to achieve a popular headline, distorting it in the process.

That said, there have been many successful attempts in recent years to present philosophy in a media-friendly way – not least the hugely popular *Philosophy Bites* series of podcasts, by Nigel Warburton and Noel Edmunds, with more than 300 interviews, in which professional philosophers explain their ideas in an immediately accessible language and format, and many millions of downloads worldwide. There are many other examples of philosophy in the media, going back to two remarkable series *Men of Ideas* (1978) and *The Great Philosophers* (1987) broadcast on British television, in which leading philosophers were interviewed by Brian Magee.

There are also online courses that reach an audience of thousands. One remarkable example is Michael Sandel's Harvard lecture series on justice, where, having watched the videos, students can then 'visit the community' to discuss the course and share their ideas.

Of course, it is never possible, within the constraints imposed by such media, to go into the detailed analysis and subtlety of serious academic philosophy, but that's not the point. The clarity with which the best philosophy is presented is immediately accessible, and many students who pick up Plato's dialogues, or dip into Hume or even Nietzsche, are surprised at just how accessible, challenging and direct their original texts can be.

Key idea for life

Philosophy is too important to be restricted to the academic department. Its appearance in the media is healthy, both for public debate, and to prevent philosophers from becoming too narrow or obscure in the presentation of their ideas. To explain something accurately and clearly, within the time constraints of modern media, is a useful challenge.

The variety of media within which ideas are conveyed may also change the style of philosophy, even when arguments remain densely packed. One of the most remarkable examples of this is the Slovenian philosopher Slavoj Zizek, the Bower Bird of the philosophical world. In a display of sheer intellectual brilliance that would have driven philosophers of the old analytic tradition to distraction, he plucks ideas and images from films, fiction, current affairs, psychology, sociology, economics, and weaves together a sort-of narrative. The problem with reading (or listening to) Zizek is that he seldom takes you through a straightforward argument. Digression follows digression as he builds up a wall of interlocking ideas. He is particularly skilled at using ideas from one discipline to apply to another. So, for example, when he comes to look at what he regards as the terminal state of capitalism (in *Living in the End Times*, 2010), he uses a five-step process of grief developed in helping those who have been bereaved. The loss of a loved one offers the pattern for understanding the loss of a familiar economic system.

Zizek's style reflects the speed and fragmented nature of our experience of the media, especially when we include social media. We are bombarded with assertions, claims, adverts, cultural presentations, personal entreaties and notes on every subject under the sun – and somehow we need to pick our way through them, assessing, discarding, using, adopting or simply passing them along to our numerous contacts.

Key idea for life

The key thing is that through broadcasting, social media and the web, philosophy is making a remarkable bid for popular attention. Brevity and clarity are valuable in philosophical argument, but do they inevitably trivialize? Perhaps, to some professional philosophers that may be the case. But it is no different from popular explanations of science, or history, or psychology in the same media. However, the benefit of allowing the skills of philosophy to be displayed within public debate is immense.

In considering language and the value of considered argument, we need to be aware of the alternative – the culture of 'fake news', 'post-truth' and bullshit. It is argued that the difference between someone who is lying and someone who is bullshitting is that the latter has no interest in whether his or her statements are true or false – they are not presented in order to convey information, but to get a result. In a 'post-truth' situation, things are said in order to engage the hearer's emotions and thereby promote a particular cause. Whether what is said is true or false is a secondary matter. As with fake news, it is often a matter of what the person presenting it would *like to be* the case, rather than what *is* the case.

That is, and will always be, the very opposite of the skills and traditions of philosophy, in assessing evidence and presenting cogent arguments, reclaiming language for personal integrity and public benefit.

5

Minds, Bodies and Brains

In this chapter you will:

▶ *Examine theories about how minds relate to bodies*

▶ *Consider the impact of neuroscience and artificial intelligence on the way we think about ourselves*

▶ *Reflect on how we get to know one another and what it means to be a person*

Why?

Are you a non-physical mind inhabiting a physical body, or simply a product of neural processes going on in your brain? If so, are you free, or directed by the physics of what is happening inside your skull? Do you control your brain, or are you entirely at its mercy? Does it even make sense to ask that sort of question? Who are 'you' anyway? Are we animated bodies, or is there something about a human being that is beyond the physical? If so, might we be able – at least in theory – to survive death? The philosophy of mind has, over the past few decades, proved a fascinating area of study, and one that links directly with advances in neuroscience, challenging many of the assumptions we have about ourselves.

As you read this book, your eyes are scanning from left to right, your fingers turn the pages, your brain is consuming energy, taking oxygen from its blood supply, and tiny electrical impulses are passing between brain cells. All that is part of the physical world, and can be detected scientifically. How does all that relate to the process of reading, thinking, learning and remembering? And how do both relate to personal identity?

▶ Where in all this is the real 'me'?

▶ Am I to be identified with my physical body?

▶ Am I my mind?

▶ Could I exist outside my body?

▶ If so, could I continue to exist after the death of my body?

▶ Is my mind the same thing as my brain?

▶ If not, then where is my mind?

▶ Can I ever really know other people's minds, or do I just look, listen and guess what they're thinking?

▶ Could a perfect neuroscience explain everything there is to know about me? If so, could a computer replicate me?

These are just some of the questions that are explored within the philosophy of mind. Its issues relate to biology, psychology, sociology, computer science, and all aspects of human thought, memory, communication and personal identity.

It is a huge subject and one that, at the moment, is arguably the most productive and interesting in philosophy. In this chapter, we can do no more than touch on some of the major issues.

Ancient minds: Plato and Aristotle

We have already looked at Plato's idea of the 'Forms' – the eternal realities by which we are able to understand and categorize the particular things that we encounter. He argued that, as they are eternal and cannot be known through the senses, we must have had knowledge of them prior to birth, and hence that there is an eternal element to the self. But, if so, how is it related to the physical body?

It is possible to trace a development in Plato's thinking on this through the various dialogues, and it is clear that he wanted to take into account both knowledge of the eternal realities and also the fact that individuals are shaped by the environment into which they are born – so the self cannot be entirely separate from the body.

In *The Republic*, Plato describes the self by way of analogy with a city. Just as a city has workers who produce its goods and services, the military who organize and defend it, and an elite of philosopher-guardians who rule it, so the self has three parts: the physical body with its appetites, the spirited element which animates and drives it, and the thinking mind that rules it. For Plato, the ideal is to have the appetites held in check by the active faculties, which are in turn guided by reason. In other words, he sees the ideal human life as integrating its three distinct elements in a hierarchy.

Key idea for life

The overall impression gained from Plato, particularly illustrated by his account of the calm way in which Socrates faced his death, is that the soul is eternal but trapped for a time within this physical body. Its home is elsewhere – and that idea was later to influence the Christian idea of the soul and its relationship to the body.

Aristotle's approach was predictably different. He rejected Plato's idea of the immortal self, but he was equally critical of the idea that the self was some kind of material substance. His great work on this is *On the Soul* (*De Anima*). Aristotle argues that everything has both physical substance and form (or essence). The form of something is what makes it what it is. The example he gives is of wax that is given a particular shape by a mould or stamp. How does the shape relate to the wax? There is no shape without wax. But, at the same time, the shape is not the same thing as the physical wax that forms it. In the same way, Aristotle sees the self (or soul) as the *form or essence of the physical body*. It is not something that is separable from the body (you don't have a shape if you don't have any wax), but it is not the same thing as the body. To use another of Aristotle's analogies, an eye is not the same thing as 'seeing', but you cannot see without an eye, and if the eye cannot 'see', then it is not an eye – for the essence of an eye is 'seeing'.

Naturally, both Plato and Aristotle have far more to say about the nature of the self, but this contrast between the two of them sets the agenda for much later debate about the relationship between the self and the physical body. However, their views have been overlaid by that of another philosopher to whom we must now turn – Descartes.

'I think, therefore I am'

In looking at the theory of knowledge, we found that Descartes – using the method of systematic doubt in his quest for certainty – could doubt everything except his own existence as a thinking being. Hence his conclusion: 'I think, therefore I am.' This provided him with a starting point from which to build up knowledge. But it also created an absolute distinction between the physical body (which is extended in time and space and which can be known to the senses), and the mind (which is not extended, and which has one function – to think).

Descartes therefore established what we now refer to as 'substance dualism', and for the next 300 years, under various forms, it was the dominant theory of how minds and bodies related to one another. Much of what has happened in the philosophy of mind over the last century has been, in one way or another, a critical response to Descartes.

Another thinker who was to influence subsequent debate was Kant (see above page 35). As we saw in the first chapter, he made an absolute distinction between things as they are in themselves and things as we perceive them to be. So how did he perceive the mind to be? He had what today would be called a 'functionalist' view; the mind is a set of functions or abilities that we possess. If you want to know a person's mind, observe their behaviour, but if you want to know your own, you need only introspect to become directly aware of yourself as a subject.

We know, by introspection, that we have desires, emotions, thoughts and so on and we can express those things through our speech and our actions. That is the given, the starting point. When we look at phenomena, however – our experience of the world, including other people – we have no such direct knowledge. We infer their minds; we do not see them.

In the next section we shall examine the general question of the relationship between mind and body, an issue with which the philosophy of mind has been preoccupied ever since. The agenda was set by Descartes' absolute mind/body dualism, and Kant's distinction between things we know by introspection (our own minds) and those we know by observation and inference (the minds of others).

The relationship between mind and body

Philosophy has explored a whole range of possible relationships between mind and body. At one extreme there is the view that what we call 'mind' is simply a way of describing the physical body and its activities (**materialism** and **behaviourism**); at the other, is the idea that everything is fundamentally mental (idealism). Between these is the view that both bodies and minds are distinct but related realities (**substance dualism**). There is also the theory that mind and body are two ways of describing the same thing (**property dualism**) or that the self is a '**bundle**' of different, and ever-changing realities.

MATERIALISM

A materialist attempts to explain everything in terms of physical objects, and tends to deny the reality of anything that cannot be reduced to them. So, for a materialist, the mind or 'self' is nothing more than a way of describing physical bodies and their activity. We may experience something as a thought or an emotion, but in fact it is *nothing but* the electrical impulses in the brain, or chemical or other reactions in the rest of the body.

This 'nothing but' is an example of the philosophical approach known as 'reductionism' (see page 15), the view that the reality of each thing lies in its simplest component parts, rather than the whole phenomenon of which they are parts. The 'nothing but' distinguishes the strictest form of materialism – termed 'eliminative materialism' – from other theories. Nobody would deny that a person's mind is related to a neural activity in their brain, in the same way that a symphony is related to air movements. The essential question is whether or not it is possible to express what a 'something more' might be, if a strictly materialist position seems inadequate.

Modern eliminative materialists tend to dismiss what they call 'folk psychology' – the ordinary ways of ascribing thoughts, emotions, wishes and so on to people. For the strict materialist, these things simply do not exist. Sensations are simply brain processes. This position has been taken by many influential philosophers, including Quine, Rorty, and Paul and Patricia Churchland, aided by the development over the last 30 years or so of *Neurophilosophy* – also the title of a book by Patricia Churchland.

For materialists, the only stuff in the universe is material. What you experience as a thought, or a sensation, is nothing more than a particular brain-state.

Key idea for life

A coffee perks you up; when really tired you can't think straight.

Brain damage, through trauma or degenerative disease, changes and may finally take from us the person we recognize physically.

Do these examples confirm the materialist view?

BEHAVIOURISM

You see people waving to you and smiling. Does this indicate that they are friendly? That they know you? That they have minds as well as bodies? That they have freely chosen to act in that way? That they have previously recognized you, had friendly thoughts towards you, and therefore decided to wave?

Let us analyse what is actually happening as you look at one of those people:

▶ You see an arm moving.

▶ Within that arm, muscles are contracting.

▶ The contraction is caused by chemical changes, brought about by electrical impulses from the brain.

▶ The electrical activity in the brain has caused the impulses.

▶ That activity depends on consuming energy and having an adequate oxygen supply via the blood.

▶ Nutrition and oxygen are taken in from the environment.

▶ And so on, and so on …

The act of waving is explained in terms of a material chain of cause and effect. That chain is, for practical purposes, infinite – it depends upon the whole way in which the universe is constructed. There is no point in that chain for some 'mind' to have its say. The world, as we experience it through the senses, appears to be a closed system, within which everything is totally determined by physical causes and conditions.

Behaviourism is the term used for the theory that mental operations are simply descriptions of physical activities. Crying out and rubbing a part of the body *is* what pain is about. Shouting and waving a fist *is* what anger is about. *All mental states are reduced by the behaviourist to things that can be observed and measured.*

Behaviourism developed out of the desire for a scientific approach to the mind that could involve measurement and experiment. Rats in cages learned to press a lever to get food, and dogs to salivate at the bell rung before its arrival – behaviourism is particularly associated with the works of Pavlov (in the then Soviet Union), Watson and Skinner (in the USA).

Key idea for life

Behind behaviourism lay the thought that human minds too could be controlled by adjusting their environment and by conditioning – with huge social and political implications.

The problem is that we experience a difference between a sensation or thought and the physical movement or the words that result from it. I can think before I speak, or before I write, but for a behaviourist there is nothing other than the words or the writing. To know a feeling, for a behaviourist, one must observe behaviour. This might be a plausible theory if one is observing rodents in a cage, but becomes more problematic when human beings are concerned. One can, for example, observe a brilliant performance by an actor – and one knows it to be a brilliant performance because it gives an illusion of (but is clearly not the same as) the expression of genuine emotions and views. The actor does not suffer; a performance is not (in this sense) painful.

IDEALISM

George Berkeley's idealist theory of knowledge has already been outlined (see page 31). He considered the world to be exactly what we perceive – the colours, smells, tastes, tangible shapes and so on – not some other physical entity, forever unknown to us, that gives rise to them.

But that does not necessarily require us to take the next step, namely to claim that all reality is somehow 'in the mind' and the physical world an illusion – although that is what idealism is generally taken to imply. We can therefore distinguish between two rather different forms of idealism. One is *epistemological*; in other words, it says that we cannot know anything *other than the experiences we have of it*. The world we encounter is one put together by our minds and sense organs (e.g. you would not see a table, if it were simply the atoms of which is it composed – its being 'a table' depends on your senses of sight and touch). The other, more extreme form, is *ontological* or *metaphysical* idealism, which takes that further step of claiming that all reality is mental.

So, for example, Kant (see page 35) was prepared to accept the first (*epistemological*) sense of idealism, but not the second. For him, the world of noumena (things in themselves) was unknowable, but it was nonetheless real, not a fantasy created by the phenomena of our experience (things as we perceive them to be).

One criticism of the idealist approach might be that, although we may not be certain of the existence of matter, for all practical purposes *we have to assume it*. However much our knowledge of other people is the result of our interpretation of the sense impressions we receive, we are forced by common sense to infer that there really *are* people, out there in the physical world, with minds and bodies like our own. Without that assumption, ordinary life would be impossible.

Although the arguments about the relationship of minds, perceptions and the objects of perception at that time are quite complex, one thing is clear: for Berkeley, the mind is that which does the perceiving. What remains in doubt for him, and why he appears to take the step towards ontological idealism is that he can't bring himself to say that physical bodies exist other than by our perception of them.

Understandably, idealism has not been a popular approach to the issue of how mind and body are related.

DUALISM

If neither the materialist nor the idealist position convinces you by its account for the relationship between mind and body, the answer may be sought in some form of dualism: that mind and body are distinct and very different things. Each is seen as part of the self, part of what it means to be a person, but the question then becomes, 'How do these two things interact?'

This question has a long history. Plato, in *Phaedo*, argued for the immortality of the soul on two grounds:

1 That the body was composite and therefore perishable, whereas the mind was simple and therefore imperishable.

2 That the mind had knowledge of the universals – the eternal Forms (such as 'goodness' or 'beauty') – but its experience during this life is of individual events and objects. Hence Plato argued that the soul itself must be immortal, having existed in the realm of the Forms before birth, and thus also able to survive the death of the body.

Few people today would wish to take up these arguments in the form that Plato presented them. However, they persist in two widely accepted features of the mind/body question:

1 That the mind is not within space/time and not material – and thus that it should not be identified with its material base in the brain.

2 That the mind functions through communication – it is not limited to the operations of a single particular body, that is, the mind is related to a network of transpersonal communication.

Key idea for life

Where does our conversation take place? Within my mouth? Within yours? Somewhere in the space between us? Or is a conversation not in physical space at all? A telephone conversation is clearly in two places at once. Where is the internet? Where is your mind? Is it elsewhere?

If you have tooth decay (a bodily phenomenon) it will lead
to pain (a mental experience): the body is affecting the mind.
Equally, if you are suddenly afraid, you may find yourself
breaking out in a cold sweat: the mind is affecting the body.
Having argued for a radical distinction between the world of
matter, known to the senses, and the mental world, known (at
least in one's own case) directly, Descartes needed to find some
point of interaction, for otherwise there would be no way in
which a mental decision to do something could influence that
otherwise closed system of cause and effect in the mechanical
world. He mistakenly located it in the pineal gland, a small
area between the hemispheres of the brain.

If mind and matter are so different, how exactly can they
influence one another? Following Descartes, there were some
curious theories to account for this, including:

- **Occasionalism**: the idea that the two systems (physical and
  mental) have no direct causal connection, but that – as
  suggested by the philosopher Malebranche – whenever he
  wanted to move his arm, it was actually moved by God.

- **Pre-established harmony**: the physical and mental realms
  are separate and independent but running in harmony.
  This view was put forward by Geulincx, a Flemish follower
  of Descartes. It is also found in Leibniz (see above page 27)
  for whom the monads of which we are comprised
  work together to produce intelligent activity through a
  pre-established harmony.

'Pre-established harmony' may seem a bizarre theory, but
for Leibniz it served a very specific purpose, and one that
has important implications for both metaphysics and the
philosophy of religion. He was concerned to preserve the idea
of **teleology** (i.e. that the world is organized in a purposeful
way) in the face of the mechanistic science and philosophy of
his day. If everything is locked into a series of causes and totally
determined by them, what room is left for a sense of purpose
or for God? Leibniz's answer is that the individual monads,
of which everything is comprised, do not actually affect one

another. Rather, God has established a harmony by which they can work together.

Then there is **epiphenomenalism**. This is the closest that a dualistic view comes to materialism. The essential thing here is that the mind does not influence the body, but is simply a product of the complexity of the body's systems. The various things that I think, imagine or picture in my mind are *epiphenomena*.

Remember this: Life-like robots

Imagine a humanoid robot. A simple version could be the source of amusement, as it attempts to mimic human behaviour. However, as the memory capacity of its computer is increased, the process of decision-making in the program is so complex that an observer is no longer able to anticipate what the robot will select to do, and the robot gradually starts to take on a definite personality or character of its own. In this case the character that starts to emerge is seen to be a product of the computer's memory, and hence it would be an *epiphenomenon*.

All of these are forms of *substance dualism* – that there are two different realities, mind and body.

Key idea for life: Animals and minds

It may be tempting, especially for a dualist, to assume that animals lack reason and therefore have no minds. This was the view taken by Descartes, who saw animals as nothing more than automata. They may appear to show emotions, for example, but this is simply the result of genetic programming. It is sometimes claimed that humans are utterly different from animals in this respect. This view, of course, allows us to treat animals very differently, not least by breeding and killing them for food. But is this difference a convenient myth?

Charles Darwin argued that:

> 'If no organic being except man had possessed any mental power, or if his powers had been of a wholly different nature from those of the lower animals, then we should never have been able to convince

ourselves that our high faculties had been gradually developed. But it can be shewn that there is no fundamental difference of this kind.'

(*The Descent of Man*, 1871, p. 35)

If, when we observe animals, we claim to see no evidence of thought or emotion, we need to reflect on the fact that, from an external point of view, we too could be seen as zombies, automata without minds, for all in us that is observable could equally be explained in terms of programmed responses, neural or social. On the other hand, one may get to know an animal, its likes and dislikes, its sense of frustration or excitement, its way of expressing affection or anger, and find that – although lacking speech – it displays a whole range of emotions and responses that are not unlike their human equivalents.

Watch the range of behaviours of animals filmed in the wild, however, and you see what, if observed in humans, would be seen as empathy, parental affection and so on. You also see planning and social co-operation – as when a pack of wolves goes hunting. Possibly, we anthropomorphize, when we take this to indicate that animals have minds and emotions similar to our own; or perhaps we simply recognize that the human range of thought and emotion is simply one example of a universal phenomenon within living things.

Key idea for life

Daniel Kahneman, in *Thinking Fast and Slow*, distinguishes between a fast, intuitive mode of thought, and a slower, reflective, logical one. Fascinating in itself as a way of examining human thought, one might also use that distinction to consider how animals communicate with one another, perhaps using only the faster mode. We may consider ourselves superior, because we have sophisticated reasoning. Might we have allowed some of our instinctual and intuitive powers to atrophy as a result?

PROPERTY DUALISM

This is the view (sometimes called the 'identity hypothesis' or the 'double aspect theory') that the complex entity that is a human being has two different sets of properties, physical and mental. You could also see this as a *non-reductive* materialist approach – in other words, it's not pretending that there is some different entity other than the physical person, but that the personal or mental description is not something that can simply be reduced to the physical. Thought or consciousness is a reality, not to be reduced to a description of brain states, but not entirely separate from them either.

A similar approach is to argue that, in a complex entity, qualities appear at a level of complexity that are not there in the simpler parts of which it is made up. Mental and personal properties therefore 'emerge' from the physical properties and 'supervene' them.

Key idea for life

Perhaps we could use an analogy and say that music is the inner cultural aspect of which sound waves of particular frequencies are the outer physical aspect. There is a profound sense that, although we are physical bodies, with all the limitations that implies, we are also something *more*.

Of course, if property dualism is correct, there is a problem with freedom. Brain activity, like all physical processes, is limited by physical laws and is in theory predictable. However, if mental events are simply another aspect of these physical events, they must also be limited by physical laws. If all my action is theoretically predictable, how can I be free?

Property dualism has something of a history. Spinoza argued that everything is both conscious and extended; all reality has both a mental and a physical aspect. The mind and body cannot be separated, and therefore there can be no life beyond this physical existence. He also held that freedom was an illusion, caused by the fact that we simply do not know all the real causes of our decisions. John Locke (1632–1710), in a letter to Bishop Shillingford of Worcester, suggested that, although the vegetable part of nature is wholly material, human nature can take on perfections and properties not found in matter in general.

The attractiveness of some form of property dualism is that it preserves the very different experiences we have of ourselves as minds and as bodies, while retaining the idea that everything is basically material.

BUNDLE THEORIES

There is an entirely different way of considering the nature of the self – that it is not a single fixed entity, or even two very different entities (mental and physical) locked together, but a bundle of different elements from which we manage to experience the reality (or illusion) of a single self.

The oldest strand of this theory comes from the Buddha, who held that we comprise five different strands – including our physical body, our emotions and wishes and our conscious thoughts – all of which are in a constant state of flux. Hence, there is no single fixed 'self'; we are constantly open to change and can be changed.

In his *Treatise on Human Nature* David Hume said '… when I enter most intimately into what I call myself, I always stumble on some particular perception or other, of heat or cold, light or shade, love or hatred, pain or pleasure. I never can catch myself at any time without a perception, and never can observe any thing but the perception.' This too reflects a bundle approach; the self we are aware of is also a self of ever-changing ideas and perceptions.

In modern discussions of the self, this approach has been taken by Derek Parfit (1942–2017) whose most influential book is entitled *Reasons and Persons*. It has also been presented in a very accessible way by Julian Baggini in *The Ego Trick*.

When we reflect on our lives, we also reflect on the way in which our conscious choices and our memory of earlier experiences gradually shape us as the years pass, mapping out for us moments of significance and change. This is explored in *Me* (see 'Taking it further').

Key idea for life: A 'place' for the mind?

All physical things are located. If the mind is not physical, it has no location. To put it crudely, you are not 'inside' your head. However, we locate another person in terms of their physical presence and we can claim to know (or not to know!) where both we and they are. So, to some extent, we treat mind as though it were located.

The concept of mind

Linguistic philosophy seeks to clarify problems by looking at the meaning and use of words, and this is exemplified by the 'concept' approach of Gilbert Ryle.

In *The Concept of Mind* (1949) Gilbert Ryle suggested that to speak of minds and bodies as though they were equivalent things was a '**category mistake**'. To explain what he meant by this, he used the example of someone visiting a university and seeing many different colleges, libraries and research laboratories. The visitor then asks, 'But where is the university?' The answer, of course, is that there is no university over and above all its component parts that have already been visited. The term 'university' is a way of describing all of these things together – it is a term from another category, not the same category as the individual components.

In the same way, Ryle argued that you should not expect to find a 'mind' over and above all the various parts of the body and its actions, for 'mind' is a term from another category, a way of describing bodies and the way in which they operate. This, he claims, is the fundamental flaw in the traditional dualistic approach to mind and body (which he attributes to Descartes and calls the 'ghost in the machine'):

When two terms belong to the same category, it is proper to construct conjunctive propositions embodying them. Thus a purchaser may say that he bought a left-hand glove and a right-hand glove, but not that he bought a left-hand glove, a right-hand glove and a pair of gloves .... Now the dogma of the Ghost in the Machine does just this. It maintains that there exist both bodies and minds; that there occur physical processes and mental processes; that there are mechanical causes of corporeal movements and mental causes of corporeal movements. I shall argue that these and other analogous conjunctions are absurd; but, it must be noticed, the argument will not show that either of the illegitimately conjoined propositions is absurd in itself. I am not, for example, denying that there occur mental processes. Doing long division is a mental process and so is making a joke. But I am saying that the phrase 'there occur mental processes' does not mean the same sort of thing as 'there occur physical processes', and, therefore, that it makes no sense to conjoin or disjoin the two.

(*The Concept of Mind*, Peregrine Books, 1949, p. 23)

For Ryle, talking about minds is a particular way of talking about bodies and their activity. Remember, however, that Ryle is primarily concerned with language – his book is about what we *mean* when we speak about the 'mind'. What he shows is that, in ordinary language, mental terms actually describe activities performed by the body, or are at least based on such activities. We speak about the mind of another person without claiming to have any privileged information about their inner mental operations.

Key idea for life

If I say that someone is intelligent, I do so on the basis of what he or she has said or done. I have no privileged access to the operation of his or her brain. Try describing the personal qualities of someone you know... You end up giving an account of what they have said and done. There is no inner 'ghost' to be described; that's Ryle's point.

Of what then does the human personality consist? Ryle's answer is in terms of 'dispositions'. These are the qualities that make me what I am; the propensity to behave in a particular way in a particular situation. If I say that someone is 'irritable', I do not mean that I have some privileged access to an 'irritability factor' in their mind. I just mean that, given a situation that is not to his or her liking, he or she is likely to start complaining, sulking, and so on. In other words, the irritability is simply a way of describing a disposition.

Thus, for Ryle, the ascription of mental predicates does not require the existence of a separate, invisible thing called a mind.

Key idea for life: Who's clever?

A small child is 'clever' if it learns to stagger to its feet and totter a few paces forwards before collapsing down on the ground again. The same is not claimed for the drunk who performs a similar set of movements. If Ryle wishes to dismiss 'the ghost in the machine' he must equally dismiss 'the ghost in the action', for mental predicates refer to, but are not defined by, individual actions.

One particular difficulty with identifying a mental phenomenon with physical actions is illustrated by the idea of pain. I may shout, cry, hold the afflicted part of my body; I may scream and roll on the ground, curl up, look ashen. None of these things, however, is actually the same thing as the pain I am experiencing. The pain is indicated by them, but not *defined* by them.

I may watch an actor on stage perform all of the above, but I do not imagine that there is any physical pain. Yet, if being in pain is to be *identified* with those physical actions (as Ryle implies) the actor *is* in pain.

Of course, Ryle is doing *linguistic* philosophy. He assumes that, when we have clarified what we mean by mental terms, we have solved the problem. But has he?

Survival?

The relationship between body and mind has implications for the idea that human beings might survive death.

If Plato was right to think that the soul was eternal, then its existence does not depend upon the physical body, and it is therefore at least logically possible for it to survive the death of the body. Similarly, Descartes' dualism of extended body and thinking mind at least leaves open the possibility of survival, as the mind is separate from the body, and cannot be reduced to anything physical.

However, if one accepts a materialist, or property dualist view of the self, it would make no sense to speak of a self that existed separately from a body, or survived physical death, as the self is an aspect of bodily activity. The only possibility would be to redefine death in some way, so that it allowed for some form of physical existence to continue, but that would beg the whole question about survival of death, as 'death' in the normal sense of the word would not have occurred.

From the religious point of view, belief in life after death is linked to two other fundamental ideas:

1 There is a deeply held view that there should be some appropriate compensation, good or bad, for what a person has done during his or her life. All religious traditions have some element of reward or punishment, whether externally imposed (as in Western religions) or self-generated (as in the 'karma' of Eastern traditions).

2 There is also a sense that human life somehow goes beyond the confines of a fragile human body, expressed in the idea that 'This cannot be everything: there must be something more.'

Neither of these constitutes evidence for survival of death. What they do show is the appropriateness of such belief for a religious person, and the reasons why he or she might hold to it in the absence of evidence.

In terms of the religious perspective on survival, we should note that there are three different possibilities: immortality, resurrection and reincarnation.

▶ **Immortality** implies that there is a non-physical element to the self that can exist independently of the physical body with which it is presently associated. This does not strictly speaking require belief in God, as a natural immortality could be seen as a logical consequence of dualism.

▶ **Resurrection**, the Christian view, is that the soul is *not* naturally immortal and the whole person – body and mind – dies, but is then raised to life by God and given a new body. This view depends on a prior belief in God, and assumes that individuality requires some sort of body in order to express itself, but it raises many questions about the nature of an embodied future life. If that life is to be endless, then what age is a person to be in such a future life? A body, after all, can vary from baby to old age. Would a resurrected child become the adult that he or she never was? Would I, in such a life, recognize my grandfather as a young man, and would he recognize me as an old one? This issue has been explored in thought experiments by, among others, Derek Parfit and John Hick – asking whether personal identity could survive being deconstructed and reconstructed again in a different place or time.

▶ **Reincarnation**, particularly associated with Hindu philosophy, sees the soul as distinct from the body, and as able, at death, to move on to take up another physical body. Personal qualities and dispositions move on from life to life, expressed through a sequence of physical incarnations. Rather like the idea of resurrection, this assumes dualism (as the self that moves on is not the same as the physical body), but still considers the self to require some form of physical body in order to live.

Key idea for life

Although illogical, the religious desire to accommodate belief in an afterlife is without doubt a significant factor in shaping some people's view of the nature of the self. A strictly eliminativist materialism implies a secular, atheist or Buddhist view.

Knowing me, knowing you

We now turn to some implications of the mind/body problem, particularly those that affect individuals in terms of their self-understanding, identity and knowledge of other people.

FREE WILL

Free will is a major feature in the mind/body debate. If the mind is simply a by-product or description of brain activity, and if brain activity is part of the material world and therefore (in theory), totally predictable, then there is no such thing as free will. We appear to be free only because we do not understand the unique combination of causes that force us to make our particular decisions.

In effect, the issue here is exactly the same as '**determinism**' within the philosophy of science. We live in a world of cause and effect. If causality is universal (or if, like Kant, we believe that the mind automatically assumes that it is), then it provides a closed loop of explanation for everything that happens. Human beings and their choices, being part of the physical world, come within that loop.

Key idea for life

There is a danger here of falling into a fallacy that the philosopher Henri Bergson called 'retrospective determinism'. Just because something *has* happened, we are tempted to assume that it *had to* happen and therefore search backwards for its necessary causes. Such a quest already rules out the possibility of genuine chance, choice and spontaneous creativity before it starts. There are always reasons why you are who you are, here and now, but – had you chosen otherwise – it might not have been so.

Many people consider freedom and morality to be an essential part of what it means to be a human individual. We do not think of ourselves as robots, even sophisticated ones. Our role in the world is proactive, not reactive. We shape the world as much as we are shaped by it. From this perspective, it is difficult to see how the mind could be 'nothing more than' a by-product of brain activity.

DISEMBODIED CONSCIOUSNESS

If you take a dualist view, it is logically possible that the mind or self could exist outside the body or survive the death of the body; in other words that it could have a disembodied existence.

Quite apart from religious beliefs about life beyond death, people may claim to have seen ghosts, or to have spoken with the dead at a séance, or to have had an 'out of body' experience – but evidence for such things is always open to interpretation, and a person who takes a strictly materialist standpoint will always seek an explanation that does not stray towards the paranormal. Thus it is possible to argue that 'near death' experiences are produced by the oxygen starvation that the brain may suffer as death approaches. So while the evidence for life beyond death may be plentiful, it is unlikely to be objective or scientific.

As in all cases where we try to evaluate the experience of individuals, a useful test is that which Hume applied to the accounts of miracles (see page 210): which is more likely, that the event actually happened as reported, or that the person reporting it is mistaken?

However, quite apart from the willingness of people to speculate about, or be persuaded by accounts of, disembodied consciousness, it presents some quite fundamental philosophical problems. Everything we know about people relates to their physical body and its activities in terms of speech and writing, the demonstration of emotions, and the stated motives for their actions. In other words, we know them as embodied. How could we start to recognize them, or ourselves display any personal characteristics, if we were disembodied?

KNOWLEDGE OF OTHER MINDS

In a strictly dualistic view of bodies and minds, you cannot have direct knowledge of the minds of others. You can know their words, their actions, their writings, their facial and other body signals, but you cannot get access to their minds. For a dualist, knowledge of other minds therefore comes by analogy. I know what it is like to be me. I know that, when I speak, I am expressing something that I am thinking. Therefore, I assume that, when another person speaks, his or her words are similarly the product of mental activity.

From Ryle's point of view, there is no problem. There is no 'ghost in the machine'; what we mean by 'mind' is the intelligent and communicative abilities of the other person. If I know his or her actions, words and so on, then I know his or her mind; the two things are one and the same.

To return to an earlier question, 'What is the difference between an actor who is playing the part of a person in pain, and someone who is actually in pain?' If I say that the one *really* feels pain, while the other only *appears* to feel pain, I have to assume some non-physical self, which exists over and above their identical grimaces, moans and verbal complaints.

But is it possible to know another mind directly? What about telepathy? Here we have the difficulty of knowing how to evaluate a phenomenon the validity of which may be challenged, and for which there is, at present, no scientific explanation. Actually, though, if we are considering what we understand by the self or mind, it makes little difference whether telepathy works between minds that are distinct from their respective bodies, or whether there is some as yet unexplained way in which brains manage to communicate with one another. So, in itself, telepathy does not help us to decide between a materialist or dualist position.

Key idea for life

If the self is not a fixed entity but a *process* – if you are your personal history of the things you have said and done – then getting to know you is simply (although far from simple!) a matter of being with you, listening to what you say and the descriptions of your thoughts, watching your habitual responses to life and getting to anticipate your wishes.

In practice, we actually get to know other people by observation, by considering what they say or write, and by judging how they deal with life. We can question them, in order to clarify their likes and dislikes, for example. In the end, however, we still depend upon the consistency and trustworthiness of our own observation.

Consider the following example:

Case study

I ask someone, whom I have invited to dinner, if he likes strawberries. He replies that he does.

If I believe he is telling the truth, I know at least one thing about his own private tastes.

He could, however, be saying that he likes them in order to be polite (seeing that I am returning home with a punnet of strawberries in my hand when I ask him the question). I need to ask myself if, in my past experience of him, he is someone who is straightforward about his views, or if he is always anxious to please and agree with people. If the latter is the case, then I am really no nearer to knowing whether he *really* likes strawberries.

I could observe him at the dinner table that evening. Does he savour the strawberries, or swallow them quickly? Does he appear to be enjoying himself, or does he suddenly turn rather pale and excuse himself from the table?

Do I subsequently observe him buying and eating strawberries?

This is a simple example of weighing up evidence for a person's private sensations. It would become far more complex if the question were, 'Did you have a happy childhood?' In this case, there are profound psychological reasons why his or her immediate response might not be the correct one. Indeed, such is the way in which the unconscious mind affects the conscious, that the person may not actually be able to remember whether he or she was or was not happy. Moments of trauma may have been blocked off and unacknowledged. The whole process of psychotherapy is one of gradually unpicking the things that a person says, in the light of their actual behaviour and physical responses.

Notice the assumption that I make in all this: that I am getting to know another person as a communicating subject. I do not explore his or her brain, nor seek for any occult 'soul'. I simply recognize that this is a person who has views, feelings, thoughts, experiences, and can communicate them. That process of communication means that getting to know another person is a two-way process. It depends upon my observation and enquiries, but also upon the willingness of the other person to be known.

If that were not the case, and if we could only know other people as we know ourselves, by direct awareness of thoughts and feelings, then we would be isolated and alone, surrounded by bodies in which we have to infer that there are other minds similar to our own. Such a view is termed **solipsism**, and this is the fate of those who think of the soul or mind as a crude, unknowable 'ghost', as caricatured by Ryle.

Knowing myself seems quite different. It is instantaneous. As soon as I stop to reflect, I can say whether I feel happy or not. It is based on sensation, not observation. I do not have to listen to my own words, or look at my facial expressions in a mirror in order to know whether I am enjoying myself. I have immediate sensations of pleasure or pain.

Even this, however, is not without its problems. Although my knowledge of myself is more reliable than the knowledge of anyone else, I may still be mistaken. If it were not so, we could never become confused about ourselves, for we would know and understand both our experiences and our responses to them. Adolescence would be negotiated smoothly, mid-life crises would never occur, psychotherapists and counsellors would become extinct. Alas, the process of really knowing oneself is just as complex as knowing another person.

In knowing myself, I have two advantages over others:

1 I have memory. My own knowledge of events and my response to them is more immediate and detailed than the accounts given by others, although my memory may let me down, and I may repress experiences if they are too painful to remember. In such a case, for example of trauma in childhood, another person may have a clearer memory of what happened and of my response at the time than I have myself.

2 I can deliberately mislead others about my feelings and responses. Generally speaking, except for cases of strong unconscious motivation, I do not mislead myself.

Key idea for life

Did I really do that? What must I have been thinking about? Reflectively understanding yourself is not so different from understanding others. You can surprise yourself, finding yourself behaving in ways you would not have anticipated, or enjoying something you assumed you would hate. Although we have immediate access to our own thoughts and feelings, we may still need to reflect on them and interpret them, as we can our dreams.

PERSONAL IDENTITY

There are many ways of identifying yourself:

▶ The son or daughter of ..., or friend of ...

▶ A member of a particular school, university, business, village, city

▶ A citizen of a country, member of a race

▶ An earthling (if you happen to be travelling through space, this might become the only relevant way of describing yourself)

At various times, each of these will become more or less relevant for the purpose of self-identity. Relationships establish a sense of identity, and the closer the relationship, the more significant will be its influence on the sense of self. Aristotle held that friendships are essential for a sense of identity, and that you should cultivate a limited number of them (he lived, of course, before Facebook!).

In general, self-identification is made easier by emphasizing those things by which one differs from others around one at the time. By contrast, those who are fearful of having their individuality exposed tend to 'blend in' with a crowd, borrowing for themselves a group 'identity' of shared values, language, dress or cultural norms.

Trying to analyse the self in order to understand what it is to be a person is problematic:

▶ **Analysis** shows your bits and pieces, of body and brain and words and behaviour, none of which, in isolation, defines 'you'.

▶ **Synthesis** shows the way in which body, mind and social function come together in a unique combination – and that is 'you'.

Identity is therefore a matter of synthesis, not of analysis, of being an integrated functioning entity comprising both body and mind. *You are the sum total, not the parts.*

Earlier in this chapter, we considered the distinction between acting and reality. This is also relevant for an understanding of 'persons'. For example, Aldo Tassi, writing in *Philosophy Today* (Summer 1993), explored the idea of a persona (or mask) that an actor puts on. The actor projects a sense of self – the self who is the character in the play. In doing so, the actor deliberately withdraws his or her own identity.

In the theatre, the actor can go off stage and revert to his or her own identity. In the real world, Tassi argues, we create a character in what we do, but we can never step outside the world to find another self 'off stage'. He refers back to Aristotle, for whom the soul is the substantial form of the body, but substance for Aristotle was not a static thing. The soul is not superadded to the body in order to make the body a living thing; rather, the body gets both its being and its life from the 'soul'. Tassi says: 'Consciously to be is to project a sense of oneself, that is to say, to "assume a mask".'

Key idea for life

Personal identity, if Tassi is right, is dynamic rather than static; it is acted out and developed; it does not exist in terms of static analysis. However, as we saw in thinking about communication and the media, we are all able to create identities for ourselves online, through tweets, blogs or websites. We automatically choose a mask as soon as we step upon the digital stage.

There is much that can be explored in terms of our understanding of 'persons'. This was particularly featured in the writings of P. F. Strawson (1919–2006), a British philosopher known particularly for his work on the nature of identity, and for his exposition and development of the philosophy of

Immanuel Kant. In 'Persons', an article first published in 1958, and 'Individuals', 1959, he argued that the concept of 'person' was prior to the popular analysis of it as an animated body, or an embodied mind. Rather, a person is such that both physical characteristics and states of consciousness can be ascribed to it (a view taken up, by the 'property dualism' approach).

The concept of a 'person' has many practical and ethical implications:

▶ In what sense, and at what point, can an unborn child be called a person?

▶ An unborn child has a brain, but cannot communicate directly. Is such communication necessary for it to be called a full human being? (Consider also the case of the severely handicapped. Does lack of communication detract from their being termed 'people'?)

▶ Does a baby have to be independent before being classified as a person? If so, do we cease to be human once we are rendered totally dependent on others, for example, on the operating table?

▶ What is the status of a person who goes into a coma or persistent vegetative state?

Key idea for life

Some notion of personal identity is crucial for many moral issues, including abortion and euthanasia. When does a bundle of cells become a person? What counts as a functioning human being, deserving respect and the protection of the law?

MEMORY

Memories are personal; they are also influential. You are what you are because you have learned from the past – and that learning depends on memory. A person who has lost his or her memory finds it difficult to function, is constantly surprised or bewildered by the response of others who claim long-established friendship or enmity. Our responses are determined by our memories.

Hume saw memories as a set of private images running through one's head. It follows that, if I say I have a memory of a particular thing, nobody else can contradict me, because nobody else has access to that particular bit of internal data. However, what if one thinks that one remembers something and then is shown that it would not be possible – for example, that I remember the Second World War, only to find that I was born after it was over? I would have to admit that my memory was faulty, or perhaps that a war film had lodged such vivid images in my mind that I genuinely believed that I had lived through it. I remember the image clearly enough, and am not lying about it, but what I have forgotten is its origin (on film, in this case, rather than in reality).

Particularly if they are strongly suggested, people may develop false memories, imagining rather than remembering what must have happened. Again, there is no doubting the mental image, what is at doubt is its origin.

Great feats of memory require sifting through the many facts and images that are habitually available to us, to more specific events: remembering a place leads to remembering a particular person who was seen there, which then leads on to remembering any suspicious actions that he or she may have made. Memory reveals bit by bit; something that was previously forgotten is now remembered because another memory has triggered it. Following serious crimes, an identically dressed person is sometimes sent to retrace the steps of the victim, hoping that it may trigger a memory in a passer-by.

Our privileged access to our own memories does not make them infallible. Four people, giving accounts of the same dinner party, may all provide quite different versions of events. Our memories are selective, providing us with recall of those sense experiences that are deemed significant, and ignoring those that are not.

Memory also serves to develop the 'background' of our actions and thoughts (to use Heidegger's term). Faced with a choice in the present, my memory searches for similar experiences in the past, and the memory of them will influence the choice I now have to make. In this sense, memory is an ever-growing means of self-definition.

Cognitive science and artificial intelligence

Much of what we have been discussing in this chapter is related to the traditional mind/body problem, which developed out of the radical dualism of Descartes and the issues raised by it. By the latter part of the twentieth century, however, these problems (without necessarily being resolved) were set in a new and broader context, provided by the development of the cognitive sciences, including neuroscience and artificial intelligence.

Cognitive science is an umbrella term for a number of modern disciplines that impinge upon ideas of the self or mind:

▶ Artificial intelligence provides a model for understanding how the human mind works, replicating the process of decision-making and data assessment.

▶ Neuroscience is now able to map out the functions of the brain, identifying areas that are associated with particular mental or sensory processes.

▶ Pharmacology is able to control behaviour by the use of drugs, bringing a whole new chemical element into our understanding of behaviour.

▶ Clinical psychology looks at the way an individual's mind functions, taking into account both its conscious and unconscious workings.

Clearly, there is no scope within this present book for examining these disciplines. All we need to be aware of is the way in which science today is far more flexible in its approach to the mind than would have been the case a century or more ago. In particular, it is able to map out mental functions such as memory, emotion, reasoning and perception, showing the way they have a physical component that can be examined scientifically, quite independent of our own personal experience of them.

Science needs data upon which to work. In the case of mental operations, one approach has been to examine the physical equivalent of the mental operation – generally in terms of brain function. Another has been to allow mental operations to provide their own physical data. For example, the behaviourist approach to gathering data was to set up experiments that involved actions and responses, and then measure those responses. Can this boxed rat learn – by rewarding it every time it does the right thing – to press a lever in order to get food?

A key term here is **functionalism**. This approach sees mental operations as the way in which intelligent life sorts out how to react to the stimuli it receives. Let us take a crude example. If I put my hand on something hot, my body receives the sensation of burning. My mind then becomes aware of the pain, remembers that if the hand is not removed from the heat damage is likely to be done, and therefore decides that I should withdraw my hand. Muscles contract, the hand is withdrawn, and the pain subsides. We may not be able to tell exactly which neurons, firing in the brain, were responsible for each step in that operation. What we do monitor, however, is the mental functions that were performed. Mind is what mind does – with inputs, processing and outputs; just like a computer.

Key idea for life: A functionalist reflection

I own several corkscrews. One is fairly straightforward: screw it into the cork, hold the bottle and pull upwards. Another, once screwed in, uses a lever function and is pulled from the side. The most sophisticated has arms that grip round the side of the bottle, and so on.

These are all corkscrews, not by virtue of how they operate, or what they look like, but simply by virtue of their function. Whatever gets a cork out for you is your corkscrew! That's functionalism.

Does it make any difference whether an action is performed by a computer or by a human brain? The mechanics by which each performs the operation may appear different, but the function is the same. There is a gap (usually referred to as the 'Leibniz' gap') in our knowledge, because we cannot see the point at which the physical and the mental interact; but, does that matter, provided that we understand how the mental and physical function together?

Hence, a functionalist is able to produce what amounts to a map of the mind; a map that shows the different functions that the mind performs. What it cannot do, and argues that it is not necessary to do, is to wait to find out what each physical or electrical component does in the chain of events, before the significance of the mental function can be appreciated.

INTENTIONALITY

The idea of intentionality predates cognitive science, but is relevant to the broad range of issues that it considers. It originated in the work of the nineteenth-century psychologist Franz Brentano (1838–1917) and influenced the philosopher and psychologist William James (1842–1910). Intentionality, put simply, is the recognition that every perception and every experience is directed towards something. I do not just experience the shape of an apple before me, but I experience it as something to eat. In other words, mental functions shape and interpret what we experience – and we cannot have experience except as experience 'of' something.

Experience is about living in the world, relating to it, getting what we need from it, influencing it. It is not a separate and detached play of passing sense data. The mind takes an 'intentional stance' towards what it experiences.

Key idea for life

We are not passive observers of the world. We have developed sense organs and brains in order to function, to find tools around us by which we can survive in a hostile environment or enjoy a comfortable one. Mind and thought is about relating and doing; when we observe, we do so with intentionality; our senses are judged by the function they perform in our life; and we take a pragmatic view of their operations. Wittgenstein said that, in order to understand it, one should look at how language is used, what function it plays in life. The same could be said of mind: intentionality, functionalism and pragmatism all suggest that we will only understand mind by considering what it *does*, not by standing back and trying to analyse what it *is*.

ARTIFICIAL INTELLIGENCE

Artificial intelligence (AI) uses computers to perform some of the functions of the human brain. It works on the basis of knowledge and response; the computer receives and stores data and is programmed to respond to requests. The faster the processor and the greater the storage, the more life-like the computer becomes.

The assumption is that, although far inferior in capacity to the human brain, artificial intelligence can show and replicate the processes by which the brain operates. However, a key difference between the human and the artificial form of intelligence is that computers are programmed while human brains learn. This is countered by creating neural networks, in which a large number of artificial neurons are linked together, in an attempt to get the system to solve problems in the same sort of way as the human brain.

The difference between AI and neural computing highlights a feature of Ryle's argument in *The Concept of Mind*. Ryle made the distinction between 'knowing that' and 'knowing how'. He argued that to do something intelligently is not just a matter of knowing facts, but of applying them. To do something skilfully implies an operation over and above applying ready digested rules. To give one of Ryle's examples, a clock keeps time, and is set to do so, but that does not make it intelligent.

We might draw a parallel with a work of art, literature or musical composition. The second-rate artist, writer or composer might follow all the established rules and apply them diligently, producing a work that follows fashion. The really creative person, however, does not appear to follow rules at all, producing work that may be loathed or controversial, but nevertheless may be said to be an intelligent production, as it attempts to express something that goes beyond all previously established norms. This is a kind of 'knowing how': knowing how to perform creatively.

Now, if a computer is fed with sufficient information, it 'knows that'. It can also follow the process that Ryle calls the 'intellectualist legend' – it can sort out the rules and apply them to its new data. What it cannot do – unless we claim that it suddenly 'takes on a life of its own' – is to go beyond all the established (programmed) rules and do something utterly original.

So, for example, Professor Roger Penrose of Oxford (in *The Emperor's New Mind*, 1989) argues that it would be impossible to create an intelligent robot because consciousness requires self-awareness, and that is something that a computer cannot simulate. He argues that consciousness is based on a 'non-algorithmic' ingredient (in other words, an ingredient that does not depend on an algorithm – a set of rules).

Key idea for life

A robot would not need *self-awareness* in order to carry out actions intelligently, merely a set of goals to be achieved. So, for example, a chess program can play chess and beat its own creator, but it only knows what constitutes winning at chess, not the *significance* of playing the game.

A hazard of unreflective living is that one may become artificially intelligent: slavishly following social programming rather than being creative.

CHINESE WRITING

A most graphic way of exploring the difference between being able to handle and manipulate information (which a computer can do very efficiently) and actually understanding that information (which, it is claimed, a computer cannot) was given by the philosopher John Searle (in his 1984 Reith Lectures, *Minds, Brains and Science*).

He presented a thought experiment in which you are locked in a room, into which are passed various bits of Chinese writing, none of which you can read. You are then given instructions (in

English) about how to relate one piece of Chinese to another. The result is that you are apparently able to respond in Chinese to instructions given in Chinese (in the sense that you can post out of the room the appropriate Chinese reply), but without actually understanding one word of it. From the outside, you appear to understand Chinese; from the inside, you are blindly following instructions.

Searle argues that this is the case with computers; they can sort out bits of information, based on the instructions that they are given, but they cannot actually *understand* the information they are given.

This touches on a key theme in modern philosophy of mind, namely how our experience of consciousness relates to brain activity.

THE INFINITE BACKGROUND PROBLEM

Also back in the 1980s, but still relevant, the philosopher Hubert Dreyfus presented a criticism of AI based on an aspect of the philosophy of Heidegger. Heidegger (and Dreyfus) argued that human activity is a matter of skilful coping with situations, and this presupposes a 'background', namely, all the facts about society and life in general that lead us to do what we do. In addition, this background is going to include all the views, experiences and impressions that we have been gathering since birth and remembering from the age of about two years, and all the skills that we have developed and tested out.

Now AI, according to Dreyfus, attempts to reduce this 'background' to a set of facts ('know-how' is reduced to 'know-that'). However, this is an impossible task, because the ever-growing number of background facts to be taken into account is, for practical purposes, *infinite*.

Upon this range of facts another is overlaid, because a person has to select *which* of those facts are relevant to the decision in hand, and the rules for *deciding* which are going to be relevant then form another set of facts that might also be infinite. It is therefore impossible to provide enough rules and facts to fill out the whole background to any human decision, and this is, according to

Dreyfus (see Dreyfus and Dreyfus, *Mind over Machine*, 1986), a problem that will continue to be formidable for AI.

Remember this: A disclaimer

Over the last three decades, there has been a phenomenal rise in the power and sophistication of computers and in the way they are used, not least in connection with the internet, with its huge impact on commerce, communication and society. Some of the material in this chapter appeared in the first edition of this *Teach Yourself* book and reflected the situation in the mid-1990s. However, reviewing it more than 20 years later, it seems to me that some fundamental issues concerning the relationship between computing and the human mind remain relevant, and those early arguments are still valid in our more computer-sophisticated environment.

Neuroscience and consciousness

It has always been assumed that the brain is intimately involved with the process of consciousness and thought, and we experience ourselves as located behind our eyes, even though we know that all we will find there is a bony skull filled with soft grey matter. We know the impact on the self and intellect of traumatic damage to the brain or degenerative disease. We recognize that human sophistication has increased over evolutionary time in line with cranial capacity. Yet it is only in the last couple of decades that neuroscience has given us the ability to see the brain working and to map out its various functions.

It's true, though, that however much neuroscience reveals, there remain fundamental questions about how the brain's activity relates to our consciousness.

David Chalmers has been a key contributor to the modern debate over philosophy of mind during the last 20 years or so. In his book *The Conscious Mind* (1996) he works on the assumption that consciousness is a natural phenomenon, and as such should be open to scientific explanation like any other. However, that does not imply that consciousness can be reduced to neural activity in the brain, or that it is 'nothing but' such activity.

The sticking point – described by Chalmers as the 'hard problem' of consciousness – is to know how to understand 'qualia'. Qualia are the introspective qualities of experience – the colour of a flower, the taste of a fruit – all the actual sensations of which we become aware. The 'hard question' is how it is that neural activity in the brain actually produces these qualia. A neuroscientist can tell me that my emotion is related to brain activity of a certain sort, but that's not how it *feels*. I know that red light is of a certain frequency, but that's not the same as the colour red that I see.

The brain sorts out all the unconscious operations of the body, adjusting blood pressure, heart rate and so on. It also processes the inputs from our senses, and – based on experience – suggests what we should welcome and what to avoid. We need the brain to be informed (or, as we experience it, 'we' need to be informed) about the sounds and sights around us, in order to survive in this world. But why does it have to produce the actual *experience of consciousness*? How does it do it?

This is not a new problem. Back in the 1970s, Thomas Nagel asked a fundamental question: 'What is it like to be a bat?' We know that bats find their way around by a form of radar, but what must it be like to 'see' through radar? What kind of experience would that be?

Two thinkers who represent different positions here are Daniel Dennett and John Searle. In 1991, Dennett published *Consciousness Explained*. He presented the brain as a computer, with inputs and outputs, and argued that consciousness is actually brain activity. We are conscious when there is, in effect, a computer turned on and operating in our brains. But what he appears not to accept is the reality of qualia – the subjective experience of what is brought about by that brain activity. In effect, Dennett's position is that whatever exists should be verifiable by scientific data, the sort of thing that can be observed and measured. However, qualia just don't fit that pattern; they are not the sort of 'thing' that can be measured. For Dennett, consciousness just *is* what is happening in the brain.

John Searle's opposition to this goes back to his 'Chinese Writing' thought experiment (see page 154). Just as the operation of sorting Chinese characters is not the same as understanding the language, so he argues that brain activity, although it *causes* consciousness, is not *the same thing as* consciousness.

The difference between Dennett and Searle can perhaps best be illustrated by considering the possible existence of a zombie – someone who appears to be human but has no internal experience at all – the imaginative possibility of which has been a feature of the consciousness question since its appearance in the work of David Chalmers, who used it to counter a completely materialist view of the self.

Searle's position suggests that there is a radical difference between the zombie and the normal human being – namely that the latter experiences conscious qualia and is not simply an automaton. However, Dennett appears to be saying that, if a zombie could be equipped with a human-like brain, able to perform all the neural functions of a human brain, then that zombie *would be human* – because having all those neural functions is what being human is all about. Searle's criticism suggests that Dennett's view, by making no distinction between the human and the zombie, makes all of us into zombies!

Very often, intuition plays an important part in philosophy, and this is true of the zombie question. Chalmers suggests that we can conceive of what it would be like to have a zombie twin – someone exactly like us but without the qualia of immediate experience. The implication, of course, is that, if we can conceive of a zombie, we intuitively know the difference between the zombie and ourselves – and hence that we have an intuition of a non-material self.

Of course, one could equally ask how anyone could know that *I am not a zombie*? After all, a complete materialist account of my life, language, brain functioning and so on would give all the information anyone else could ever have about me. Yet if this is not the same thing as *what it is like to be me*, there is nothing that the observer could use to distinguish me from my zombie twin!

As you may imagine, current debates in the philosophy of mind are fascinating and can get rather complex; the comments here do no more than touch on some of the key issues.

Key idea for life

In *Consciousness Explained* (and other popular books on this subject), Daniel Dennett, taking a materialist position, suggests that, at some point in the future, a perfect neuroscience will tell us all we need to know about the mind. My own view is that it will tell us nothing more than we already know about who we are as persons – it will simply show which neurons fire when we think, experience or do various things. It may provide observable and measurable correlates to our experience and thought, but that simply provides us with the digital equivalent of a biography. Our mind, changing and growing out of its infinite background, will remain – even if it surprises us at times – accessible to reflection rather than measurement.

NEUROPLASTICITY

In broad outline, the debates about how, or whether, neural activity produces the qualia of our conscious experience tend to assume that the material brain is fundamental and gives rise to mind or consciousness. The key question is whether that consciousness is distinct from the neural activity or simply a description of it.

However, in recent years, studies of the brain have revealed a far more interesting phenomenon – neuroplasticity. This tracks the way in which the brain develops and grows in response to mental activity.

Remember this: Growing your memory

Before they can qualify to work as a London 'cabbie', drivers have to take and pass an examination in 'the knowledge'. They have to learn the locations of and directions to a vast number of roads and buildings within the London area. It requires a remarkable exercise in remembering names and places. It has been found that those who succeed in gaining 'the knowledge' increase the volume of their hippocampus (the part of the brain concerned with memory and learning) in the process of doing so.

We know that physical exercise increases the flow of blood to the brain, bringing it supplies of oxygen and glucose, and this triggers hormones, including serotonin, which is a mood enhancer and dopamine, which stimulates attention and learning. These and other hormones are also known to play a role in the growth of new brain cells. We also know that techniques such as meditation and yoga can influence brain activity.

One implication of this is that any dualist perception suggesting that the material brain and an immaterial mind are linked only problematically (or not at all!) is no longer tenable. Whatever the relationship of mind and body, we know now that it is subtle and all pervasive. Our brains grow and adapt to our lives – we can change them as much as they can change us.

Conscious experience, mediated through the senses and interpreted by the brain, is a process by which neural pathways are forged or reinforced. At an unconscious level, our bodies work automatically, and the brain continues to regulate our various physical systems. But beyond that, once we become conscious, a whole new process comes into play – a process in which *subjective experience is mapped onto the physical brain*. Skills and habits reflect that mapping; memory and recognition brings it into play.

If our brain were a vehicle, we would be the driver rather than a back-seat passenger. True, we may sometimes drive it off the road, it may break down or its steering mechanism may fail, but we cannot pretend to be mere passengers.

Key idea for life

It is consciousness that makes us proactive, giving us a basic level of awareness that takes priority over a slower process of rational thinking and enables us to survive, find food, mate and avoid predators (of the carnivorous, social or economic sort!). Consciousness shapes the brain, etching neural pathways and thereby establishing habits and skills. It is only illusory or problematic for those who take a very narrow, empirical and reductive view of reality.

A personal postscript

My personal view is that the self is not the conclusion of an argument, nor the answer to a question. The self is the *starting point* of all experience. It is that which makes all our discussion about the world and about existence possible. It is the means by which I encounter the world, the sense of agency by which I am able to act.

Hence I find it curious that some will argue that the self is reducible to neural experience, for, as an entity in the world, the self does not exist; it is not to be found in any description of the world or of my brain.

The mind/body issue, perhaps more than any other, illustrates the problem of a reductionist approach to complex entities. The experience of being a thinking, feeling and reflecting person is not susceptible to analysis or reduction, because *it is not part of the world we experience*. Wittgenstein was right in saying that the self was the *limit* of the world, rather than part of it.

Nor is the self a fixed entity. Hume could never see his mind except in the procession of thoughts that passed through it. From birth to death, there is constant change, and our thoughts of today shape what we will be tomorrow – an observation made by the Buddha, two and a half thousand years ago.

Key idea for life

Throughout life, we leave our imprint on the world around us: words we speak, actions we perform, roles we assume. These form the unfolding story of our life, material for a biographer. However, at the same time, these same words, actions and thoughts leave their imprint upon our brains, constantly reshaping the neural pathways that influence our character from moment to moment. Having habitually behaved or thought in a particular way, I am predisposed to follow that pattern in the future. To understand our present, we need to reflect on our past; to understand our future, reflect on our present. In addition, if we want to change, we will need to make a conscious effort.

Even our process of reflection, the most private of activities, is dependent upon the outside world. It is extremely difficult to experience something with absolute simplicity or purity, for we immediately categorize it and understand it 'as' something. We cannot help doing that, because the way we think is shaped by our common language, common culture and the whole range of ideas and experiences that we share with others. As soon as we explain ourselves, we are engaged in a social activity; private language is meaningless.

Philosophers and scientists tend to *think* – that is their job, but it is also their problem! They cast about for ideas, concepts, theories and evidence and inevitably find it difficult to locate the self or explain its nature. Just as a camera can photograph anything but itself, or the eye see anything but itself (leaving mirrors aside for the moment), so the senses – designed to engage consciously with the external world – are ill-equipped to turn in upon the mind. What they see instead is brain activity, behaviour, dispositions, language: the traces of our conscious life.

By contrast, those who *meditate* (or who simply give quiet attention to any object), stilling the mind until it is gently focused on a single point, become aware of something very different. The self becomes empty, becomes nothing and everything at the same moment. There is no separate 'self' or 'mind' waiting to be discovered, only an ongoing process to be observed.

Without some sense of self – not necessarily a fixed entity, but more likely a bundle of thoughts, emotions, intentions and responses – we could not function as human beings, nor could we effectively relate to others; we may not know exactly what the mind *is*, but we know we cannot make sense of life without it. The mind (as a separate, definable thing) is a convenient illusion, a shorthand term we use for the ongoing personal process of experiencing, thinking and responding that is our life as an intelligent being.

6

Art and Creativity

In this chapter you will:

▶ *Consider what makes something a work of art*

▶ *Explore the nature of aesthetic appreciation and the sublime*

▶ *Look at the impact of postmodernism*

Why?

Consider the visual arts, music, drama, literature, mime, film. If you want to explore the reality of life, its values, meaning, hopes, dreams and frustrations, these may well guide you more effectively than any logical argument. They may evoke emotion and a sense of purpose, or may challenge the way you see things. Their examination leads us into the philosophy of art, aesthetics, and an appreciation of the sublime. They also invite us to understand the potential of creativity, both in art and in ourselves.

The philosophy of art

Most areas of philosophy spring from simple but fundamental questions: epistemology asks 'What can we know?' and political philosophy asks 'What is justice?' or 'How should we be governed?' In the same way, the philosophy of art addresses the question 'What is art?' and follows through the various answers that can be given to it.

You can trace questions about the nature and function of art through the whole history of philosophy, from Greek ideas of art, through mediaeval and Reformation debates about religious images (whether they pointed beyond themselves, or were in danger of being themselves worshipped in an idolatrous way), through Hume's attempt to get a norm of taste and Kant's analysis of the aesthetic experience, to Marxist critiques of art in terms of its social and political function, and on to existentialist and postmodernist views of art.

However, it is far from straightforward to say exactly what makes something a work of 'art'. One could define art as in some way a 'picturing' of reality; however, then one would need to leave out music or architecture, which are arts, but which create something that has no direct external point of reference in the natural world. (Both may, of course, suggest or hint at things in the natural world, but that is another matter.) Another approach is to start from the artist, rather than from the work of art. Hence art is the product of a certain kind of human activity, related to the expression of emotion, or the enhancement of perception.

Think of the range of artistic activities that go into producing an opera, for example. There is the designing and painting of sets, the production of costumes, the libretto, the music and the quality of voices that perform it. A single experience results from the very special combination of a whole range of 'arts'. Here, as with the appreciation of a 'person', more is understood by synthesis (seeing how everything works together) rather than by analysis (isolating and trying to define each component separately).

The same could be said of literature. Individual words in a work of fiction may well have a straightforward, literal meaning, and the individual events they describe might well be factual (indeed, this leads on to the debate about how much fact can rightly be incorporated into a work of fiction), yet the overall effect – the synthesis – is to create something which reflects, but does not copy, real life.

So what is art?

Art may surprise and shock – indeed, many works of art are designed to do just that. To be confronted in a gallery with a pile of bricks, a urinal or a rather disgusting, unmade bed (to take three well-known examples of twentieth-century art) leads to the basic question 'What is art?'. What do such things have in common with a work by Constable, or Titian, or Picasso? How can something that is not deliberately created as such be termed 'art'?

One possibility is to search for what all genuine works of art have in common, but that is particularly difficult because they are so varied. It could be argued, however, that they exhibit 'significant form' (to use a term introduced by Clive Bell in his book *Art*, 1914). He considered that a sensitive viewer would appreciate a certain balance of line, colour, shape or similar qualities in a work and would therefore declare it to be art. What the art actually depicts (if it depicts anything) is almost irrelevant; what counts is that it should be artistic. The problem with any such approach, however, is that it tends to promote a kind of elitism, whereby an inner circle of art critics effectively decide what counts as significant form.

Another approach would be to say that something becomes art because of the creative input of the artist, and it expresses his or her vision or emotion. This was key to the work of the Oxford philosopher R.G. Collingwood (1889–1943) and the Italian Bernadetto Crose (1866–1952), both of whom emphasized the way in which art could express the emotional engagement of the artist.

You could argue that an appreciation of art involves both significant form and an expression of the emotions. A landscape photograph by Ansel Adams – as, for example, his wonderful images of the Yosemite National Park – is not just a photograph, in the sense of a technical reproduction of light and shade, but an expression of his way of seeing, his attention to detail, to light, to balance (significant form, if you like) which also expresses his love for the scene he is capturing. Yet at the same time, he takes care to balance the photograph, with lines that lead the eye towards the points of most intense interest. Choosing exactly the position from which to take a photograph, arranging its composition, and printing it with attention to light and shade, are all elements of form. Yet at the same time, they are a natural expression of emotional engagement with the beauty of the landscape. Adams always claimed that one does not 'take' a photograph but 'makes' one; his careful work in developing his images to bring out their full tonal range reflects this. In the final image, you see exactly and uniquely his own engagement with the scene as he originally saw it.

Of course, it may not be possible, because of the wide range of artistic media, to give any definitive account of what makes something 'art.' Perhaps art should be seen as an umbrella term for a whole range of loosely related forms, their common factor being no more than the fact that people take them to be art.

In practical terms, art may perhaps be defined in terms of what the art establishment (or art world) is prepared to accept as art. As with the process of selecting of images for an exhibition, or putting together the programme for a concert, something is considered art, or music, if it is what people are prepared to go and look at or listen to. It may not be to everyone's taste, people may be provoked to laugh, may walk out of a performance, may find an exhibit offensive – but it remains art or music if it is treated as such by those who run the gallery or concert hall. Would the pile of bricks remain art, even if nobody appreciated it as such and it was located on a building site rather than in a gallery?

Art may thus be defined in terms of its function; in other words, something is art if it is treated as art, or if it works as art for us, even if the medium is entirely new. Alternatively, it may be defined by the procedures that *lead* to its production and use; does this particular thing or event follow an established tradition (or writing, drawing, composing and so on) and is it accepted as such within the community of those engaged in the arts?

Key idea for life

Perhaps the most immediate way to engage with these issues is to confront various works of art and monitor your response to them. What do they 'say' to you? Would you consider them to be art at all? Those wanting to explore further the question of what constitutes art, might find Nigel Warburton's *The Art Question* (Routledge, 2003) a useful starting point.

What does art do?

How you see the function of art depends in part on how you understand experience and reality. Plato, for example, saw individual things as poor copies of timeless realities (his 'Forms'), and therefore criticized art for taking this a stage further, producing copies of copies. Art therefore, for Plato, is presenting something 'unreal' and therefore further from the truth, whereas for Paul Tillich and Susanne Langar it is a necessary way of encountering transcendent reality, and therefore supremely 'real'. Art functions as a means of allowing us to see reality that cannot be conveyed by literal description or direct perception.

The richness of art has produced a variety of responses from philosophers. Plato feared that art in general, and dramatic poetry in particular, had the power to corrupt people by stirring up their emotions. He was hostile to art and in favour of strict censorship. He saw art as subversive, replacing reality with fantasy, manipulating the emotions. Yet his dialogues are great works of literature; they are art!

Nietzsche, by contrast, welcomed this aspect. In *The Birth of Tragedy* (1872) he contrasted the Dionysian and Apollonian spirit within humankind, the former bringing elation, intoxication and a stirring of the emotions, the latter bringing cool rationality. Art has the positive function of holding the two together.

How can you allow art to have its full effect on the person who sees, reads or hears it, and yet maintain some rational control on what art says? Should art be politically correct? Marx saw art as having a social and political function. Good art, from a Marxist perspective, is that which reflects the values of social revolution, and which stirs the emotions in line with certain political values and attitudes.

Many, by contrast, would argue that art should not be determined by political correctness, and that maintaining its ability to challenge conventional opinions is essential. In that case, should a work of art be its own justification? If so, does it make sense to speak of good or bad art?

The work of the artist links to questions about the nature of the self, the nature of language and the nature of perception. A novelist, for example, may use language in a rich and subtle way in order to convey a whole range of emotions and intuitions, and not just to convey them, but to evoke them in the reader. A work of fiction thus invites an emotional and imaginative response. No two readers 'picture' the events described in the novel in exactly the same way.

Key idea for life

Contrast this function of literature with the ideal of analytic philosophy, which presents each argument with as much literal clarity as possible, or logical positivism, which insists that a statement can only have meaning if backed up by evidence. That approach seeks language which is clean, precise and straightforward, while a novel or poem may be rich in meaning, evocative, symbolic and often deliberately ambiguous. They function in utterly different ways, although both may seek to aid our understanding of life. One might argue that philosophy and art are two sides of the creative human coin; the one focusing on reflective thought, the other on creative expression.

In recent years there has been an increase in interest in the philosophy of film, both as a way of expressing philosophical ideas (seen particularly in films like *The Matrix*, which asks about the nature of perception and reality), and in the way in which it can present moral and existential challenges. When immersed in watching a film, we are engaging with the experiences on screen, interpreting them and responding emotionally to them. Yet at the same time, because it is a film, we are aware that what we are experiencing has already been interpreted – by the scriptwriter and director – in order to present ideas and narrative. So film and television are popular media for presenting *interpreted* reality, and it is then up to us to *interpret those interpretations*, as we explore and evaluate what the film or the television programme is 'saying'.

Aesthetics and the sublime

Whether through works of art or by the direct experience of the natural world, people appreciate beauty. But what exactly is beauty? Can it be defined? The study of beauty is termed 'aesthetics' (although that term is sometimes used more generally of the philosophy of art) and it goes hand in hand with another experience, that of 'the sublime'.

Although a number of earlier philosophers had written on aesthetics, including David Hume and Edmund Burke, and the question of beauty had been explored from the time of the ancient Greeks, a key figure for any discussion of aesthetics is Immanuel Kant, and particularly his *Critique of Aesthetic Judgement*, written in 1790, at a time when matters of taste were not thought of as exclusively subjective and personal, but as indicating genuine features of our experienced world.

Philosophical effort warning

Reading Kant and unpicking his arguments is difficult in the extreme, and going through academic commentaries on his work is almost as bad. However, the gist of what he has to say is relevant to our understanding of our judgements of taste, beauty and the sense of awe we may experience in nature. For those determined to try it, be aware that the *Critique of Aesthetic Judgement* is the first part of his work known as *The Critique of Judgement*.

By 'aesthetic judgement' Kant means that, when he looks at or listens to that object or event, he is pleased by the experience of it, and says that it is beautiful or sublime – and that, of course, can apply to a natural object as well as an art object.

In exploring this, Kant suggests that there is no objective test by which we can judge beauty; no single feature that applies to everything that we can describe as beautiful. But that does not mean that all beauty is a matter of subjective preference. Rather, he sees our idea of the beautiful as a reflective judgement that we can make.

He argues that we see such judgements as *universal*. In other words, the beauty is real and potentially recognized as such by everyone. We may be mistaken about it, but we think it is real and belongs to the object itself. If I say that a flower is beautiful, I refer to its form, colour and so on – and my appreciation and relationship to it. It is also *disinterested*. It would be wrong to say that something is beautiful simply because I have just created it myself, or paid good money for it, or in some way stand to gain by it. It is beautiful only if I can stand back from my own interests and make that judgement.

A judgement of beauty is also a matter of *common sense*, in that it is to do with the sort of sense experiences that everyone and anyone can have, and it is also *purposive*, in a way that is not defined by its intended end. In other words, something is beautiful in itself, not simply because an artist was commissioned to paint it for a wealthy customer, or a flower is beautiful in itself not simply because it needs to attract insects for purposes of pollination.

Through these criteria, Kant explores the way in which we make judgements of beauty, and these therefore impact on our understanding of art. However, art and beauty are not one and the same thing. Some art can be challenging and ugly. But equally, when we think of aesthetics, we consider natural beauty as well as the beauty of artistic creations, and this takes aesthetics beyond art. For one thing, if art is a matter of 'significant form' as Bell argued (see page 165), then the beauty of nature is certainly not art, unless we project onto it natural forms in our admiration of it. So, with Kant, we are dealing with a sense of the sublime that is closer to a religious experience than any formalized structures of art.

Kant also, in the second part of his *Critique of Aesthetic Judgement*, examines 'the sublime'. This refers to those moments when nature tends to overwhelm us by its sheer size or power – moments that render us speechless, moments of awe, moments often interpreted in religious terms. We cannot take it all in; we feel helpless before it.

A key feature of the sublime, in contrast to the beautiful, is that it goes beyond the bounded sense of form that a beautiful object can have. There is no way that the mind can grasp and understand the sublime.

There is far more to be said about both the beautiful and the sublime, but these comments on Kant should just alert us to the fact that the description of something as beautiful or sublime is not the same as saying that it has particular qualities of colour or size or shape. It is to do with our relationship to that object or that aspect of nature. It is what we say when we reflect upon our experience of it.

Key idea for life

Life is full of things that are beautiful or awe-inspiring; we know them when we encounter them. Our experience of them is personal, but it does not feel limited to a matter of taste. We sense that we are in the presence of something that goes beyond simple factual description. I know that sunset is simply bands of orange and red, but just LOOK at it! The beautiful and (particularly) the sublime also relate to the religious experience of awe at that which is encountered within nature, but somehow goes beyond any factual description. In spite of Kant's best efforts, we cannot define it, but we are enriched by it.

Aesthetics links with other areas of philosophy. For example, writing in the USA in the 1950s, both the theologian Paul Tillich and philosopher Susanne Langer spoke of art as symbol, as pointing beyond itself to some other transcendent reality. This links aesthetics with the philosophy of religion. Indeed, Tillich held that all religious ideas and images were symbols, pointing to 'being-itself', and that religious truths could not be conveyed other than by symbols. A work of art could therefore be seen as in some sense 'religious', however secular its context, as it pointed to that which was beyond ordinary experience.

For those wanting to follow up on aesthetics and the philosophy of art in the twentieth century, other philosophers of particular importance in this area include R. G. Collingwood, who published *Principles of Art* in 1925, written at a time when philosophy was much concerned with literal description (as in logical positivism), and, from the 1960s, E. H. Gombrich's *Art and Illusion* (1960) and N. Goodman's *Languages of Art* (1968).

The relationship between art and nature is illustrated by considering garden design – the very point at which the two interlock, with the attempt to give 'significant form' to nature. One may contrast the formal French gardens of the eighteenth century, with their geometric shapes outlined with neatly trimmed box hedges, with the romantic gardens of the nineteenth, where a slight tweaking of the landscape attempts to improve on nature while excluding any sense of the artificial.

Key idea for life: Art, culture and change

Art reflects the particular self-understanding of each age: wander through any art gallery and it becomes clear that the concerns and values of each period are clearly reflected in its visual art. It is not just a matter of style, but of the changing sense of what it is appropriate to depict in art. There is also great variety in the self-consciousness of creativity; in one period, the aim appears to be to render such an accurate depiction of external reality that the artist disappears from immediate view; in another period, perceived image is distorted in order to reflect the self-conscious intentions of the artist.

In the eighteenth century, for example, primacy was given to natural beauty, and a sense of balance between nature and the mind perceiving nature. Kant saw a 'formal purposiveness' in those things that produced an aesthetic experience: art objects creating a sense of harmonious pleasure in the mind. The twentieth century has been more concerned with the nature of artistic production, and the process of artistic creativity has often become its own subject matter.

Thus, although aesthetics and the philosophy of art may be studied as a separate branch of philosophy, their real fascination comes from interlocking them with questions about the nature of perception, the self and its creativity, the self-transcending quality of religious experience or the ethics of what is expressed or depicted. This touches on a key question that has haunted philosophy since Plato: How do the particular, changing and ephemeral images that dance before us, relate to what, if anything, we may take to be an enduring or eternal reality?

Postmodernism

Postmodernism is a rather vague term for a number of approaches to philosophy, literature and the arts that have in common a rejection of an earlier 'modernist' view. The 'modern' view, against which postmodernism reacts, is one that sees the image as the production of the unique human subject and was itself a self-conscious rejection of older cultural and religious traditions that occurred in the late nineteenth and early twentieth centuries. This broad movement paralleled existentialism in its focus on the self, its freedom, and the choices by which it creates itself and its world. Its hallmarks are innovation and self-expression.

Postmodernism, as a general approach to culture, goes beyond the writings of Derrida, Lyotard and others who work in the fields of philosophy and literary criticism, for it can apply to all the arts. Indeed, the ideas were explored in architecture, literature and the fine arts before transferring to philosophy. Previously, an image could be taken to refer to something external to itself, either something in the physical world or in human consciousness. In postmodernism, however, an image reflects only other images and has no fixed reference. There is, therefore, no such thing as an 'authentic' image – authentic, that is, in the sense that an existentialist would use the term. It can't be checked against reality or declared to be right or wrong. It is understood simply in terms of a network of similar ideas or images, part of a broad swathe of human creativity.

A piece of writing is, for postmodernism, no longer a message sent from a creative author to a receptive reader. Rather, it is bound up with a mass of reduplication. We shuffle and arrange images, but do not have any creative control over them. In a work of art, a novel or a film, a postmodernist approach undermines the modernist belief in the image as the production of an individual consciousness. We, and all that we produce, are products of our cultural environment; our language and concepts are borrowed, re-arranged and presented as something new.

A postmodern image often sets out to display its own artificial nature; it may represent something, but without pretending to give it any new depth. So, for example, in the art world, one might contrast Picasso (who, as a 'modernist' strove for a unique view and form of communication) with Warhol's use of mass-produced public images. An interesting discussion of this is found in R. Kearney's 'The crisis of the postmodernist image' in *Contemporary French Philosophy* (A. Phillips Griffiths (ed.), Cambridge, 1987).

For reflection:

▶ **Modernism:** The dilemma and existential agony of the blank sheet of paper, a set of paints and brushes, and the desire to express oneself through a unique image.

▶ **Postmodernism:** The word-processing package comes to the rescue, for it contains a great variety of pieces of 'clip art', which can instantly be printed out and arranged on the paper.

Postmodernism is encouraged by the developments in technology, particularly mass communication and the ability to reproduce images. The individual subject is no longer considered to be the creator of his or her images. What we appear to create is what is already there around us. We produce consumer items.

It is not so much philosophy that is postmodern, but the whole of society. There are many images to be shuffled, but there is no metaphysical insight to be had, and no transcendental reality to represent.

Key idea for life

For postmodernism, you cannot get *behind* the images, symbols and reproduced goods of a technological age in order to discern individuality, purpose or meaning. They are exactly what they are, nothing more and nothing less, except that you are invited to give them your attention.

This is also reflected in the postmodernist view, explored by Jean-Francois Lyotard, that statements about the overall purpose of life or society (for example, society exists for the benefit of its members), sometimes called 'meta-narratives', are losing their credibility. It is no longer realistic to make general statements of a metaphysical nature about life, as they do not reflect the fragmented nature of modern society.

Case study

I am the author of this book: I address you, the reader, directly in order to illustrate some of the issues connected with the postmodern outlook.

What do you think of me as an author? You could say: 'He's just stuck together bits of information that others have given him.' That is true. You could go on to say: 'There is absolutely nothing original in it!' This is a more serious charge, but made complicated because there is a certain originality in the way that the ideas of others are selected, analysed, arranged and presented.

But suppose I claim to have said something original. Can that claim be justified?

What of the words I use? Their meanings are already given by the society that uses this language (if they weren't, you would not understand them). They do not originate in my mind.

What of the climate of opinion within which I write? Does that not shape my views? Am I responsible for it, or shaped by it?

What of comments for which I claim originality? If you knew everything that I had read, everyone whom I had spoken to, could you not predict my views? Could you not analyse my views, show influences, categorize the style, and place my views within a particular tradition? A literary critic often shows that what seems to be a unique expression of a thinking self is in fact an intellectual patchwork of influences.

This book is being written to fit a certain number of printed pages of a particular size, and in a particular style. Its chapters reflect the range of philosophy taught in some university departments; what is included is determined by the constraints of space, purpose and market.

Thus the author of this book can vanish!

However, although I may keep within the overall structure of language, I feel that, from time to time, I am entitled to peer round the side of the structure and address you, the reader, directly. It is this that structuralism and postmodernism deny, and indeed, the idea of an author making a personal appeal to a reader is just another literary device. I disappear again!

The self as art

Michel Foucault once said 'We have to create ourselves as a work of art.' Nietzsche's advice: 'Live dangerously!'; 'Go beyond!'

We each have a variety of views – of society, of morals, of religion, of what is worthwhile, of particular people. We have hopes and fears about the future. These, lumped together, distinguish us and give each of us a means of interpreting and responding to our circumstances; they make us who we are, and they are expressed in the choices that we make as we go through life.

One of the possible benefits of philosophy is that it offers a set of tools by which to examine these views and relate them to one another. In the theory of knowledge, one of the ways of assessing truth is by examining its 'correspondence' with other views we hold. We will generally perceive something as being correct if it reflects and reinforces those other beliefs or views. Ideas that contradict everything we know so far are either an opportunity for some great moment of enlightenment and conversion, or they are likely to be rejected, swamped by those things to which we are already committed.

Yet if we are to retain, or shape, our integrity, or even simply progress and mature as we go through life, it is essential that we are at least open to the ideas that will shift our network of assumptions. This is a characteristic of being open to the impact that philosophy can have upon us – we may be challenged.

What does all this have to do with art? Well, some philosophers have argued – as did Foucault and Nietzsche – that our task in life is to shape and direct our lives so that they 'say' something; in effect that they become works of art – not in the sense of expressing physical beauty (although, from body art to cosmetic surgery, there is plenty of scope for doing just that), but as making a statement about what life is about.

Key idea for life

Just as some works of art are simply beautiful while others are puzzling or challenging, so there is no standard way of sculpting your life into an artwork. The philosophical hope is that the examined life will present its own distinctiveness.

Clothes may say it all. In the introduction to his fascinating book *The Dandy: Peacock or Enigma?*, Nigel Rodgers says 'The fop and the flashily-dressed are always with us. The true Dandy – sardonic, aloof, independent – is a much rarer phenomenon. For him clothes are merely the outward visible form of an inward self-discipline, never to be wholly relaxed.'

Uniforms make an obvious statement about the role a person has in life, but are generally used to hide rather than enhance the individual. In a military context, a uniform expresses and reinforces the commitment of the man or woman wearing it, with personal preferences set aside.

Key idea for life: Art, self and shopping?

As consumers, we seek out products that signify for us the good life. Brand loyalty, strengthened by every purchase, tends to define us. Personally, at a superficial level, I might be branded as 'Mercedes, Apple, Nikon', and you'll immediately get some idea of my interests. The success of a 'lifestyle' approach to promoting of brands, shows the extent to which we understand ourselves in terms of symbols, and seek to present our lives as works of art – 'saying something'.

Narratives can also express the self as art – seeing your life as an unfolding story. At a funeral, the eulogy seeks to present the story of a life, summing it up, making sense, showing qualities. Daniel Dennett, rejecting any dualistic sense of the self as separate from the body, describes the self as the 'narrative centre of gravity', the notional point around which the story of our life turns.

Remember this: Social media and self-image

Through social media, everyone can now create an image of themselves to present to the world. We live at two levels: the physical and the digital. Should we be radically honest about ourselves in the digital world? There is a danger that the personal blog or website can become like the more irritating form of Christmas letter, offering nothing but a list of family successes during the past year. The photograph on my website is already eight years old. Should I change it, or quietly leave it as it is?

This ability to create of ourselves a digital work of art impacts on our understanding of the nature of the self (am I the person you see, or am I really the person who expresses himself or herself online, through a blog or website or Twitter feed?), and on the nature of artistic creativity.

Art, in the broadest sense, is the creative exploration of life. As such, it touches on – and is used by – another way of understanding the self in its relationship to the whole of reality: religion.

Nietzsche, art and religion

In *The Genealogy of Morals*, Nietzsche describes creative artists as having a telephone link with the 'above' and of being the 'ventriloquists of God'. In other words, he is open to the idea of art as a vehicle for exploring transcendence (the sense of going 'beyond' the mundane or surface experience of things) that does not require any of the metaphysical beliefs normally associated with religion. From this starting point, it would be possible to explore the idea that art may take over functions that have traditionally been performed by religion.

In early societies, the development of art runs parallel with the development of religious rites, associated particularly with the burial of the dead, or the celebration of the animals upon which human life depended. As we now look at early cave drawings, it is widely assumed that they were seen, not merely as decorative, but as having religious and existential significance.

In taking up a brush to paint, or an instrument to play music, one engages the creative imagination, bringing out a personal sense of meaning – very much the equivalent of the spiritual explorer within religion. Equally, in looking at visual art or listening to great musical performances, there can come a sense of a tingle of excitement or a moment of insight, that are also features of religious experience (see page 189). In both cases, we feel a distinction between the superficial and the profound, the glib and the serious.

Nietzsche's distinction between Apollonian formalism and Dionysian ecstasy (see above page 168) reflects the double nature both of artistic creativity and religion. On the one hand there is the desire to see formal structures, to make sense, to organize; on the other the feeling of being taken completely out of oneself, away from all predictable order and into an area of experience that an artist might refer to as inspiration and a religious person as an encounter with the numinous, the mystical or the ineffable. In both cases there is an immediate, emotional and expressive engagement with a level of reality that defies rational explanation. If you want to kill art or religion, reduce it to a set of rational propositions!

Key idea for life

Why is it that, at a time when commitment to formal religion is on the decline in the West, there seems to be a remarkable resurgence of interest in the arts? Galleries are full of people who look, give attention, emotionally engage, and seek to find meaning in art. Might this be a way in which a secular society provides an outlet for an inherently 'religious' cast of mind?

7

The Philosophy of Religion

In this chapter you will:

- ► *Consider religious experience and how it may be described*
- ► *Learn about the arguments for the existence of God*
- ► *Examine miracles, the problem of evil and other key issues*

Why?

Whether you are a believer, an agnostic or an atheist, there is no escaping the fact that religion still plays an important part in the lives of many people, and religious ideas and images have contributed hugely to our cultural heritage. However, can religious beliefs be rationally justified? Should they be? Are they simply a way of expressing intuitions about the meaning and purpose of life or a commitment to live by certain moral principles? The philosophy of religion is relevant for everyone, whether religious or not, simply because it raises fundamental questions about life and its meaning.

In Western thought, the philosophy of religion is concerned with:

▶ Religious language: what it means, what it does and whether it can be shown to be true or false.

▶ Metaphysical claims (e.g. that God exists): the nature of the arguments by which such claims are defended, and the basis upon which those claims can be shown to be true or false.

In addition to these basic areas of study, there are many other questions concerning religious beliefs and practices which philosophy can examine:

▶ What is faith? How does it relate to reason? Is it ever reasonable to be a religious 'fundamentalist'?

▶ What is 'religious experience' and what sort of knowledge can it yield?

▶ Is the universe such as to suggest that it has an intelligent creator and designer?

▶ Are miracles possible? If so, could we ever have sufficient evidence to prove that?

▶ Is belief in a loving God compatible with the existence of suffering and evil in the world?

▶ Can psychology explain the phenomenon of religion?

▶ Is life after death possible? If so, what difference does it make to our view of life?

Faith, reason and belief

Should religious belief be based on reason? If it were, it would be open to change if the logic of an argument went against it. However, experience tells us that most religious people hold beliefs that, while they may be open to reasonable scrutiny, depend on a prior commitment or wish to believe, and therefore belief may persist in the face of reasonable criticism.

Within Christianity, there is a tradition – associated particularly with the Protestant Reformation and Calvin – that human nature is fallen and sinful, and that human reason is equally limited and unable to yield knowledge of God. Belief in God is therefore a matter of faith, and any logical arguments to back up that belief are optional and secondary.

Key idea for life: Reasonable believing 'in'?

This last sentence speaks of belief 'in God' and not just belief 'that God exists'. That is a crucial difference, especially when discussing the existence of God. Belief 'in' something implies an added element of commitment and valuation. One might, after all, believe 'that' God exists, but think that such belief is quite trivial and of no personal significance, which is not what believing 'in' something is about. This explains the frustration that arises during some debates between atheists and believers. The one expects that reason and evidence will settle the matter; the other has deep emotional and intuitive 'reasons' for believing. But the key question is: can you believe 'in' something, if you do not also have reasons to believe 'that' it exists?

The quest for certainty sometimes leads to **foundationalism** – the attempt to find statements that are so obviously true that they cannot be challenged. We have already seen that Descartes came to his incontrovertible statement 'I think, therefore I am'. Some modern philosophers of religion, notably Alvin Plantinga, argue for a 'Reformed Epistemology' – a theory of knowledge founded on basic beliefs that are self-evident to the person who holds them, even if they are not open to reasoned argument.

An example of this would be the belief that the universe is designed by God, based on a sense of wonder and beauty. We shall look at the 'design argument' on page 201; what is different here is that Plantinga thinks that such belief is not a logical *conclusion* to an argument, but is held *prior to* engaging with that argument.

A related idea is **fundamentalism**. Originally used as a term for those who wished to set aside the superficialities of religion and return to its fundamental principles, it is now more commonly used for those who take beliefs, as they are found in the Bible or the Qur'an for example, in a very literal and straightforward sense and apply them without allowing them to be challenged by reason. A basic problem with this is that the scriptures were written using particular language and in a particular context, and if statements are taken literally and out of context, the original intention of the writers may be lost. Of course, the fundamentalist would not accept this, believing that the words of scripture are given directly by God and are therefore not open to any form of literary or contextual analysis.

That something more than logic is needed if we are to understand the nature of religious statements was highlighted by the Danish philosopher Søren Kierkegaard (1813–55). He argued that a 'leap of faith' was necessary, and that it was not so much the *content* of a belief that made it religious, but the *way* in which it was believed – with subjectivity and inwardness.

PASCAL'S WAGER

Blaise Pascal (1623–62) put forward what must count as one of the saddest pieces of logic ever employed within the philosophy of religion. His *Pensées* were published posthumously in 1670. In them, Pascal battles (as did his contemporary, Descartes) with the implications of **scepticism** – the systematic challenging of the ability to know anything for certain. Pascal was a committed Catholic and wanted to produce an argument that would both justify and commend belief.

To appreciate the force of his argument, you need to be aware that his view of human nature was rather bleak: without God's help, people were inherently selfish, and would only do what seemed to be in their own self-interest.

His starting point is that reason alone cannot prove that God exists; to believe or not believe therefore involves an element of choice. Which choice is in line with enlightened self-interest, and therefore likely to appeal to the non-believer? His argument runs like this:

- **IF** I believe in God and he does indeed exist, I stand to gain eternal blessings and life with God after my death.

- **IF** I believe in God and he does not exist, all I lose is the negligible inconvenience of having followed the religious life.

However:

- **IF** I do not believe in God and he does indeed exist, I stand to suffer eternal punishment in hell, banished forever from his presence.

- **IF** I do not believe in God and he does not exist, I have lost nothing, but gained some benefit from not having had to lead a religious life.

On balance, therefore, Pascal claims that self-interest suggests that it is best to believe in God and follow the religious life!

I called this the saddest piece of logic because it takes a rather grim view of God (as one who will punish or reward according to a person's belief), and a less-than-attractive view of the religious life (regarding it as a mild inconvenience, rather than something of value and enjoyable in itself). Fear of hell may drive people to believe, but that is hardly wholehearted belief in God.

Key idea for life

Pascal saw people as caught between dogmatism and doubt, and hoped that he had found a way to overcome the latter without imposing the former. My personal view is that he ended up with the worst of both worlds – self-deception motivated by self-interest! In any case, a philosopher might challenge the very idea that one can *choose* to believe; one either does or one does not, anything else is pretence.

In the rest of this chapter, we shall be looking at reasoned argument concerning religious ideas. However, we need to recognize that there is more to religious faith than the intellectual assent to propositions.

Religious language

If you describe a religious event or organization, the language you use need not be especially religious. Consider the following:

▶ The Pope is the Bishop of Rome.

▶ The Jewish religion forbids the eating of pork.

The first of these is true by definition, since 'Pope' is a title used for the Bishop of Rome. The second can be shown to be true by looking at the Jewish scriptures. (It would not be made invalid by evidence that a non-practising Jew had been seen eating a bacon sandwich, for the moral and religious rules remain true, even if they are broken.) Provided that the terms are understood, such descriptive language presents few problems.

However, religious people use language in a variety of ways. They may pray, give thanks, hold moral discussions and – most importantly – make statements about what they believe. The problem is that these belief statements sometimes make claims about things that go beyond what can be known of the ordinary world that we can experience and examine scientifically. We have already seen that some philosophers want to dismiss all metaphysics as meaningless, and along with it they would therefore discard most statements of religious belief.

However, here's the problem. Religious statements are not simply bad science or superstition, because, even when they appear to make supernatural claims, they are also about experiences, values, community, commitment and a sense of meaning and purpose in life. They are not simple, factual statements. So, if we are to make a serious attempt to understand religious claims, if we are to take religion seriously, we need to examine the character of religious language and the function that it performs.

HOW? AND WHY?

One way of expressing a distinctive flavour of religious language is to highlight the difference between 'how?' questions and 'why?' questions. Science answers 'how?' questions by explaining how individual parts of the world relate to one another. Religion, however asks 'why?'; not 'How does the world work?' but 'Why is there a world at all?'

A 'why?' question asks about meaning and purpose. It cannot be answered in terms of empirical facts alone. This is illustrated by a story devised by John Wisdom (1904–93) and widely used in discussions about the existence of God. It runs like this:

Two explorers come across a clearing in the jungle. It contains a mixture of weeds and flowers. One claims that it is a garden and that there must be a gardener who comes to tend it; the other disagrees. They sit and wait, but no gardener appears; they set up various means of detecting him, but still nothing. One explorer continues to deny that there is a gardener. The other still claims that there is a gardener, but one who is invisible and undetectable. How – and this is the central point of the argument – how do you distinguish an undetectable gardener whose activity is open to question, from an imaginary gardener or no gardener at all?

Key idea for life

Of course, there is another relevant question: 'What difference does it make to you if you choose to see the clearing as a garden?' In other words, how might your view of life be changed by seeing the world as controlled by a loving God (whether or not such a God exists)?

As originally presented, this story was used to show that a good idea could 'die the death of a thousand qualifications'. In other words, when all obvious qualities that the gardener might have are eliminated, nothing of any significance remains. However, the story also illustrates the idea of a **blik** – a particular 'view' of things. In the story, the same evidence is available to both explorers, but they choose to interpret it differently. We have our own particular blik and interpret everything in the light of it. It can be argued that religious belief is just one such blik; one way of organizing our experience of the world. As such it is no more or less true than anyone else's blik, and every argument ends with someone saying: 'Well, if that's the way you want to see it …'

THE PERSONAL ASPECTS OF LANGUAGE

In *Religious Language* (1957), the British theologian I.T. Ramsey points out that there are elements of both discernment and commitment in religious statements. They are not simply detached, speculative comments. Although they include facts, they are far more complex than that. He makes the essential point that the word 'God' is used to describe a reality about which the believer feels strongly.

We should therefore distinguish between the philosopher who examines arguments for the existence of God in an objective and disinterested way, and the religious believer who uses 'God' to express a sense of direction, purpose and meaning that comes through religious and moral experience.

Ramsey used the terms *models* and *qualifiers* to explain the way in which religious language differs from ordinary empirical language. A 'model' is like an analogy – an image that helps a person to articulate that which is rather different from anything else. For example, if God is called a 'designer', it does not imply that the religious believer has some personal knowledge of a process of design carried out by God, simply that the image of someone who designs is close to his or her experience of God. Contrariwise, having offered the 'model', it is then important for the religious believer to offer a 'qualifier' – God is an 'infinite' this or a 'perfect' that – the model is therefore qualified, so that it is not mistakenly taken in a literal way.

Key idea for life

Belief in God involves commitment to a particular way of looking at life. It should not be reduced to simple statements of fact, to be checked against evidence. That mistake led it to be branded 'meaningless' by the logical positivists (see page 101). But if religion is exclusively a matter of the way in which we look at life, the issue is not whether it is true or false, but whether it is healthy or unhealthy, helpful or unhelpful.

Religious experience

If nobody had religious experiences, there would be no basis
for the idea of a 'god', nor would there have been any reason
for religions to have developed. So what is it that makes an
experience religious?

The nineteenth-century religious writer and philosopher
Schleiermacher described religious awareness in terms of a
'feeling of dependence' and of seeing finite things in and
through the infinite. This was rather like mystical experience – a
sudden awareness of a wider dimension, throwing new light on
the ordinary world around us. What Schleiermacher was trying
to express was that religion was not a matter of dogma or logic,
but was based on a direct experience of oneself as being small
and limited, against the background of the eternal. It was also
an identification of the self with the whole: a sense of belonging
to the whole world. Feelings like that do not depend on logic;
they are not the result of reasoning but of intuition.

Rudolph Otto, in *The Idea of the Holy* (1917), argued that
the religious experience was essentially about the *mysterium
tremendum*, something totally other, unknowable; something
that is awesome in its dimensions and power; something which
is also attractive and fascinating; something that makes the
spine tingle or the flesh creep.

For example, you may feel overwhelmed at the sight of a range
of snow-capped mountains looming above you. Their sheer
size and bulk, contrasting with your own minuscule body,
give you a 'tingle', a sense of wonder, a sense that, faced with
this scene of absolute and almost terrifying beauty, your life
cannot ever be quite the same again. However, when you try
to describe that experience to a cynical friend, you cast around
for suitable words, but cannot fully convey that 'tingle', unless,
as a result of your description, he or she too can start to sense
'the holy'.

However, such experiences can only be described by using
words that have a rational, everyday meaning – language
that, if taken literally, could not do justice to their special
quality. Many words seem to describe the feelings and express

ideas that are close to this experience of the 'holy' (goodness, wonder, purity, etc.) but none of them is actually about the holy itself. Such words, which attempt to describe the holy, are (to use Otto's term) its **schema**. The process of finding words by means of which to convey the implications of the holy is **schematization**. Religious language is just such a schema, whereas the 'holy' itself is an *a priori* category; in other words, the holy cannot be completely described or defined in terms of the particular experiences through which we encounter it. It is conveyed by means of these terms but is always elusively beyond them and cannot be contained by them.

Key idea for life

The holy cannot be fully explained, only experienced, and its subsequent 'religious' interpretation is optional. In secular terms, it comes close to the experience of the 'sublime' (see page 169).

Otto's idea of schematization is important for understanding the nature of the philosophy of religion. Philosophy examines the rational concepts by means of which the religious experience is schematized. The proofs of the existence of God are, following this way of thinking, not proofs of the actual existence of a being which is known and defined as 'God', but are rational ways of expressing the intuition about 'God' that comes as a result of religious experience.

Thus, the idea of God as the designer of the universe is not open to logical proof but is a schema. It invites us to think what it would be like if this whole world had been designed for a particular purpose, with everything working together as it should. Such a schema suggests what it is like to believe in God.

We can see, therefore, that the pattern of religious language and the analysis of religious experience point in the same direction – that of an experience and a level of reality which transcends, but springs out of the literal, the empirical or the rational. All of these things can suggest the object of religious devotion, but none can define or describe it literally.

TRANSCENDENCE

One way of describing religious experience is in terms of 'transcendence' – that an experience goes beyond ordinary perception to give some sense of what is 'beyond' or 'absolute' even if that cannot be described in itself. Clearly, great works of art, or a beautiful landscape, or simply the awesome power of nature (whether benign or threatening) can give rise to a sense of transcendence. However, that raises a fundamental question. Just because an experience is transcendent – just because it gives that sense of awe, or wonder, or a new view of oneself – does that imply that there has to be a transcendent *object* of which we become aware? If not, it might be possible to have the same transcendent experience that inspires the believer, but to have it entirely within a secular context. This is explored in a chapter entitled 'Transcendence without God' by Anthony Simon Laden in *Philosophers without Gods* (ed. Louise Antony, 2007).

Does God exist?

Before looking at some traditional arguments for the existence of God, we need to have some working idea of what is meant by the word 'God'.

As we are concerned with Western philosophy, the relevant concepts have come from the Western theistic religions – Judaism, Christianity and Islam. For these, God may be said to be a supreme being: infinite, spiritual and personal; creator of the world. He is generally described as *omnipotent* (all-powerful), *omnibenevolent* (all-loving) and *omniscient* (all-knowing). Although pictured in human form, he is believed to be beyond literal description (and is thus not strictly male, although 'he' is generally depicted as such).

Remember this

✳ Belief in the existence of such a god is **theism**.

✳ The conviction that no such being exists is **atheism**.

✳ The view that there is no conclusive evidence to decide whether God exists or not is **agnosticism**. (This term is also used for the more general view that no beliefs should be accepted unless they can be supported by evidence.)

✷ An identification of God with the physical universe is **pantheism**.

✷ The belief that God is within everything and everything within God (but God and the physical universe are not simply identified) is **panentheism**. (Most interpretations of theism include the idea of everything being 'within' God; indeed, if he is infinite, there is nothing external to him.)

✷ The idea of an external, designer God who created the world, but is not immanent within it, is **deism**.

There is a problem with taking the idea of the existence of God too literally. The thirteenth-century philosopher and theologian Thomas Aquinas described God as being *supra ordinem omnium entium* – beyond the order of all beings. In other words, God is not a being who might or might not exist somewhere; indeed, he is not *a* being at all. *So we should not be tempted (as are some atheists) to assume a crude idea of God and then show that there is no evidence for his existence. On those terms, Aquinas and most serious religious thinkers down through the centuries would certainly have qualified as atheists. The meaning of God is far more subtle than that.*

In his *Critique of Pure Reason* (section A, 590–91), Kant argued that there could be only three types of argument for the existence of God:

1 Based on reason alone

2 Based on the general fact of the existence of the world

3 Based on particular features of the world

They are called the **ontological, cosmological** and **teleological** arguments. Kant offered a critique of all three, but then introduced a rather different approach: the moral argument.

The traditional arguments for the existence of God form the central core of the philosophy of religion – not necessarily because they are convincing as arguments, but because they help to illustrate what religious belief is about.

Key idea for life

Before getting into these arguments, one thing needs to be absolutely clear. 'God' does not and cannot exist in the sense that anything else can be said to exist. The God of theism is neither part of the universe nor somehow 'outside' the universe. The key question is: to what aspect of reality (if any) does the word 'God' refer? That may not be what you expect when you ask 'Does God exist?', but it is the only intellectually legitimate way of trying to understand what religious people claim to believe.

THE ONTOLOGICAL ARGUMENT

The ontological argument for the existence of God is not based on observation of the world, or on any form of external evidence, but simply on a definition of the meaning of 'God' that implies that he must exist. It is of particular interest to philosophers because it raises questions about language and metaphysics that apply to issues other than religious belief.

The argument was set out by Anselm (1033–1109), Archbishop of Canterbury, in the opening chapters of his *Proslogion*. He makes it clear that he is not putting forward this argument in order to be able to believe in God, but because his belief leads him to understand God's existence as *aliquid quo nihil maius cogitari possit* – 'that than which nothing greater can be thought' – in other words, it expresses his idea of 'perfection', 'the absolute', the most real thing (*ens reallissimum*).

In the second chapter of *Proslogion*, the argument is presented in this way:

> Now we believe that thou art a being than which none greater can be thought. Or can it be that there is no such being, since 'the fool hath said in his heart, "There is no God"'? [Psalm 14:1; 53:1] But when this same fool hears what I am saying – 'A being than which none greater can be thought' – he understands what he hears, and what he understands is in his understanding, even if he does not understand that it exists. For it is one thing for an object to be in the understanding, and another thing to understand

> that it exists ... But clearly that than which a greater cannot
> be thought cannot exist in the understanding alone. For if
> it is actually in the understanding alone, it can be thought
> of as existing also in reality, and this is greater... But
> obviously this is impossible. Without doubt, therefore, there
> exists, both in the understanding and in reality, something
> than which a greater cannot be thought.
>
> (translation as in *The Existence of God*,
> John Hick, Macmillan, 1964)

In other words, Anselm assumes that something is greater
if it exists than if it doesn't. So, if God is the greatest thing
imaginable, he must exist.

One of the clearest criticisms of this argument was made by
Kant (in his *Critique of Pure Reason*) in response to Descartes',
version of the argument, in which he had argued that it was
impossible to have a triangle without its having three sides and
angles, and in the same way it was impossible to have God
without having necessary existence. Kant's counter-argument
may be set out like this:

▶ **If** you have a triangle

▶ **Then** it must have three angles (i.e. to have a triangle without
three angles is a contradiction)

▶ **But** if you do not have the triangle, you do not have its three
angles or sides either.

In the same way, Kant argued:

▶ **If** you accept God, it is therefore logical to accept his
necessary existence.

▶ **But** you do not have to accept God.

To appreciate the force of Kant's argument, it is important to
remember that he divided all statements into two categories –
analytic and synthetic:

▶ **Analytic statements** are true by definition.

▶ **Synthetic statements** can only be proved true or false with
reference to experience.

For Kant, statements about existence are synthetic; definitions are analytic. Therefore, the angles and sides of a triangle are necessary because they are part of the definition of a triangle. However, that says nothing about the actual existence of a triangle – necessity (for Kant) is not a feature of the world, but only of logic and definition.

Kant gives another way of expressing the same idea. He says that *existence is not a predicate*. In other words, if you describe something completely, you add nothing to that description by then saying 'and it has existence'. Existence is not an extra quality, it is just a way of saying that there is an example of the thing you have described.

Norman Malcolm (in *Philosophical Review*, January 1960) pointed out that Kant's criticism failed in an important respect. You can either have a triangle or not, but (on Anselm's definition) you simply cannot have no God, so the two situations are not exactly parallel.

For Anselm, then, 'God' is a unique concept. This was something that he had to clarify early on, in the light of criticism from Gaunilo, a fellow monk, who raised the idea of the perfect island, claiming that, if Anselm's argument were true, then the perfect island would also have to exist. Anselm rejected this. An island is a limited thing, and you can always imagine better and better islands. But he holds that 'a being than which a greater cannot be thought' is unique. If it could be thought of as non-existent, it could also be thought of as having a beginning and an end, but then it would not be the greatest that can be thought.

This is another version of the argument that he had already introduced in Chapter 3 of the *Proslogion*:

> Something which cannot be thought of as not existing … is greater than that which can be thought of as not existing. Thus, if that than which a greater cannot be thought can be thought of as not existing, this very thing than which a greater cannot be thought is not that than which a greater cannot be thought. But this is contradictory. So, then, there truly is a being than which a greater cannot be thought – so truly that it cannot even be thought of as not existing.

In other words, Anselm claims that necessary existence is implied by the idea of God. But he goes one step further. In Chapter 4 of *Proslogion*, he asks how the fool can still claim that God does not exist, and concludes:

> For we think of a thing, in one sense, when we think of the word that signifies it, and in another sense, when we understand the very thing itself. Thus in the first sense God can be thought of as non-existent, but in the second sense this is quite impossible. For no one who understands what God is can think that God does not exist ... For God is that than which a greater cannot be thought, and whoever understands this rightly must understand that he exists in a way that he cannot be non-existent even in thought.

So what did Anselm mean by speaking of God as 'that than which none greater can be thought'?

In another work, *Monologion*, he spoke of degrees of goodness and perfection in the world, and that there must be something that constitutes perfect goodness, which he calls 'God', which causes goodness in all else. This idea of the degrees of perfection was not new. Aristotle had used it in *De Philosophia*, and it is also closely related to Plato's idea of 'Forms'. Anselm's idea of God comes close to Plato's 'Form of the Good'.

There are several general philosophical issues to be explored here, which is why this argument has been set out at greater length than others in this book.

It touches on the idea that, without a sense of perfection, or of 'the highest quality', we have no means of judging relative value. Even if our judgements are entirely subjective, we need to have some concept of perfection in order to make them. Therefore our experience of meaning and value suggests the existence of an ultimate reality of some sort.

This has parallels with Plato's 'cave' (see page 22). The 'greatest thing' for Anselm is an intuition, necessitated by seeing lesser values as merely shadows or copies of something greater.

This approach to the ontological argument was taken by Iris Murdoch, the well-known novelist and Oxford philosopher, in her book *Metaphysics as a Guide to Morals* (1992). She held that an argument about necessary existence can only be taken in the context of this Platonic view of degrees of reality. She pointed out that what the proof offers is more than a simple logical argument, for it points to a spiritual reality that transcends any limited idea of God. It is also something that goes beyond individual religions:

> An ultimate religious 'belief' must be that even if all 'religions' were to blow away like mist, the necessity of virtue and the reality of the good would remain. This is what the Ontological Proof tries to 'prove' in terms of a unique formulation.
>
> (p. 427)

And this, she claimed, is a necessary part of our understanding of life:

> What is perfect must exist, that is, what we think of as goodness and perfection, the 'object' of our best thoughts, must be something real, indeed especially and most real, not as contingent accidental reality but as something fundamental, essential and necessary. What is experienced as most real in our lives is connected with a value which points further on. Our consciousness of failure is a source of knowledge. We are constantly in process of recognizing the falseness of our 'goods', and the unimportance of what we deem important. Great art teaches a sense of reality, so does ordinary living and loving.
>
> (p. 430)

To sum up:

If we simply think of the ontological argument in terms of 'existence is a predicate' then Kant was probably right, and Anselm wrong – for to say that something 'exists' is quite different from anything else that can be said about it.

But Anselm's argument suggests that some idea of 'the greatest that can be thought' is a necessary part of the way we think, because, every time we ascribe value to something, we do so on the basis of an intuition of that which has supreme value.

Key idea for life

At its heart, the ontological argument is about how we relate the ordinary conditioned and limited things we experience to the idea of the perfect, the absolute and the unconditioned – and that is a key question for philosophy. How can we say that anything is good or beautiful without having some general conception of what goodness or beauty is about? We may never encounter perfect goodness, but perhaps we need to have some such concept in order to make sense of our intuitions about goodness. Perhaps God also functions in that regulative way – not as something that exists, but as a necessary idea to express our ideals.

THE COSMOLOGICAL ARGUMENTS

Thomas Aquinas (1225–74) was probably the most important philosopher of the mediaeval period, and has certainly been the most influential in terms of the philosophy of religion. He sought to reconcile the Christian faith with the philosophy of Aristotle, which in the thirteenth century had been 'rediscovered' and was being taught in the secular universities of Europe.

Aquinas presented five ways in which he believed the existence of God could be shown. They are:

1 The argument from an unmoved mover

2 The argument from an uncaused cause

3 The argument from possibility and necessity

4 The argument from degrees of quality

5 The argument from design

The fourth of these has already been considered, for a version of it came in Anselm's *Monologion*. The last will be examined in the next section. For now, therefore, we need to look at the first three, which are generally termed 'cosmological arguments'.

These arguments are based on the observation of the world, and originate in the thinking of Aristotle, whom Aquinas regarded as *the* philosopher. The first may be presented as follows:

▶ Everything that moves is moved by something.

▶ That mover is in turn moved by something else again.

▶ **But** this chain of movers cannot be infinite, or movement would not have started in the first place.

▶ **Therefore,** there must be an unmoved mover, causing movement in everything, without itself actually being moved.

▶ This unmoved mover is what people understand by 'God'.

The second argument has the same structure:

▶ Everything has a cause.

▶ Every cause itself has a cause.

▶ **But** you cannot have an infinite number of causes.

▶ **Therefore,** there must be an uncaused cause, which causes everything to happen without itself being caused by anything else.

▶ Such an uncaused cause is what people understand by 'God'.

The third argument follows from the first two:

▶ Individual things come into existence and later cease to exist.

▶ **Therefore,** at one time none of them was in existence.

▶ **But** something comes into existence only as a result of something else that already exists.

▶ **Therefore,** there must be a being whose existence is necessary – 'God'.

One possible objection to these arguments is to say that you might indeed have an infinite number of causes or movers. Instead of stretching back into the past in a straight line, the series of causes could be circular, or looped in a figure of eight, so that you never get to a first cause, and everything is quite adequately explained by its immediate causes. This image of circularity does not really help us to understand the force of Aquinas' argument, for it is unlikely that he was thinking of a series of causes (or movers) stretching into the past. His argument actually suggests a hierarchy of causes here and now. Every individual thing has its cause: Why should the whole world not have a cause beyond itself?

However, if the world itself had such a cause, that cause too would require a cause, for it would have become part of the known world. Kant argued that causality is one of the ways in which our minds sort out the world – we impose causality upon our experience. If Kant is right, then an uncaused cause is a mental impossibility.

A rather different objection came from Hume. He based all knowledge on the observation of the world. Something is said to be a cause because it is seen to occur just before the thing that is called its effect. That depends on the observation of cause and effect as two separate things. *But*, in the case of the world as a whole, you have a unique effect, and therefore cannot observe its cause. You cannot get *outside* the world to see both the world and its cause, and thus establish the relationship between them. If, with Hume, you consider sense impressions as the basis of all knowledge, then the cosmological proofs cannot be accepted as giving proof of the existence of a God outside the world of observation.

Perhaps this gives a clue to a different way of approaching these cosmological arguments. If we follow them in a literal and logical way, they do not *prove* that there is an uncaused cause or unmoved mover. However, they show how a religious person may use the idea of movement or cause to *point to the way in which he or she sees God* – as a being that in some way stands behind yet causes or moves everything.

Remember this: Note

Although Aquinas' is the best-known version of the cosmological argument, it was not the first. An argument from the existence of the universe to its first cause, known as the *Kalam Argument*, was put forward by the Muslim scholars al-Kindi (ninth century) and al-Ghazali (1058–1111).

THE TELEOLOGICAL ARGUMENT – THE ARGUMENT FROM DESIGN

Although Aquinas has a form of this argument, the clearest example comes from William Paley (1743–1805). He argued that, if he were to find a watch lying on the ground, he would assume that it was the product of a designer, for, unlike a stone, he would see at once that it was made up of many different parts worked together in order to produce movement, and that, if any one part were ordered differently, the whole thing would not work. In the same way he argued that the world is like a machine, each part of it designed so that it takes its place within the whole. If the world is so designed, it must have a designer whose purpose is expressed through it.

This argument, reflecting the sense of wonder at nature, was most seriously challenged by the theory of evolution. Darwin's 'natural selection' provided an alternative explanation for design, and one that did not require the aid of any external designer. At once, it became possible to see the world not as a machine, but as a process of struggle and death in which those best adapted to their environment were able to breed and pass their genes on to the next generation, thus influencing the very gradual development of the species. Adaptation in order to survive became the key to the development of the most elaborate forms, which previously would have been described as an almost miraculous work of a designer God.

Actually, the challenge of natural selection was anticipated in the work of Hume, who set out a criticism of the design argument some 23 years before Paley published his version of it. He argued that, in a finite world and given infinite time, any combination of things can occur. Those combinations that work together harmoniously can continue and thrive, those that do not will fail. Therefore, when we come to observe the world as it is now, we are observing only those that *do* work, for those that don't are no longer there to be observed. The implication of this is that we observe a world populated by survivors, but that does not mean that it is so ordered by an external designer; it is merely the result of a long period of time and endless failures.

Notice that the most this argument can claim is that the world shows features of design. Whether that is a natural phenomenon, or one caused by some external agency is another matter. Hence, arguments about the very precise ways in which complex entities work, or the difficulty of seeing how some elaborate arrangements can come about by natural selection alone, simply highlight *the appearance of design*. They do not, in themselves, prove that there is any *external agency* bringing about that design. Even if they did, such an external agency could not necessarily be identified as the 'God' of traditional theism.

Key idea for life

A sense of purpose and direction appears to be important for individual human happiness. Yet is it essential for a satisfactory (or comforting?) understanding of the world as a whole? Theists tend to think that it is, call it God, and respond accordingly. Existentialists tend to suggest that we are responsible for creating our own sense of purpose and direction, and that the natural world may well be indifferent to us. It's a bit like Pascal's wager: you choose how you see yourself and the world.

THE MORAL ARGUMENT

Kant believed that the traditional arguments could never prove the existence of God, and therefore hoped to go beyond them by presenting an understanding of God based on faith rather than reason.

He did this by examining the idea of moral experience, and in particular the relationship between virtue and happiness. In an ideal world they should follow one another – that is, if there is a 'highest good' to which a person may aspire morally, doing what is right (virtue) should ultimately lead to happiness. Clearly, however, there is no evidence that virtue automatically leads to happiness. Why then should anyone be moral?

Kant started from the fact that people do have a sense of moral obligation: a feeling that something is right and must be done, no matter what the consequences. He called this sense of moral obligation the **categorical imperative**, to distinguish it from a 'hypothetical imperative' (which says: 'If you want to achieve this, then you must do that'). (See Chapter 8 for further discussion of this idea.)

In *The Critique of Practical Reason*, Kant explores the presuppositions of the categorical imperative. What do I actually believe about life if I respond to the absolute moral demand? (Not what must I rationally accept before I agree with a moral proposal, but what do I actually feel to be true, rationally or otherwise, in the moment when I respond to the moral imperative?) He argued that three things – God, freedom and immortality – were **postulates** of the practical reason. In other words, that the experience of morality implied that you were free to act (even if someone observing you claimed that you were not), that you would eventually achieve the result you wanted (even if you would not do so in this life, as when someone sacrificed his or her own life), and that, for any of this to be possible, there had to be some overall ordering principle, which might be called 'God'.

The way in which Kant saw the world obliged him to go beyond the traditional arguments for the existence of God. After all, if the idea of causality is imposed on external reality by our own minds, how can it become the basis for a proof for the existence of God? We can only know things as they appear to us, not as they are in themselves (see page 35):

▶ **If** we contribute space, time and causality to our understanding of the world

▶ **Then** to argue from these to something outside the world is impossible.

▶ God, freedom and immortality are therefore not **in** the world that we experience, but have to do with **the way in which** we experience the world.

▶ Therefore, **God is a 'regulative' concept (part of our way of understanding) not a 'constitutive' concept (one of the things out there to be discovered).**

In effect, Kant turned the old arguments on their head. If all we know are the phenomena of our experience, speculative metaphysics cannot give us evidence that God exists. On the other hand, our minds need the idea of God in order to make sense of our moral experience.

THE MEANING OF 'GOD'

In considering the arguments about the existence of God, we should keep the whole exercise in perspective by reminding ourselves that any 'God' who might or might not exist is not what theism is about; at best it is a caricature. Thus, the American theologian Paul Tillich, in his *Systematic Theology* (Vol. I, p. 262), said:

> The question of the existence of God can be neither asked nor answered. If asked, it is a question about that which by its very nature is above existence, and therefore the answer – whether negative or affirmative – implicitly denies the nature of God. It is as atheistic to affirm the existence of God as to deny it. God is being itself, not a being.

This reinforces what has been implied throughout the ontological and cosmological arguments: that what is being claimed is not the existence of one entity alongside others, but a fundamental way of regarding the whole universe. It is about the structures of *'being itself'* (to use Tillich's term, which he took over from Heidegger), not the possible existence of *a* being.

Tillich insisted that religious ideas could only be expressed by way of symbols. A symbol is something that conveys the power and meaning of the thing it symbolizes, in contrast to a sign, which is merely conventional. He argued that the religious experience has two elements: the material basis (the actual thing seen, which could be analysed by science) and the sense of ultimate value and power that it conveys, which makes it 'religious'.

For him, there were two essential features to the God that appears through religious experience or a religious symbol:

1 That God is 'being itself' rather than a being. In other words, an experience of God is not an experience of something that just happens to be there, an object among others, but is an experience of life itself, of being itself, an experience which then gives meaning to everything else.

2 That God is 'ultimate concern'. This implied that 'God' could not be thought of in a detached and impartial way.

For the religious believer, God demands total attention and commitment, covering all partial concerns, all other aspects of life. This sense of God as the most important thing in life is seen in the nature of religious experience.

Language about 'God' need not be religious. You can have a statement about the structure of the universe which includes the idea of God, but that does not make it religious, only cosmological. In order for something to be religious, it has to use religious language in a way that reflects religious experience and/or religious practice. The personal aspect of this was emphasized by Martin Buber (1876–1965), who introduced the important distinction between 'I – Thou' and 'I – It' language. 'I – Thou' language is personal, while 'I – It' is impersonal. Religious language is about an 'I' addressing a 'Thou', not speculating about an 'It'.

Key idea for life

Take Wittgenstein's advice – don't just ask about a word's meaning, look at how it is used. That applies to 'God' as much as any other word. What use do religious people make of that word and concept?

The most stringent test of the meaning of a statement is that given by logical positivism (see page 101). Under this set of rules, a statement has a meaning if it pictures something that can be verified by sense experience. If no evidence is relevant to its truth, a statement is meaningless. In language about God, such verification is not possible. Most definitions of 'God' are such as to preclude any explanation in terms of what can be directly experienced. This would lead a strict logical positivist to say that statements about God are meaningless.

The broader perspective – as illustrated by Wittgenstein's view of language as a 'form of life' (see page 107) – seeks to understand language in terms of its function. Religious language finds its meaning in terms of what it does. So, for example, 'God' (for a religious believer) may be a way of expressing the sense of wonder or holiness that is encountered in religious experience.

We therefore need to guard against the 'existence trap':

► **If** you prove that God 'exists' in a way that would satisfy a logical positivist (i.e. testable by empirical evidence)

► **Then** 'God' becomes part of the world

► **So** he is no longer 'God'.

A religious person might argue that belief in that rather simplistic idea of God is no more than idolatry – for idolatry is not simply a matter of worshipping a *physical* image, but may apply to worshipping a particular *idea* of God, rather than the source of reality itself. Religious wars have come about when conflicting ideas are elevated to divine status, and people feel the need to defend them as though they were defending 'God' himself, which does seem a particularly silly thing to try to do!

Key idea for life

In popular devotion and a literal reading of scriptures, God appears as a separate entity, external to the world and with human characteristics – a being who might or might not exist. For many people, it is difficult to switch from this image to an understanding of 'God' as a word used to describe reality itself. But unless that switch is made, it is difficult to see how theistic religion can be understood rationally and reconciled with science.

TO SUM UP ...

So far in this chapter we have looked at the nature of religious language and religious experience and the traditional arguments for the existence of God, and have thereby started to examine what the word 'God' can mean.

We now turn to some key issues in the philosophy of religion: whether the world is created and designed by God; miracles; the problem of evil; and whether life after death is possible. We shall also look briefly at explanations of religion offered by sociology and psychology. In all these topics, philosophy uses rational arguments to assess the truth of beliefs that people may hold for deeply personal reasons. This is not to denigrate the value of personal commitment, but simply to see whether such beliefs hold up to rational scrutiny, irrespective of their personal value.

The origin and design of the universe: religion or science?

The origin and the nature of the universe are subjects to be examined by science. There is broad agreement that the most likely theory for the origin of the universe as we know it, is that it has expanded out of a space–time singularity, just as – on Earth – there has been an evolution of species along the general principles of natural selection. Naturally, because these are scientific theories, they are open to be revised and might eventually be replaced although, given the weight of evidence, that seems unlikely.

However, from what we have seen from an outline of religious experience, and also from our brief look at the cosmological arguments (page 198) and the argument from design (page 201), it is clear that a sense of wonder at the nature of the universe is a very common feature of religious awareness, and has given rise to the arguments for the existence of a creator and designer god.

The problem is that, once God is given a role in the origin and design of the universe, any alternative scientific theories that explain the same things without requiring any supernatural agency, may be seen as threats to religious belief. Hence, at a superficial level, religion would seem to have a vested interest in the failure of science to give a complete explanation of the universe. On the other hand, it is clear that many scientists – in the past and also today – do hold religious beliefs and certainly do not see their scientific work as in any sense incompatible with them.

So we need to ask: Are the religious and scientific approaches to these topics compatible?

In *The Blind Watchmaker*, Richard Dawkins makes the point that the argument for the world being made by an intelligent designer is based on the assumption that complexity cannot arise naturally. His central theme is that the process of natural selection gives us a mechanism which explains how complexity can arise from original simplicity. Once you accept that, there is no need to look for an external cause for design. Dawkins' point is not that belief in a creator can be *disproved*; rather, he shows that *the idea is superfluous*. This has been the principal threat to religious belief in a designer-god ever since Charles Darwin put forward the theory of natural selection – for that theory provided the first genuinely independent explanation of the appearance of design.

However, that argument does not deny the sense of wonder at the beauty and complexity of the world. Indeed, Dawkins himself (in *Unweaving the Rainbow*) expresses amazement at what can arise from what is basically a mathematical sequence. Light and colour is no less impressive for being susceptible to scientific analysis.

Key idea for life

A religious person may ascribe the origin of a beautifully designed natural object to an external deity, whereas an atheist (whether scientist or not) celebrates the same beautiful design without seeking any external cause. The difference is not a matter of fact, but of personal interpretation.

The fundamental question therefore is:

'Can the world, as examined by science (in theory, if not in practice), provide us with an explanation of itself?'

If it can, this aspect of religion appears superfluous.

If it cannot, is that because:

▶ Our minds are incapable of understanding any overall cause for that within which we are immersed?

▶ Or, the explanation can only come through religious intuition (or the direct revelation of God) rather than through human reason and science.

However, this assumes that, for both scientist and religious believer, the world is such as to display design and intelligence. That can be challenged. One of the key nineteenth-century criticisms of the 'argument from design' came from John Stuart Mill. He argued that the world was not a particularly benign place, and that evolution (for he was writing after Darwin's theory had been published) progressed only at the price of immense suffering.

It is clear that any objective assessment of nature is going to reveal the scale of suffering, as species prey on one another in the struggle to survive. If design were the product of an intelligent and loving God, why all this suffering? This leads into two related issues that may be addressed in the philosophy of religion – whether God, if he exists, can and does intervene selectively in the operating of the world through miracles, and whether a rational argument can show the compatibility of an omnipotent and loving God with the fact of suffering and evil.

Key idea for life

Even Kant, who saw logical problems with the argument from design, nevertheless said that it deserved to be treated with great respect, since it gave life to the study of nature. In other words, it suggested that the world was a fascinating and wonderful place, worthy of our attention, and that may be an inspiration for science, as much as for a this-worldly theology. The key question is: 'Do you see it as wonderful and inspiring *in itself*, or as pointing *beyond* itself?'

Miracles

The cosmological arguments for the existence of God were an attempt to lead the mind from an understanding of the physical world to a reality that lay behind it and was responsible for it. The arguments led from ordinary movement and causes to the idea of an unmoved mover or uncaused cause. But Western theistic religions have tended to go beyond this, and have claimed that God can act in particular events, which may be called miracles.

Initially, we will be looking at miracles in terms of events for which it is claimed that there is no rational or scientific explanation. This is not the only way to interpret miracles, but it will suffice as a starting point.

If you want to find an argument against this idea of a miracle, the logical place to look is among those philosophers who take an empiricist position, for an empiricist will want to relate everything to evidence, and this is precisely what is not possible if an event is to be a miracle.

Hume examines the idea of miracles in the tenth book of his *Enquiry Concerning Human Understanding*. His argument runs like this:

► A wise man proportions his belief to the evidence; the more evidence there is for something, the more likely it is to have been the case (see page 34).

► Evidence given by other people is assessed according to their reliability as witnesses.

► He then turns to the idea of miracles and offers a definition.

► A miracle is the violation of a law of nature.

► But a law of nature is the result of a very large number of observations.

He therefore concludes from this:

> A miracle is a violation of the laws of nature; and as a firm and unalterable experience has established these laws, the proof against a miracle, from the very nature of the fact, is as entire as any argument from experience can possibly be imagined. Why is it more than probable, that all men must die; that lead cannot, of itself, remain suspended in the air; that fire consumes wood, and is extinguished by water; unless it be, that these events are found agreeable to the laws of nature, and there is required a violation of these laws, or in other words, a miracle to prevent them? Nothing is esteemed a miracle if it ever happen in the common course of nature … The plain consequence is … That no testimony is sufficient to establish a miracle, unless the testimony be of such a kind, that its falsehood would be more miraculous, than the fact, which it endeavours to establish.

In other words, *it is always more likely that the report of a miracle is mistaken, than that a law of nature was actually broken, for the evidence against the miracle will always be greater than the evidence for it.*

Strictly speaking that does not preclude something being a miracle, it simply says that *there can never be sufficient evidence* for a wise man to accept it as such.

Hume's argument is based on the assumption that a miracle appears to be a violation of a law of nature and therefore inexplicable in terms of present scientific knowledge. But is that necessarily the case for an event to be a miracle?

Take the example of a 'black hole' in the middle of a galaxy. It is a violation of what are generally called 'laws of nature' (according to Newtonian physics). Yet it is not seen as a miracle, merely an extreme case, which suggests that the existing 'laws' of physics need to be modified to take it into account.

So we need to ask: What distinguishes a miracle from a rare or unique occurrence?

Generally, in order to be termed a miracle, something needs to be seen as displaying *positive purpose*. If a life is saved, against all expectations, that may be regarded as a miracle by those for whom that life was dear, but if a person suddenly drops dead, his or her friends are unlikely to call it a miracle. However, a long-lost relative, who had no emotional connection with the deceased, and who is suddenly saved from financial ruin by an unexpected legacy, may well find it miraculous.

A unique occurrence is therefore unlikely to be called a miracle unless it had some personal relevance and apparent sense of purpose. Equally, an ordinary event – in other words, one for which there is a perfectly reasonable explanation – may still be regarded as a miracle if its timing is right, or it has particular significance.

In other words:

With a miracle, it's not just *what* happened, but *why*. Is the physical world impersonal, or can it display a sense of purpose or agency? Without direct evidence, the problem is proving either purpose or agent.

UNIQUE OR UNIVERSAL?

There is an important sense in which the idea of the miraculous and that of the cosmological and design arguments work against one another. The whole essence of the earlier arguments is that the world is structured in a way that displays an overall purpose. Those arguments only work on the basis of regularity, for only in regularity does the sense of design and purpose appear. Yet the literal idea of a miracle violates that regularity, introducing arbitrariness and unpredictability into our understanding of the world, thereby undermining those arguments.

In other words, you can't have it both ways. *Either* God is seen to exist because the world is a wonderful, ordered place, *or* his action is seen in individual events because the world is an unpredictable, miraculous place. It's illogical to argue for both at once!

The problem of evil

In its simplest form, the problem can be stated like this:

▶ **If** God created the world

▶ **And** if God is all-powerful and all-loving

▶ **Then** why is there evil and suffering in the world?

Conclusion:

▶ **Either** God is not all-powerful

▶ **Or** God is not all-loving

▶ **Or** suffering is either unreal, necessary or a means to a greater good

▶ **Or** the whole idea of an all-loving and all-powerful creator God was a mistake in the first place.

An important book setting out suggested answers to this problem is *Evil and the God of Love* (1966) by John Hick (1922–2012), a philosopher and theologian notable for his contribution to the problem of evil and to the issue of religious pluralism. In that book he gives two main lines of approach, the Augustinian and the Irenaean:

The Augustinian approach is named after St Augustine (354–430), and reflects his background in neo-Platonism. In Plato's thought, particular things are imperfect copies of their 'Forms'. Imperfection is a feature of the world as we experience it. Therefore evil is not a separate force opposing the good, but is a lack of goodness, a deprivation. The world as we experience it is full of imperfect copies, and suffering and evil are bound up with that imperfection.

But Augustine had a second line of argument, coming from the Bible and Church teaching, rather than from Plato. The biblical account of the Fall of the Angels and of Adam and Eve in the Garden of Eden led to a 'fallen' state for all creation. Because of human disobedience, the world is a place of suffering rather than innocent bliss. Hence moral suffering (the pain caused by humans) can be seen as a consequence of sin, and natural evil (earthquakes, tsunami, diseases and the like) can be seen as a just punishment for sin.

The Irenaean approach is named after Bishop Irenaeus of Lyons (c. 130–c. 202). It presents the idea that human life is imperfect, but having been made in the image of God, human beings are intended to grow and develop, aspiring to be what God intended them to be. Through free will and all the sufferings of life, people have an opportunity to grow and learn.

In other words, it is only by having a world in which there is both good and evil that we can have moral choice and develop spiritually. In this way, Irenaeus can justify the presence of natural evil, for a world that includes sickness and natural disasters is one in which people grow through facing real challenges.

> How, if we had no knowledge of the contrary, could we have had instruction in that which is good? ... For just as the tongue receives experiences of sweet and bitter by means of tasting, and the eye discriminates between black and white by means of vision, and the ear recognizes the distinctness of sounds by hearing; so also does the mind, receiving through the experience of both the knowledge of what is good, become the more tenacious in its preservation, by acting in obedience to God ... But if any one do shun the knowledge of both kinds of things, and the twofold perception of knowledge, he unaware divests himself of the character of a human being.
>
> Irenaeus, *Against Heresies* iv, xxxix.1, quoted in John Hick, *Evil and the God of Love*, Fontana, 1968

Hick's own approach is to treat evil as something to be tackled and overcome, with the hope that, ultimately, it will be seen as part of an overall divine plan.

Key idea for life: Compensation after death?

Pascal's wager (page 184) assumed that there was heaven to gain and hell to avoid, and that prospect made religion the safe bet. Similarly now, both Augustine and Irenaeus, each in his own way, looks beyond this life for an ultimate justification for suffering. Whether suffering is a just punishment or a means of developing, it only makes sense – as the prescription offered by a loving God – if there is some form of compensation beyond death.

The crucial difference between the religious and non-religious evaluation of life, is that – in general – the non-religious approach is that life (with its unequally distributed mixture of pleasure and pain) is of value *in itself*, not as a preparation for anything beyond this world.

To say 'Yes' to this life, just as it is, and to be prepared to live this life over and over again, is the hallmark of someone radically free from the consolations of religion. Indeed, Nietzsche made such 'Yes-saying' a key feature of his *übermensch* (superman), the higher form to which humankind is challenged to evolve.

That said, a psychologist might argue that it is exactly the consolations of religion (as opposed to those of philosophy) that explain the continuation of religious belief in the face of rational criticism.

Psychological and sociological explanations of religion

In one of the most quoted passages of all time, Marx claimed, in his *Contribution to the Critique of Hegel's Philosophy of Right*, that:

Religion is the sign of the oppressed creature, the heart of the heartless world, just as it is the spirit of the spiritless situation. It is the opium of the people.

The abolition of religion as the illusory happiness of the people is required for their real happiness. The demand to give up the illusions about its condition is the demand to give up a condition which needs illusions. The criticism of religion is therefore in embryo the criticism of the vale of woe, the halo of which is religion.

(as quoted in Paul Helm, *Faith and Reason*, OUP, 1999)

In other words, Marx wants people to turn their attention to their present situation and to struggle for real happiness. The assumption he makes is that the sort of happiness associated with life after death is illusory. However, at the same time, if such an illusion is believed, the fact of suffering and the longing for a life free from it, is a powerful motivation for continuing to be religious in the face of present adversity.

A parallel explanation for religion is given by sociologists such as Emile Durkheim. From the sociological perspective, religion provides a cohesive force within society. If a community is bound together by its religion, then the continuation of that religion does not depend so much on the intellectual acceptance of its articles of belief, but the perceived value it offers society. For the same reason, governments and political parties may promote a religious tradition if it helps to give a sense of national identity. Most religions have found themselves used for political purposes in one way or another.

Freud's criticism of religion was partly based on the parallels he saw between religious behaviour and obsessional neuroses, like repeated handwashing or tidying routines. In both cases, repeated actions (for example, confessing sins, attending worship) were an attempt to escape from a sense of unworthiness and guilt. More significant, though, for our argument here are the supposed benefits of religion that he sets out in *The Future of an Illusion* (1927). Just as a child depends on an adult for protection, so he sees religion as offering God to adults as a substitute, heavenly Father – a comfort and protection in the midst of the threatening nature of life and the eventual inevitability of death.

These explanations of religion, mentioned briefly here, but well worth exploring further, are a reminder that the sort of rational arguments examined by the philosophy of religion are far from being the whole story. Religious beliefs may claim to be rational, and may be backed up by rational argument, but religion does not ultimately depend on any of these arguments for its continued existence. As the widespread increase of fundamentalism and literalism in religious circles shows, it is often the rejection of an intellectually sophisticated approach to these issues that appeals.

This is not to suggest that these explanations of religion necessarily invalidate religious beliefs. Those beliefs (examined rationally) may be true or they may be false. What is clear, however, is that – as a phenomenon – there are many reasons for religion to continue and even to flourish, quite apart from them.

It is also possible to argue that belief in God is simply a projection outwards of all that is best in humanity – the view taken by Ludwig Feuerbach (1804–72). In effect, religion then becomes a way of dealing with issues that face humankind and the values to which people subscribe. God embodies all that we would wish to be – loving, kind, merciful and so on. His key work *The Essence of Christianity* (1841), offered a positive explanation of religion in terms of human self-transcendence and provided an intellectual underpinning for a period when religious belief was increasingly being challenged. Not only did Feuerbach influence Karl Marx in his criticism of religion, but he has had a positive influence on theology, opening up discussion of the personal dimension of what people mean by 'God', as, for example, in Paul Tillich's view of God as our 'ultimate concern'. Feuerbach was the original de-mythologizer!

Key idea for life

If Feuerbach is right, then to say 'God is love' is to elevate love as the highest of all human qualities; that it is 'love' we experience as supremely important in ourselves and our relationships. If the supernatural idea of God is seen as incredible or irrelevant, religious language may still, in this non-projected form, have value in exploring human values.

Locating what is most real?

There are two very different approaches to belief in God, miracles and so on. One (sometimes referred to as 'onto-theology') tends to describe God as a being who exists and interacts with the world; the other ('expressive theology') sees God and religion as a way of exploring and expressing value in this world. The problem – as clearly set out by Simon Blackburn in, for example, *Philosophers Without Gods* (ed. Louise Antony, 2007), – is that the latter, even if more compatible with secular atheism, is not in line with the sort of impetus that beliefs need to have in order to sustain religion. In other words, if you don't believe that God actually, literally exists, it's difficult to be committed to obeying him.

WHERE DO WE FIND REALITY?

Is the world fundamentally an imperfect copy of something more real, as Plato argued? As we look at the world, do we see it as a half-empty glass, forever lacking fullness and perfection? In order for life to be worthwhile, does it need some compensation after death?

Or is the world still developing, working towards a perfection that lies in the future? Is the structure of the world (along with everything in it, good and bad) the means by which growth can take place? Is its reality still in the future, at the end of a process of natural selection or class conflict?

Or do we simply accept and affirm the reality of life exactly as it is, with its mixture of joy and suffering, pleasure and pain, and make of it what we can?

Key idea for life

These are practical, moral and political as well as religious questions. But they raise an enormous psychological and philosophical problem: *Everything that we experience is in a process of change.* Birth, death, suffering and evil are inescapable. How can you engage with anything so mobile and ambiguous? How can you love it? That is the challenge posed by Nietzsche, by modern atheism and humanism, and also by Buddhism, which has always seen life as fragile and subject to change, but has nevertheless proposed insight and compassion as a recipe for overcoming human suffering.

The key question and challenge: How can you, with conviction and intellectual honesty, say 'yes' to life?

8

Ethics

In this chapter you will:

- ▶ *Consider how the balance of facts and values shapes our morality*
- ▶ *Reflect on whether or not we are free to decide what to do*
- ▶ *Learn about some major ethical theories*
- ▶ *Explore the relationship between ethics and the values held by society*

Why?

In Ethics, philosophy turns from general questions about how we understand the world, science, language, religion or art, to the most personal and essential of all matters – how we decide what is right or wrong, how we should act, whether we are genuinely free to choose what to do, and to what extent our morality is shaped by the society in which we live: issues that are universally relevant.

Facts, values and choices

Fundamental to all sentient creatures is conscious awareness of their environment, enabling them to act, to find food, to recognize danger, to mate and thereby to survive and produce offspring. Human beings are no different, except that their intellectual ability presents them with a range of choices. What should we do? How should we organize society? What is right? How should we understand the idea of justice? On what basis can we choose between different courses of action? These lead to a study of ethics and political philosophy.

These practical aspects of philosophy have a long history. Although the pre-Socratic philosophers of ancient Greece had probed many questions about the nature of reality – questions to which their answers are still interesting in terms of both epistemology and the natural sciences – with Socrates, Plato and Aristotle, the emphasis shifted towards issues of morality. So, for example, Plato's *Republic* is not based on the question 'What is society?' but 'What is justice?', and it is through that question that many other issues about society and how it should be ruled are explored.

Aristotle (in *Nicomachean Ethics*) asked about the 'good' that was the aim of every action, and about what could constitute a 'final good' – something worthwhile for its own sake, rather than for the sake of something higher. He came to the view that the highest good for man was *eudaimonia*, which literally means 'having a good spirit', but perhaps can be translated as 'happiness' or 'living well'. He saw it as the state in which a person was fulfilling his or her potential and natural function.

It expressed a form of human excellence or virtue (*arete*). This tied in with his general view that everything had a 'final cause': a goal and a purpose to which it moved. If you understand the final cause of something, you also understand its fundamental essence. If a knife had a soul, Aristotle argued, that soul would be 'cutting' – that is what makes it a knife; that is what it is there to do. What then is the essence of humankind? What is it there to do? What is its goal?

Aristotle linked his ethics to his whole understanding of human life. He refused to accept that any simple rule could cover all situations, and he also considered human beings in relation to the society within which they lived, recognizing the influence this has on human behaviour. Aristotle saw man as both a 'thinking animal' and a 'political animal'. It is therefore not surprising that ethics becomes the study of rational choice in action, and that it should have a social as well as an individual aspect. In this chapter we shall take a brief look at some of the main philosophical approaches to moral issues and in the following chapter we shall examine issues of a social and political nature. Although, for convenience, ethics and politics are separated, it is important to remember that ethics is more than the justification of personal choices. It is equally possible to examine morality in terms of the requirements of the state and the place of individuals within society; in ethics the personal and the social cannot be separated.

'IS' AND 'OUGHT'

Once you start to talk about morality, or about the purpose of things, you introduce matters of value as well as those of fact. An important question for philosophy is whether it is possible to derive values from facts, or whether facts must always remain 'neutral'. In other words:

▶ Facts say what 'is'.

▶ Values say what 'ought' to be.

Which leads to the question:

▶ Can we ever derive an 'ought' from an 'is'?

In other words, can facts alone determine what should be done or what course of action should be judged to be right? David Hume thought they should not, and this view was later described as the 'naturalistic fallacy' by G. E. Moore (1873–1958) in his influential book *Principia Ethica* (1903). In other words, to say 'These people are starving' is simply to state a fact. It does not, in itself, imply 'So you ought to feed them.' For that to follow, you would need to add another step in the argument, namely the general principle that, 'When you see people who are starving it is right to feed them.'

Ethical theories – which form the core of what we shall be examining in this chapter – seek to establish the principles by which, when confronted with an 'is', one can decide what 'ought' to be done.

Am I free to choose?

It is illogical to tell someone that they **ought** to do something, unless we believe that it is at least **possible** for them to do it and that they are free and able to choose to do it. But are we ever genuinely free?

If (as Kant argued) space, time and causality are categories used by the human mind to interpret experience, it is inevitable that we shall see everything in the world as causally conditioned – things don't just happen, they must have a cause!

This process of looking for causes, which lies at the heart of the scientific quest, has as its logical goal a totally understood world in which each individual thing and action is explained in terms of all that went before it. In theory, given total knowledge of all that has happened in the past, everything that will happen in the future can be predicted. This reflects what we may call the Newtonian world-view, that the universe is like a machine, operating by means of fixed rules.

We saw that this created problems in terms of the relationship between mind and body. If everything is causally conditioned, then even the electrical impulses in my brain are part of a closed mechanical system and my freedom is an illusion. I may feel sure that I have made a free choice, but in fact everything that has happened to me since my birth, and everything that has made the world the way it is since the beginning of time, has contributed to that decision.

Key idea for life

'I just knew you'd say that!' One of the annoying things about people who claim to predict our choices is that we like to think we are free, but are forced to recognize that we may not always be the best judge of that.

The question of freedom and determinism is a fundamental one for philosophy and is closely related to what happens when we reduce complex entities (like human beings) to the simpler parts of which they are composed. If we are nothing more than the individual cells that comprise our bodies, and if those cells are determined by physical forces and are predictable, then there seems no room for the whole human being to exercise freedom.

For now, dealing with ethics, one distinction is clear:

▶ If we are free to make a choice, then we can be responsible for what we do. Praise or blame are appropriate. We can act on the basis of values that we hold.

▶ If we are totally conditioned, we have no choice in what we do, and it makes no sense to speak of moral action springing from choices and values, or action being worthy of praise or blame.

By the same token, there are levels of determinism. It is clear that nobody is totally free:

▶ We have physical limitations. I cannot make an unaided leap 30 metres into the air, even if I feel I have a vocation to do so. Overweight middle-aged men do not make the best ballet dancers. It's not a matter of choice, merely of physical fact.

▶ We may be psychologically predisposed to act in certain ways rather than others. If you are shy and depressed, you are unlikely to be the life and soul of a party. But that is not a matter of choice, merely of present disposition.

- We may be socially restrained. I may choose to do something really outrageous, but know that I will not get away with it.

- We may also be limited by the financial and political structures under which we live. There are many things that I cannot do without money, for example.

So, in considering moral responsibility, we have to assess the degree of freedom available to the agent.

Case studies

Is a soldier who is *ordered* to shoot prisoners or unarmed civilians thereby absolved of moral responsibility? Is he free to choose whether to carry out that act or not? Does the fear of his own death, executed for refusal to obey an order, determine that he must obey?

If a person commits a crime while known to be suffering from a mental illness, or if a psychiatric report indicates that he or she was disturbed at the time, that fact will be taken into account when apportioning blame. But how many people who commit crimes could be described as clear-headed and well balanced? How many have no mitigating circumstances of some sort when family background, education, deprivation and other things are considered?

If we are all obeying orders, even those that have been lodged in our unconscious mind since childhood, or influenced by circumstances, are we ever responsible for our actions? Are paedophilia or kleptomania crimes, or illnesses, or both? Do they require punishment or treatment?

There is no doubt that our actions are influenced by many factors. The difference between that and determinism is that determinism leaves no scope for human freedom and choice (we are automata), whereas those who argue against determinism claim that there remains a measure of freedom that is exercised within the prevailing conditions. But keep in mind that everything we are, everything we believe, and everything we understand about the world is there in the moment when we make a moral choice; not necessarily consciously, but there in the background, exerting an influence.

Not all philosophers have presented the issues of freedom, determinism and moral choice in quite this way. A notable exception is Spinoza. He argued that freedom was in fact an illusion, created because we do not know all the causes of our actions. Things that happen to us produce in us either passive or active emotions. The passive emotions, such as hatred, anger or fear, lead a person into bondage, whereas the active ones, those generated by an understanding of our real circumstances, lead to a positive view of life, and an ability to be ourselves. Spinoza held that the more one understood the world, the more the negative emotions would diminish and be replaced by positive ones. One might perhaps say of this that freedom (and the only freedom that Spinoza will accept) is the ability to see life exactly as it is and say 'yes' to it.

Key idea for life

The philosopher Isaiah Berlin made the distinction between 'freedom from' and 'freedom to' in a lecture entitled 'Two concepts of Liberty' given in Oxford, 1958. In *On Liberty*, John Stuart Mill (1806–73) had suggested that human creativity would be crushed without a suitable level of freedom. In other words, freedom 'to' do things required freedom 'from' constraints. Isaiah Berlin disagreed with that, arguing that creativity can flourish even within the most repressive of regimes. This distinction is important for ethics, political philosophy and existentialism. It is a big issue and worth exploring further; too often (in the personal as much as the political sphere) people assume that they will be free 'to' do something only when they are free 'from' other things.

Ethical language

What does it mean to say that something is 'good' or that an action is 'right'? Do these words refer to a hidden quality in that action, something over and above what is actually observed? What sort of evidence can be given for such a description?

I can show you what I mean by 'red' by pointing to a range of red objects, and relying on your ability to identify their common feature. Can I do the same by pointing to a range of actions that I consider to be morally right? Take for example:

- A loving couple having sexual intercourse
- Someone helping a blind person across a road
- Paying for goods in a shop (as opposed to stealing them)

We may describe each of these actions as good or moral, but in terms of *factual description* they have nothing in common. So how do you set about defining moral values?

DESCRIPTIVE ETHICS

This is the most straightforward form of ethical language. It is simply a description of what happens: what moral choices are made and in which particular circumstances. Rather than making a statement about the rights or wrongs of abortion, for example, descriptive ethics simply gives facts and figures about how many abortions take place, how they are carried out, and what legal restraints are placed on that practice. *Descriptive ethics is about 'is' rather than 'ought'.*

NORMATIVE ETHICS

Normative ethics deals with the norms of action, in terms of whether an action is considered good or bad, right or wrong. It expresses values, and makes a moral judgement based on them. It may relate to facts, but it is not wholly defined by facts. It may be justified in a number of ways that we shall examine shortly. *Normative ethics is about 'ought'; it makes judgements.*

META-ETHICS

When philosophy examines the claims made in normative ethics, a number of questions are raised:

- What does it mean to say that something is right or wrong?
- Can moral statements be said to be either true or false?
- Do they express more than the preferences of the person who makes them?
- What is the meaning of the terms used in ethical discourse?

These questions are not themselves moral statements; they do not say that any particular thing is right or wrong. Meta-ethics does to normative ethical statements what philosophy does to language in general. It examines ethical language to find what it means and how it is used. So let us look briefly at some meta-ethical theories.

INTUITIONISM AND DEFINING 'GOOD'

Ethical intuitionism is the view that people are naturally aware of moral values. They may not be able to say exactly what they mean by 'good', but they know it when they see it.

In *Principia Ethica*, G. E. Moore argued that the term 'good' could not be defined, and that every attempt to do so ended in reducing goodness to some other quality that was not common to all 'good' things. Goodness may involve kindness, altruism, generosity, a sense of social justice – but it is not actually *defined* by any of these. Moore therefore claimed that:

> Everyone does in fact understand the question 'Is this good?' When he thinks of it, his state of mind is different from what it would be, were he asked 'Is this pleasant, or desired, or approved?' It has a distinct meaning for him, even though he may not recognize in what respect it is distinct.
>
> *Principia Ethica*, Chapter 1

Moore likened this to describing the colour yellow. In the end you just have to point to things and say that they are yellow without being able to define the colour. You know what yellow is by intuition. In the same way, you know what goodness is, even though it cannot be defined. Although his view is often described as intuitionism, Moore himself was not happy with that term; he regarded 'good' as simply an irreducible, non-natural property. However, he was quite prepared to say that, in making a moral judgement, one could argue to a conclusion (from basic intuitions) in order to achieve the best result for all concerned, so one's moral choice also depended upon rational argument and was not simply known intuitively.

Of course, Moore could not define 'good' in terms of a natural property because to do so would have been to commit his 'naturalist fallacy' of trying to derive an 'ought' from an 'is'. The good cannot be equated with any fact or thing – hence his view is described as 'non-naturalist'.

NATURALISM AND METAPHYSICAL ETHICS

In spite of Moore's view that you could not get an 'ought' from an 'is', it is clear that, from Plato and Aristotle onwards, there have been philosophers who have argued that moral principles and values should be derived from the examination of human beings, their society and their place within the world as a whole. This task is termed 'naturalism' or 'metaphysical ethics', and it implies that what you 'ought' to do has some close relation to what 'is', in fact, the case about yourself and the world. In other words, that morality should be more than an expression of personal choice; it should be rooted in an overall understanding of the world. Natural Law ethics (see page 229) is one example of this approach – it is based on a rational understanding of the nature of human life, its essence and its purpose.

EMOTIVISM

According to this theory, saying that something is good or bad is really just a way of saying that you approve or disapprove of it. In Chapter 4 we saw that, early in the twentieth century, logical positivism argued that statements were called meaningless unless they either corresponded to empirical data, or were true by definition. Hence moral statements were meaningless.

One response to this challenge was to argue that moral statements were not factual descriptions, but were simply expressing approval or otherwise. They were therefore not true or false by reference to that which they described, but according to whether or not they correctly reflected the emotions or preferences of the speaker. A. J. Ayer, who popularized logical positivism in the English-speaking world, took this view.

PRESCRIPTIVISM

This is another response to the challenge of logical positivism. It claims that moral language is actually recommending a course of action. If I say that something is good, I am actually saying that I feel it should be done – in other words, I am prescribing it as a course of action. This argument is particularly associated with the philosopher R. M. Hare (1919–2002).

Remember this: From language to theory

So far we have been looking at the status of moral language as it developed within the philosophical debate about the nature of language in general. This was a key feature of philosophical ethics through the middle decades of the twentieth century. However, if we want to argue for a particular moral view, we need to consider how we are going to justify it rationally, and that is helped by considering the various ethical theories, to which we now turn.

Natural law

In Book 1 of *Nicomachean Ethics*, Aristotle says:

> Every art and every enquiry, and similarly every action and pursuit, is thought to aim at some good; and for this reason the good has rightly been declared to be that at which all things aim.
>
> (p. 1094a)

Aristotle develops this into the idea of the supreme good for human beings: happiness (*eudaimonia*). If you agree with Aristotle that everything has a final cause or purpose, a 'good' for which it exists, or if you accept with Plato that the 'Forms' (especially the 'Form of the Good') have a permanent reality, independent of our own minds and perceptions, then it should be possible to specify which things are 'good' and which 'bad', which actions are 'right' and which 'wrong' in an independent and objective way.

Aristotle's natural law ethics follows from the second and fourth of his four causes (see page 25), applied to human life. To know what is right, good, beautiful or fine (for which he used the term *kalon*) for us, we need to know what we are (our essence) and what we are for. He saw people as both rational and political (or social) and argued that they would flourish only if they cultivated qualities (or virtues) in line with their rational and social nature. This is the basis of his natural law ethics.

Natural law is the approach to ethics that claims something is right if it fulfils its true purpose in life, wrong if it goes against it.

Case study: sex

Natural law, based on the idea of a natural purpose inherent in everything, might seem particularly appropriate for dealing with issues of sex, since it is clear that sex does have a natural purpose that is essential for life. In natural law terms, a simple argument might run like this:

- The 'natural' function of sex is the reproduction of the species.
- Therefore non-reproductive sexual activity, which cannot fulfil that function, is wrong (or at least a misuse of the natural function of sex). Masturbation, contraception and homosexuality could all be criticized from this standpoint.

Of course, if that conclusion seems unreasonable, one may challenge its premise. Just because sex can lead to procreation, does that imply that it is its *only* function or *only* purpose?

Natural law is *not* based on what we can observe in nature, but on *nature as seen through the eyes of reason*. It is essentially an *interpretation* of nature and its purpose.

This point is crucial for understanding natural law arguments. For many species, murder and rape are a normal part of life, as males seek to dominate one another in order to mate with as many females as possible and therefore increase their genetic offspring. Natural selection – the basis upon which life evolves – is a cruel business, and no pattern for an acceptable moral code.

Natural law, however, is never simply about what is 'natural' in the observed sense, but is based on a reasoned understanding of natural purpose.

Many see natural law arguments as reflecting the religious view of the world as purposeful and comprehensible by human reason, because created by God. As such, this theory may be seen as the ethical aspect of the traditional argument from design (see page 201). In recent years, natural law has declined in popularity, except among Roman Catholic thinkers, where (as presented by Aquinas) it is seen as establishing a first step to an understanding of the eternal law of God.

There are many issues within medical ethics that have a 'natural law' component, particularly those that concern decisions about life and death. So, for example, a natural law approach tends to go against euthanasia, since it sees the desire to maintain one's life as rational and natural.

Another example is that of an infertile couple who may seek IVF or other treatments to help them to conceive a child. It is 'natural' (and reasonable) that they should want to do so. But what about the nature and purpose of the treatments involved? Should they be approved by natural law, in the sense that they facilitate the 'final purpose' of having the child? Or is it an unnatural attempt to 'play God'.

A major issue with all natural law arguments, and why they mainly feature now in religious approaches to morality, is that they presuppose that the world can be interpreted rationally in terms of purpose and direction. If that is challenged, the force of these arguments is severely restricted.

Key idea for life

Natural law argues that morality should help each person to fulfil his or her own nature. It presents us with a rational challenge: if you want to know what you should do, first discover who you are and what your life is for.

Virtue ethics

Rather than looking at actions, and asking whether they are right or wrong, one could start by asking the basic question 'What does it mean to be a "good" person?' and develop this to explore the qualities and virtues that make up the 'good' life. This approach had been taken first by Aristotle who linked the displaying of certain qualities with the final end or purpose of life.

As it developed in the 1950s (particularly as a result of the work of Philippa Foot and Elizabeth Anscombe) this approach appealed to feminist thinkers, who considered the traditional ethical arguments (mainly Kant's ethical theory and utilitarianism, which we shall examine in a moment) to have been influenced by particularly male ways of approaching life, based on rights and duties, whereas they sought a more 'feminine' approach and a recognition of the value of relationships and intimacy.

Virtue ethics was also seen as *'naturalistic'*, in that it moved away from the idea of simply obeying rules, to an appreciation of how one might express one's own fundamental nature, and thus fulfil one's potential as a human being. In other words, it aims at that which would enable human beings to flourish.

In general, it looks at qualities and dispositions rather than the morality of particular actions. It asks, in effect, what sort of behaviour we associate with the terms 'good' or 'generous' or 'courageous', building on the 'cardinal' values of classical Greek philosophy: temperance, justice, courage and prudence. In other words, it is *agent-centred*, concerned with the person, rather than *act-centred*, and this sets it apart from both Kant's ethics and utilitarianism (see below pages 234 and 238).

Notice also that, by promoting virtues such as kindness, compassion and generosity, virtue ethics points to the benefit of these qualities both for the person who practises them, and for those on the receiving end. Cultivating generosity is thus a win-win practice; you do not sacrifice yourself by helping others, but actually enhance and fulfil your own potential in doing so.

Virtue ethics raises some basic questions (which are also relevant to natural law):

▶ Do we have a fixed **essence**? Are there particular masculine or feminine qualities that give rise to virtues appropriate to each sex? Or is our nature the product of our surroundings and upbringing?

▶ If our nature has been shaped by factors over which we have no control (e.g. the culture into which we have been born, traumatic experiences in childhood), **are we responsible for our actions?**

▶ How should we relate the expression of an individual's virtues to the actual needs of society?

▶ How are you able to decide between different ways of expressing the same virtue? For example, a sense of love and compassion might lead one person to help someone who is seriously ill to die, yet another might find that love and compassion lead them to struggle to keep that same person alive.

Notice that beneath some of these 'virtue ethics' approaches lie the basic questions raised by Aristotle about the end or purpose of human life. Whereas 'natural law' generally examines an action in terms of its 'final cause', virtue ethics examines human qualities in terms of their overall place within human life, and the appropriate ways in which they may be expressed.

Key idea for life

The idea of having a bad conscience is linked to both natural law and virtue ethics. If we do have some fundamental sense of the nature and purpose of human life, and the qualities that enable it to flourish, we are likely to have a bad conscience if we go against that inner sense of what is right. Ask the question: Why should I have a bad conscience over this? The answer tends to be framed in terms of not living up to what you believe you are made to be or capable of being.

Utilitarianism

Utilitarianism is a moral theory set out by Jeremy Bentham (1748–1832), a philosopher, lawyer and social reformer, involved particularly with the practical issues of prison reform, education and the integrity of public institutions; it was further developed by John Stuart Mill (1806–73), a campaigner for individual liberty and for the rights of women. Its roots, however, are found earlier in the basic idea of hedonism.

Hedonism is the term used for a philosophy that makes the achievement of happiness the prime goal in life. Epicurus taught in Athens at the end of the fourth century BCE. He took an atomistic view of the world (everything is composed of indivisible atoms), regarded the gods as having little influence on life, and generally considered the main purpose of life to be the gaining of pleasure, in the broad sense of well-being. Pain, he held, was of shorter duration than pleasure, and death was nothing but the dissolution of the atoms of which we are made, with no afterlife to fear. He therefore considered that the wise should lead a life free from anxiety, and if morality had any purpose it was to maximize the amount of well-being that life can offer.

To be fair to Epicurus, this crude outline does not do justice to the fact that he distinguished the more intellectual pleasures from the animal ones, and that Epicureans were certainly not 'hedonists' in the popular sense. He advocated a life of simple pleasures, seeing the craving for material goods as insatiable and inevitably leading to frustration and unhappiness. Nevertheless, Epicurus did establish the maximizing of happiness as the prime purpose of morality.

This principle (though far removed from the way in which Epicurus presented it) was to become the basis of utilitarian theories of ethics: that the right thing to do on any occasion is that which aims to give maximum happiness to all concerned. This may be expressed in the phrase 'the greatest good for the greatest number' (a phrase used by Francis Hutcheson (1694–1746) who used it to assess political systems), and Bentham made the point that everyone should count equally in such an assessment – a radical point of view for him to take at that time. Utilitarianism is therefore a theory *based on the expected results of an action, rather than any inherent sense of right or wrong.*

This is very much a common-sense view of ethics; to do what is right is often associated with doing what will benefit the majority. From a philosophical point of view, however, there are certain problems associated with this: you can never be certain what the total effects of an action are going to be. To take a crude example: you may save the life of a drowning child who then grows up to be a mass murderer. In practice, there always has to be a cut-off point beyond which it is not practicable to calculate consequences. Added to this is the fact that we see the result of actions only with hindsight; at the time, we might have expected something quite different. Thus, although utilitarianism seems to offer a straightforward way of assessing moral issues, its assessment must always remain provisional.

The definition of what constitutes happiness may not be objective. Other people may not want what you deem to be their happiness or in their best interests. The utilitarian argument appears to make a factual consideration of results the basis of moral choice, but in practice, in selecting the degree or type of happiness to be considered, a person is already making value (and perhaps moral) judgements.

A quantitative assessment of beneficial results raises a crucial question: How do you judge between pain caused to a single individual and the resulting happiness of many others? Would global benefit justify the inflicting of pain on a single innocent person?

Case study

A perfectly healthy young visitor innocently walks into a hospital in which there are a number of people all waiting for various life-saving organ transplants. Might a utilitarian surgeon be tempted?

But more seriously:

In allocating limited healthcare budgets, choices have to be made. Do you spend a large amount of money on an operation that may or may not save the life of a seriously ill child, if the consequence of that choice is that many other people with debilitating (but perhaps not life-threatening) illnesses are unlikely to receive the help they need? How do you assess the relative happiness or benefit of those concerned?

Consider the situation of an unborn child known to be seriously handicapped but capable of surviving. Is the potential suffering of both child and parents as a result of the severe handicap such that the child's survival does not add to the total sum of happiness? And who could possibly make such an assessment objectively?

FORMS OF UTILITARIANISM

▶ *Act utilitarianism*. This makes moral judgements on the basis of the likely consequences of particular acts (this is the form in which it was introduced by Jeremy Bentham, who presented a 'hedonic calculus' – a means of calculating the benefit of any action, based on its intensity, immediacy and so on).

▶ *Rule utilitarianism* additionally takes into consideration the overall benefit that will be gained by society if a particular rule is followed. In other words, breaking a rule may benefit the individual concerned, but allowing that rule to be broken may itself have harmful consequences for society as a whole. This was a form of utilitarianism put forward by John Stuart Mill in the nineteenth century. There are two forms of rule utilitarianism: strong and weak. A strong rule utilitarian will argue that it is never right to break a rule if that rule is to the benefit of society as a whole. A weak rule utilitarian will argue that there may be special cases in which breaking the rule is allowed, although the overall benefit to society of not doing so should also be taken into consideration.

▶ *Preference utilitarianism* is based on taking the preferences of all those who are involved into account. (In other words, the basis on which the 'good' is to be assessed in a particular situation is not impersonal, but takes into account the views and wishes of all concerned.)

Utilitarianism is a popular ethical theory today – and one that many people consider to be common sense. After all, if you are told that something is wrong, the natural thing to ask is what harm it is likely to cause, and conversely that doing what is right implies doing what is beneficial. It can be used to present radical moral challenges, as for example in the many books by Peter Singer (b. 1946), who argues that you should give equal consideration to others as to yourself. Thus, if you are able to prevent something bad from happening to another person, without thereby sacrificing anything morally significant to yourself, you should always do so. This has huge implications for tackling the issue of world poverty. He asks how one can morally justify retaining wealth in a situation where one is aware of the benefits that sharing it could offer others. The problem, of course, is that it seems 'natural' to care for yourself and your family and friends more than those who live at a distance and are not known personally, but *it is difficult to give a rational justification for the resulting disparity in wealth and chances in life*.

Key idea for life

This touches on a huge issue – is reason 'natural'? Is someone motivated by reason likely to behave in ways that are noticeably different from those who are primarily motivated by their hormones and appetites? Plato clearly thought so – he argued that only philosophers should rule. Singer implies it, in presenting a clear challenge to the radical selfishness that inhibits people from wholeheartedly doing what is in the common good. Two fundamental questions: Are people motivated by reason rather than emotion? Are people by nature selfish or co-operative? How we answer these will shape both our morality and our politics.

Both utilitarianism and natural law appear to give rational and objective bases for deciding between right and wrong. Both of them, however, have presuppositions that are not accounted for by the theory itself. One depends on the idea of a rational final cause, the other on the acceptance of shared well-being as the highest good.

The categorical imperative

We have already looked at the work of the eighteenth-century German philosopher Kant in connection with the radical distinction he made between things as we perceive them and things as they are in themselves, and the categories of space, time and causality by which we interpret our experience. However, Kant also made an important contribution in the field of ethics. He sought to formulate a general and universally applicable principle by which pure practical reason could distinguish right from wrong.

He started with the fact that people have a sense of moral obligation – what he calls the **categorical imperative**. In other words, we all know that there are things we 'should' do, irrespective of the consequences. This is the alternative to a 'hypothetical' imperative, which says what you need to do in order to achieve some chosen result. Thus:

▶ You should work hard (categorical imperative).

▶ You should work hard if you want to succeed in this business (hypothetical imperative).

Key idea for life

Of course, you might want to argue that all categorical imperatives are really hypothetical imperatives in disguise – prompted by the unconscious programming of your childhood and social pressure. Can your moral intuitions be independent of your upbringing?

Kant's aim was to express this experience of the categorical imperative in the form of universal principles of morality. These principles are generally referred to as the three forms of Kant's categorical imperative. He expressed them using various forms of words, but they amount to this:

▶ Act only on that maxim (or principle) which you can – at the same time – will that it should become a universal law.

▶ Act in such a way as to treat people as ends and never as means.

▶ Act as though you were legislating for a kingdom of ends.

The first of these expresses the idea that, whatever one wishes to do, one should be prepared for everyone else to act upon that same principle. If you are not prepared for the maxim of your action to become a universal rule, then you should not do it in your individual circumstances. Here you have the most general of all principles and one that, on the surface, has a long pedigree. It follows from the golden rule – to do to others only that which you would wish them to do to you.

One problem with this, however, is that there may be circumstances in which a person may want to kill or lie, without wishing for killing or lying to become universal. Suppose, for example, that the life of an innocent person is being threatened, and the only way of saving him or her is by lying, then a person would wish to do so. In this case, following Kant's argument, one would need to argue that you could wish that anyone in an *identical* situation should be free to lie, without thereby willing that anyone in *any* situation should be free to do so – and here we are back to the most general of all moral problems, how you relate a particular action and set of circumstances to the general moral principle. Notice that it is the overall *principle* (or maxim) of the action that Kant wants to universalize, not the action itself.

Case study

If I argue that I should have the right to end my own life if suffering from a terminal illness that inflicts on me intolerable pain or indignity, that does *not* imply that *everyone* with such an illness should be euthanized, only that *they should, in principle, have the right to make that choice* for themselves.

The second form of the categorical imperative follows from the first. If you want to express your own moral autonomy, you should treat all others on the basis that they would want the same. So you should not treat them as 'means' to your own end, but as 'ends' in themselves. In other words, it is always wrong to 'use' people. That is what distinguishes slavery from fair and just employment – a slave is merely a 'thing', whereas an employee deserves rights.

The third form suggests that you should make your moral judgements as though you had responsibility for legislating in a kingdom in which everyone was an 'end'; in other words, respected as an autonomous moral being.

Kantian ethics, because they are based on pure practical reason, rather than a utilitarian assessment of results, seems to establish universally applicable moral principles. However, in practice, there are a relatively small number of such principles that can be applied without qualification, not least because society and its values vary so much from place to place – what is allowed in one is forbidden in another, often because of deep cultural or religious reasons. Morality is also shaped by the 'social contract' by which individuals, directly or implicitly, agree to give up some of their autonomy in order to work together and establish laws for the common good (see below page 258). So we always need to consider how general moral principles are to be applied in different situations and whether *all* such principles should be open to modification for social and political reasons.

Absolute or relative morality?

If moral rules are absolute, then a particular action may be considered wrong no matter what the circumstances. So, for example, theft may be considered to be wrong. But what is theft? In one sense, the definition is straightforward: theft is the action of taking what belongs to another without that person's consent. The problem is that 'theft' is an interpretation rather than a description. You may take something that belongs to another person without their consent, and yet do so for the best of reasons – they may have dropped something inadvertently and you have picked it up in order to restore it to them. At the moment you stoop and take it, that action might equally be theft or an act of kindness, depending upon your intention.

One example of this dilemma might be 'mercy killing', where someone who is seriously ill and facing the prospect of a painful or lingering death is helped to die by a relative or close friend. If you take a view that there are moral absolutes, you may say: 'Murder is always wrong.' The next question then becomes:

'Is mercy killing the same thing as murder?' In other words, you start with absolute moral principles and then assess each particular situation in terms of which of these moral principles are involved (a process that is generally termed **casuistry**).

In 1966, Joseph Fletcher published a book entitled *Situation Ethics*, which reflected a reaction against the perceived narrowness of traditional Christian morality at a time of rapid social change. Rather than simply obeying rules, he argued that one should always do what love required in each and every situation. He claimed that his view represented a fundamental feature of the Christian approach to life, as seen in the emphasis on love in *I Corinthians*, the rejection of Jewish legalism, or St Augustine's view that, if you love, what you want to do will be what is right.

By following the law of love and the demands of each situation, this approach suggested that it would sometimes be right to set aside conventional moral rule or go against the expectations of society. Although critics tended to accuse **situation ethics** of leading to moral anarchy, it was a genuine attempt to combine an overall moral principle (love) with a recognition of the uniqueness of every situation.

Very much a book of its time, *Situation Ethics* was widely criticized for presenting something of a caricature of moral theory. Its aim, amid the heady days of 1960s rebellion against authority, was to attack conventional, legalistic morality. However, whatever its limitations, it showed the need for flexibility, at a time when obedience to moral rules was seen a less than ideal way of promoting peace and love.

VALUES AND SOCIETY
There is a broader sense in which we need to be aware of relativity in ethics. Each society has its own particular way of life, along with the values and principles that are expressed through it. This has come to be focused on the issue of **multiculturalism.** What might be considered right in one society may be thought wrong in another. A set of moral rules may be drawn up that are valid for one society, but cannot be applied universally. Equally, a person may find that they live within more than one cultural circle – defined by race, religion,

class and nationality – each with its own set of values and implied moral principles.

However, if we live in a multicultural and complex society, we have to face the relativity of moral judgements. To this may be added the general sense in a postmodernist era (see page 173) that everything depends upon taking, using and mixing the cultural, linguistic and mental ideas that we find around us. In such a situation, it is very difficult to impose uniform moral principles. Apart from anything else, they may be rejected on the grounds of their origin – in the Catholic Church (in the case of natural law) or in the words of a long-dead, male philosopher (in the case of Kant).

Of the theories we have examined so far, preference utilitarianism gets round this problem most straightforwardly, as individual preferences (and therefore the cultural and social factors that give rise to them) are taken into the utilitarian assessment.

Kantian ethics has the greatest problem with relativism. On the one hand, it wants to establish universal moral principles (which relativism will not allow) and on the other it wants to treat each individual as an autonomous moral agent (of which relativism approves). Kant may perhaps be forgiven for not appreciating the scale of the relativist challenge in a multicultural society, as he spent his whole life in his native Königsberg.

Key idea for life

The real problem for many ethical thinkers today is with a full-blown *relativism* that simply refuses to accept *any* general moral norms. In other words, it becomes increasingly difficult to make any moral judgements that may not be challenged on the basis of the gender, race, religion or social position of the person making that judgement. Sensitivity to social norms or particular circumstances has always been a key feature of ethics – and even the much maligned process of 'casuistry' attempted to apply moral principles to particular situations. However, at some point, if moral discussions are to be effective, there needs to be a shared set of values, and that implies a limit to relativism.

The values and life you choose

Is morality something discovered, or something created? Some approaches – natural law for example – clearly see morality as linked to objective facts about the world, moulding human morality to fit an overall sense of purpose. There is another approach, however, which suggests that we are free to choose the basis for our morality.

This approach is illustrated by Nietzsche, particularly in the title of his book *Beyond Good and Evil*. For Nietzsche, humankind has a responsibility to develop towards something higher, to say 'Yes!' to life and affirm the future. He saw both Christianity and democracy as fundamentally a morality for slaves, attempting to protect the weak at the expense of the strong, and thereby weakening the species. Rather, he looks to a master morality, deliberately choosing the *übermensch*, or higher man, as the meaning of the Earth.

Equally, existentialism (see page 51), in emphasizing person authenticity, tends to see morality in terms of the affirmation of the self. I shape my life by the choices I make, and take responsibility for that shaping. Choices, though, have ethical implications; so existentialism gives a particularly self-referential approach to morality.

Key idea for life

How do you balance the determination to act with integrity, seeking self-fulfilment, with the relationship you have with those around you and with society as a whole? Is altruism necessarily a form of slave morality? Is it always right to act in your own self-interest (enlightened or otherwise)? If you want to take charge of your life, do you also need to take charge of your morality? If so, what consequences might follow?

Applying ethical theories

Throughout history, philosophers have sought to apply their ideas, and this has been most obvious in the field of ethics. Applied ethics started to come to the fore again during the last three decades of the twentieth century, after a number of years during which philosophers had been rather preoccupied by linguistic questions and assumed that they had no special qualification, as philosophers, to speak out on practical moral issues.

A key to a successful argument in applied ethics is to achieve a balance between facts and values. Thus, for example, in questions of abortion, it is important to know at what point the bundle of cells that would naturally grow into a human being actually takes on human characteristics. At what point does the brain start to exist? When does consciousness arise? At what point should the growing baby be considered as a human being separate (and separable) from its mother? Whatever one's views on the morality of abortion are, such facts need to be known in order to make a moral case. The skill is to use them effectively within the framework of a moral theory, whether of the natural law type or utilitarian. In turn, each of those theories will be based on fundamental views about the nature of morality and the value of life. This makes applied ethics particularly demanding, but immensely worthwhile.

In putting together an ethical argument, here are some points to consider:

▶ Do I have a basic intuition about what is right or wrong here? If so, reflect on exactly what it is that you feel strongly about. (This will decide how you are going to shape your argument.)

▶ What are the facts?

▶ What are the possibilities? (In other words, if you have a moral dilemma, or want to take a moral stance, it implies that something *could* be done to change or improve the situation.)

▶ Which of the ethical theories supports the point I want to make?

So, for example, if you are going to make a case for or against euthanasia, you might want to consider a natural law argument about the natural impulse to keep living, or a virtue ethics argument about the qualities that constitute good medical care, or a utilitarian argument about whether it would benefit the person to be euthanized, or a categorical imperative argument about the absolute respect for the autonomy of the individual, or whether you would want everyone to be free to decide on euthanasia in similar circumstances.

So, just as there are a variety of different moral views, so there are different ways to support any one of them rationally.

THE SCOPE OF APPLIED ETHICS

There is no scope in an introductory text of this sort to do more than point to some of the major areas within which ethics is applied today.

Professional ethics has been concerned with standards of conduct expected of members of the professions and with drawing up guidelines for situations in which there are difficult moral choices to be made. The medical, nursing and legal professions most obviously provide a whole range of moral dilemmas that need to be examined.

Sometimes advances in technology raise issues that require ethical examination. The rise of information technology, for example, raises issues about privacy, identity theft, and the limits to what can be done with stored information. Should the state be responsible for, and have control of, whatever data it manages to gather on its citizens? Should I have a right to see what information is held about me? Of course, issues of privacy have been around for a long time, but they are brought into sharper focus by the ability to store and retrieve data in digital form. Equally, genetic manipulation of the food we eat is an old issue presented in a very new form. These are matters that affect everyone, and are therefore not limited to those who work in the relevant industry.

Business ethics is an important and growing area of interest, with the conflict between those who favour a free-market approach and those who want more political and social control. Equally, media ethics is relevant to everyone, since assumptions are made about the veracity of news items, the morality of public humiliation or deception, and whether the media should have social and political responsibilities.

Key idea for life

You will find that most arguments in this area are fundamentally utilitarian, with a clash of interest between the short-term economic benefits to the relative few and the potential long-term benefits for the many. As we shall see below, economics (combined with an implied impulse to self-interest) tends to be an unquestioned background to many ethical and political issues, particularly in what is generally termed the 'neo-liberal' agenda.

In addition, there is of course the huge issue of the ethics of warfare, raised in recent years particularly by the wars in Iraq and Syria and the resulting debates about when, if ever, it is right to intervene to seek regime change in a sovereign nation. Traditionally, the ethics of war and peace has been divided into issues over *when* it is right to go to war, and *how* wars should be fought, once they have started. Hence morality examines both the right of a nation to defend itself and the types of weapons that are used in battle.

Modern technology increases the possibilities for presenting us with new moral dilemmas. So, for example, through drugs or genetic manipulation it would be possible to try to enhance human beings – not just physically (that already happens illegally in sport) but mentally, perhaps even socially or morally. If you could change people, to make aggression and war less likely, or to enhance empathy, should you do so? Should we experiment with interventions to boost our intellectual capacity? Would that be a positive step in human evolution or a dangerous interference with the natural order?

With any such question, we can apply the theories explored above – natural law might have something to say about whether such interference is inherently wrong, utilitarianism might try to weigh its potential harms and benefits, virtue ethics might consider whether one can be made virtuous artificially, and we might need to consider whether it would be socially acceptable.

Key idea for life

Hanging over this and similar questions is a moral issue that relates to the 'problem of evil' in the philosophy of religion: Would it be better to live in a world where everyone was artificially forced to be good, or in one where there was the freedom to be selfish or cruel?

Environmental ethics

How we treat the natural world springs most obviously from how we understand our place within it. This gives environmental ethics a rather different character from most other ethical issues, because it links so directly with our understanding of who we are as conscious, self-conscious and thinking human beings living on a finite planet.

Much representational art has been concerned with displaying, giving attention to, or reinterpreting the natural world and a sense of wonder at nature has inspired both religion and art – with a sense both of natural beauty and the overwhelming, threatening nature of the sublime. However, there are two very different ways in which we can relate to the natural world – we see ourselves either as detached observers or as engaged participants – and which of these we adopt has a profound effect on how we see nature and how we treat it.

If we try to stand back from the world, regarding it as something 'out there' with which we have to deal, there will always be a temptation to 'enframe' it (a term used by Heidegger) – in other words, the tree is not just a tree, but a source of shade, or fruit, or wood, or a place into which one might climb to escape a predator, or an attractive thing to photograph or paint. In other words, we give it a *function in relation to ourselves*.

The danger of this approach, as Heidegger pointed out, is that it can encourage us to exploit natural resources for our short-term benefit – and there have been plenty of examples of that, including most obviously the destruction of rainforests for logging. Such exploitation is opposed by those who are concerned that the natural world should be preserved for our long-term benefit and delight. Thus, for example, the saving of rainforests and the variety of the flora found in them, is often argued on the basis of medicines that may in the future be derived from such plants. The arguments here are generally utilitarian.

To step out of that way of thinking, and to recognize that we are engaged participants in the world, encourages us to be aware of the interconnected nature of all life, including human life. We are one species among others, only recently dominant on this planet. The question is then not framed in terms of 'To what extent is it right or prudent to maximize our use of natural resources?' but rather 'How can we preserve and enhance the environment within which we live, both for our own long-term benefit and for that of all other species?'

Key idea for life

Exploitation of natural resources is linked to the human desire to consume more and more by way of material goods, on the assumption that increased consumption brings happiness. This idea has been challenged by some philosophers, notably Epicurus (see pages 59 and 234) who advocated the enjoyment of simple pleasures, freed from the burden of an insatiable appetite for consumption. The theme of his ethics and lifestyle is, in effect, 'Enjoy more by consuming less!'

The central issue in any ethical argument concerning the relationship between humans and other species, or humans and the environment in general, is whether other species have *inherent worth*, or whether their value is bound up with their *usefulness to the human species*.

The distinction is often made between an approach in which the environment is cared for simply in order to make conditions better *for humankind*, and **deep ecology** (a term introduced by the Norwegian philosopher Arne Naess) in which the environment is preserved for its own sake, and in which we have no right to privilege humankind over other species. This distinction gives rise to another pair of terms. The environment is said to have **extrinsic value,** if its value is based on what it can do to benefit humankind, and **intrinsic value**, if it is of value in itself, quite apart from any relationship it has with humankind.

The philosophical approach to ecology has been built on the basis of research that has shown the impact that humans have upon other species. In 1962, Rachel Carson (1907–64) published *Silent Spring*, in which she highlighted the damage done to birds through the pesticide DDT and other chemicals. It was hugely controversial at the time because it challenged the assumed progress that pesticides could achieve, but eventually it led to the banning of DDT.

Part of the problem in establishing environmental ethics is how you see the significance of humankind as a species. The biblical idea that humankind had a right to use and subdue nature tended to favour an anthropocentric view of the environment – it was there for the sake of humankind, and should only be taken into consideration where human welfare was threatened. This view was opposed by Peter Singer in *Animal Liberation*, 1976, an influential book for considering the rights of animals, and one that deliberately tried to steer ethical thinking away from an exclusively anthropocentric viewpoint. Singer argues that – just as we have realized that sexism and racism are wrong – so we should recognize that 'speciesism' is wrong. In other words, we should not limit consideration to members of our own species.

Here, from a humanist and Buddhist perspective, is the view of Matthieu Ricard:

> The realization that all sentient beings, from the simplest to the most complex, are part of an evolving continuum, and that there is no basic rupture between the different degrees of evolution, should naturally lead us to respect other species and to use our superior intelligence not to profit from them as if they were simply instruments in the service of our well-being, but to promote their well-being at the same time as our own.
>
> (*Altruism*, p. 207)

Since the Enlightenment and the emergence of liberal economics, it has also been assumed that humankind had a natural right and expectation that society would enjoy 'growth' and an ever-rising standard of living. However, on a finite planet, with limited resources and a rising population, unlimited growth is simply not possible. Hence there has been a fundamental difference in perspective between those who promote indefinite growth and development (often with the assumption that technology will eventually come to the rescue of humankind as energy and other resources diminish), and those who recognize the need to switch to a sustainable lifestyle, seeing humankind within an environment that it needs in order to survive, but which it is in danger of destroying.

Key idea for life

Our thinking about the environment is not just a matter of ethics, but of self-awareness. How you see yourself will determine how you treat your world. Are you part of the natural order, or only an observer?

Ethics is a huge subject, both in terms of the range of ethical theories and the way in which these may be applied to moral and social issues. It has provided the impetus for much work in philosophy as a whole, and is the single largest area of study within departments of philosophy (judging by the number of papers published). It is particularly valuable as an area of philosophical study, as the benefits of clear thinking, analysis and the clarification of concepts and presuppositions can be seen to have immediate relevance to practical aspects of life.

9

Political Philosophy

In this chapter you will:

▶ *Learn about some traditional political theories*

▶ *Consider key issues of equality, justice, fairness and human rights*

▶ *Explore questions relating to freedom and the law*

Why?

Nothing is more relevant than the question 'What is the good life, and how may it be achieved?' Whether or not you take an active interest in politics, you cannot avoid being caught up in the laws, traditions and values of the society within which you live. We are all political animals, so it is always useful to reflect on the values we hold and the sort of society we want to live in. We live in uncertain times; to guide and make sense of where we are going, politics needs to be underpinned by clear thinking. Philosophy can help sort out conceptual muddles (and there are plenty of them in the political world) and is generally non-dogmatic, which is of great value when it comes to the critical examination of both legislation and political arguments.

Philosophers do not always live in ivory towers. Plato sailed to Syracuse, hoping to tame a tyrant, and failed; Aristotle became tutor to Alexander the Great; Marcus Aurelius ruled the Roman Empire; Machiavelli offered cynical advice for any aspiring ruler; Hobbes responded to the chaos of the English civil war; Locke influenced the American Constitution; Rousseau's ideas contributed to the French revolution; Paine was radical, Burke conservative; Marx changed much of the world; Sartre joined the Resistance and later backed the communists; Popper attacked Marxism; Ayn Rand inspired the American right-wing; and today, Michael Sandel's hugely popular course on justice is available world-wide. Welcome to the world of political philosophy!

Politics is about the way we organize the running of a village, city, state, nation, or the international community. It applies principles such as equality, fairness, security and freedom to day-to-day questions of defence, law and taxation and economic organization. However, politics only exists because people work together in order to achieve certain basic ends – in other words, to seek 'the good life' for society as a whole, whatever they conceive that to be. That's where political philosophy comes in; it discusses the values and principles in which the practical operation of politics may be grounded.

Key idea for life

Unless you know where you want to go and why you want to go there, there's little point in discussing routes and means of transport. Political philosophy is about the where and the why; politics is about the routes and the transport.

We saw in the previous chapter that ethics is largely *normative*; it is about the norms and values by which people live, not just about what they *actually* do, but what they *ought* to do. Political philosophy applies ethical principles (including many of the arguments that we considered in the last chapter, particularly utilitarianism) to public life. What is the equivalent of the 'good' person when it comes to the way in which nations behave, both towards one another and in the treatment of their own citizens? What are the norms by which we can assess whether a nation is doing what is right?

If asked what we expect from our national government, we might suggest some or all of the following:

▶ The ability to live in peace, free from the threat of war, or terrorism or crime.

▶ The provision of basic services, including health, education and the protection of the vulnerable.

▶ The freedom to live as one wants, within reason and without hurting others in the process.

▶ The security and stability to enable us to plan ahead, to make provision for our families, to buy and keep a home and so on.

▶ The ability to earn money, the value of which is not eroded by excessive inflation, and of which not too much is taken in tax to pay for the rest of this list.

▶ A sense of fairness in the way in which people are treated.

▶ The ability to have our say in the way in which the country is run, particularly in those things that affect us personally.

Yet *how much* of this is the responsibility of government and how much should be left to the individual? Should you opt for minimal government interference? Or would it be fairer to pay more tax and rely on the state to provide for the basic, practical needs of all its citizens? Your answer to that, of course, may depend on whether you are relatively wealthy and liable to tax, or unemployed, vulnerable and dependent upon health care and social provision.

The other fundamental question with which political philosophy is concerned is about how and to what extent we should be involved with the process of government. Almost everybody agrees that some form of democracy is ideal, because it suggests that everyone has an opportunity to vote and therefore to influence what happens in government. But how should that be organized?

2016 provided an interesting range of issues illustrating the relevance of political philosophy, with the Brexit vote in the United Kingdom, the election of a businessman and television personality, Donald Trump to the presidency of the United States, the continuing problems with refugees and economic migrants seeking to enter Europe from the Middle East and Africa, and increasing concerns about global warming. Beneath these events lie some fundamental issues:

▶ How do you ensure that a 'democratic' system is able to take account of and reflect the wishes of all citizens? (It is clear that both in the USA and the UK, a large number of working people did not feel that the 'establishment' were taking notice of their needs and concerns.)

▶ How do you reconcile globalization of trade with the needs of working people, for whom the availability of jobs in their part of the world is crucial?

▶ In addition, underlying many other issues is the fundamental one about the neo-liberal economic and political agenda, driven by free-market capitalism, globalization, and the general desire to minimize government expenditure, imposing austerity on many rather than increasing taxes or seeking a more equitable distribution of profits and resources.

Turn from surveying the modern world to read, for example, Aristotle's *Politics*, and you find there a serious discussion about justice and equality within society and how to ensure stability that is utterly relevant to present concerns. All we can hope to do in this chapter is to touch on some of these fundamental issues.

Key issues in political philosophy include:

▶ the concepts of freedom, justice, liberty and equality
▶ the role of the state
▶ the relationship between the state and the individual
▶ the nature of authority
▶ the status of law
▶ the role of power
▶ human rights.

Only individuals?

Does the state exist? Is there any such thing as society? If I were suddenly to declare that the USA did not exist, I would be thought insane, but is it that obvious? There are two ways of looking at individuals and society:

1 Society, or the nation, is a reality over and above its individual citizens. It is 'real' in the sense that it can exert its power over them, forcing them to take part in a war, claiming taxes from them, imposing laws on them. Patriotism depends on the idea that the nation is real, and worth fighting for.

2 There is no such thing as society. There are just individuals who decide on rules and regulations for their mutual benefit and who band together to do things that are beyond the abilities of any one person or family. In this case, Great Britain or the USA are just names: they have no reality other than the millions of people who happen to live in those parts of the world, and the various institutions by which they organize their lives.

If you tend towards the first of these, you might take a further step and claim that individuals can only exist as part of larger social groups. You could argue, for example:

▶ You are part of a family and circle of friends: you are a mother, father, child or friend by virtue of your relationships. Without other people, you would be none of these things.

▶ You speak a language that is not of your own devising. You share in a common store of words and thoughts. Without society, there would be no language. You have 'rights' as an individual only because they are given to you by society.

Therefore, although you would continue to be a human being, you would not really be an 'individual', with a name, rights, responsibilities, education, a language and a stock of inherited ideas, without society. Individual rights and obligations are not discovered in nature, but are devised by society. Without society, there would be no laws and no morality. Therefore it is unrealistic to think that everything is reducible to the perspective of the self-interest of individuals.

By contrast, Margaret Thatcher, Britain's first female prime minister, famously declared in 1987:

> And, you know, there's no such thing as society. There are individual men and women and there are families. And no government can do anything except through people, and people must look after themselves first.

Such a view minimizes the role of government and puts individuals centre-stage. We shall see that this has become a key feature of modern free-market economics and the controversial neo-liberal economic and political agenda.

The idea of the individual or citizen is closely linked to that of society or the state. Each is defined with reference to the other. A central issue for the philosophy of politics is to find an acceptable balance between these two things. Individualism, democracy, totalitarianism, socialism, cultural imperialism, regionalism, internationalism: these are all about the balance between individuals or groups and the larger social wholes of which they are a part.

An example:

Case study

Is the United Nations an emerging global 'state' of the future, within which individual nations subsume their own interests for the sake of a greater good? Or is it simply a group of individual nations banded together for mutual benefit, within which each will seek to gain as much for itself as is compatible with retaining membership?

There was no doubt about the nature of society for Aristotle. He presented what we would today call a progressive, even socialist view of the correct functioning of political systems. In *The Politics*, a hugely important collection of his teachings on this area, he argues that a democratic statesman should seek how best to achieve a lasting prosperity for all the population, and certainly that he should seek to ensure that the majority of citizens should not slip into extreme poverty. Hence, for him, the prime responsibility of a ruler, apart from securing peace and order, is to ensure fairness and justice – and that requires government legislation and engagement with the world of finance and commerce. He regarded superintendence of the market as an indispensable function of government, in order that the desire on the part of the wealthy to consolidate their position should not happen at the expense of the less fortunate. He would have been baffled by the idea that there was no such thing as society, only individuals. For Aristotle, society is the context within which individuals can flourish, and regulating it is the responsibility of government.

Much modern discussion in political philosophy, like that of ancient Greece, centres on the key ideas of freedom, equality, fairness and justice. However, it is also important to be aware of some of the broad theories about how social and political life should be organized, as these continue to exert a significant influence.

The social contract

Self-preservation is a fundamental human need. Born in 1588, Thomas Hobbes knew first-hand the traumas of civil war in England and used such a lawless and dangerous state as the starting point for his political theory. In Chapter 13 of

Leviathan, published in 1651, he considers what life is like when a person can rely only on his or her own strength for protection:

> In such condition, there is no place for industry, because the fruit thereof is uncertain; and consequently no culture of the earth; no navigation, nor use of the commodities that may be imported by sea; no commodious building, no instruments of moving or removing such things as require much force; no knowledge of the face of the earth; no account of time; no arts; no letters; no society; and, which is worst of all, continual fear and danger of violent death; and the life of man solitary, poor, nasty, brutish, and short.

Hobbes considered that the need for self-preservation was so fundamental to human life, that (using a 'natural law' form of argument) it should be the basis of political science and that, illustrated by the passage quoted above, society and civilization would be impossible without personal security.

In this situation, Hobbes argued that people would band together for their mutual protection, and would set up a ruler who would maintain order. The value of the state is seen in its ability to protect and benefit the individuals of which it is comprised. His political theory, the start of what is called the 'social contract' tradition, springs from this need for self-preservation. Hobbes believed, however, that the ruler so appointed should be given absolute power, and that only by doing so could the security of the state be maintained.

John Locke (1632–1704) argued from a similar starting point. Laws should be based on the need for the preservation of life and private property within the state, and defence from foreign threats. However, he went beyond Hobbes, arguing that the people who entered into their social contract should have the right, if the rulers did not benefit them, to replace them with others. In other words, he argued for a representative democracy, with rulers accountable to those who have put them in power. Thus we have a constitutional government, where rulers have power, but only to the extent that they are given it by the people, and within principles that are set out within a constitution.

For Hobbes and Locke, the moral justification for the actions of the state is utilitarian, the moral theory that seeks 'the greatest happiness for the greatest number' as formulated by both Jeremy Bentham and John Stuart Mill (see his essays *On Liberty* and *On Representative Government*). Government is established by the people and for the benefit of the people.

Key idea for life: Reason or rhetoric?

Plato describes Socrates as criticizing the Sophists for using rhetorical skills, rather than reason, to persuade people. Today, we have a similar problem, with politicians frequently making claims that appeal to the emotions, swaying public opinion, but sometimes doing so on the basis of a selective use of evidence and without sound reasoning. For a social contract to be effective, people need to be persuaded by means that will secure their future co-operation; false promises tend to produce only short-term gains. Equally, spreading unfounded fear only achieves its end until people realize that the threatened future disaster has not come about.

Political philosophy protects politics from the threat posed by unprincipled rhetoric.

The social contract is based on the agreement that people will act together for their mutual benefit. The problem arises over exactly what is to the benefit of society as a whole, and who is to decide it. To what extent can an individual, on the basis of a social contract, act on behalf of all? Do all have to agree before some action is taken? On what basis is there to be arbitration between conflicting interests. Locke is clear that decisions must reflect the wishes of a majority, and any minority must accept that judgement:

> Every man, by consenting with others to make one body politic under one government, puts himself under an obligation to every one of that society to submit to the determination of the majority, and to be concluded by it; or else this original compact, whereby he with others incorporates into one society, would signify nothing, and be no compact if he be left free and under no other ties than he was in before in the state of Nature.
>
> *The Second Treatise of Government*, Chapter 13, section 97

Thus a government can act as long as it has the consent of a majority. But what if a government seeks to act in a way that the rulers consider to be in the interests of the people, even if that is not what people as individuals actually want?

Locke raises some fundamental questions here:

▶ When (if at all) might it be right to disobey the law?

▶ Can civil disobedience ever be justified in a democracy?

▶ Does its support by a majority of people itself justify the actions carried out by a democratic government?

These are as relevant now as in the seventeenth century. Of course, in Locke's day, only men of a certain wealth were given the vote, and women were excluded. So, although he put forward the principle should be established by 'the people', democratic rights were, in practice, very limited.

Key idea for life

If the interests of all citizens are to be taken into account, should it be legal for a politician to promise something that cannot realistically be delivered, simply in order to secure votes? Elections and referenda are seldom clear-cut. Have 'the people spoken' if a minority of the population (given that not everyone votes) have secured a slim majority in a poll? Is it right, in a democracy, to act exclusively on behalf of a winning majority, against the interests of a substantial minority? This is a particularly relevant question, today, both in Britain and in the USA.

Social contract theories apportion *responsibilities*, setting out what can reasonably be expected of people in terms of their relationship with others. They also set out the *rights* to which individuals are entitled. Many areas of applied ethics have focused on rights and responsibilities, especially in the area of professional conduct. For example, they might ask what responsibility a doctor has to patients, to the society within which he or she practises, and to the development of medicine – and from this a code of professional conduct can be drawn up. Equally, it can ask what basic expectations a person should have in terms of the way in which he or she should be treated by other people or by the state.

The general will

Jean-Jacques Rousseau (1712–78), was a Swiss philosopher who, in spite of having little formal education and a hard and colourful personal life, produced ideas about democracy that were to be hugely influential, particularly at the time of the French revolution.

Rousseau, recognizing that all existing states were imperfect, sought to start from first principles and establish the basis of a legitimate political system. Like Hobbes and Locke, he looked back to man in a state of nature but, unlike them, he thought that in such a natural state people's needs would be few and relatively easily satisfied, and would be unlikely to lead to conflict.

By contrast, once society becomes established, people enclose property and deprive others of the use of it. The basic requirements of food and shelter become commodities, which people have to get through barter, and many may thereby be reduced to misery. With private property, inequality increases and this may lead to civil strife. Thus, where Hobbes and Locke saw private property as a natural right to be defended, Rousseau saw it as something artificially imposed by society. *He saw society as tending to corrupt natural man rather than improve him.*

Key idea for life

For Rousseau, natural human feelings and instincts are fundamentally good, but society ruins our innocence by offering temptations and highlighting inequalities. In other words, you become deprived by being unable to get what you are now offered, but previously had no idea you wanted. On that basis, advertising promotes deprivation by promising a satisfaction not available to all. Yet is it not natural for us to *want* things, even if we don't *need* them?

Rousseau presents a social contract theory, but one that differs significantly from that set out by Hobbes or Locke. A central issue for Rousseau is how an individual can retain his or her freedom, while at the same time accepting the terms of a social contract, with the requirement that an individual is bound by the wishes of society as a whole. He does this through the idea of the 'general will'. He argues that an individual must give himself or herself totally, including all his or her rights, to the whole community. *The general will is sovereign, and individuals find their own freedom by conforming to it.*

For Rousseau, natural freedom is, in fact, a slavery to individual passions. By contrast, to set aside one's individual, personal will, and to accept the general will, is to discover one's higher aspirations and moral freedom. There will be occasions when individuals will oppose the general will, but on those occasions the individual concerned should be *forced* to accept it, for the good of all.

In any political system, someone has to decide how general laws should be applied to individual situations. Rousseau held that there should be a legislator, someone who would know instinctively what the general will was and be able to apply it.

One might say that, whereas for Hobbes and Locke individuals are freely able to decide what is in their own best interests (although are sometimes required to set these interests aside for the benefit of the majority), for Rousseau, individuals are not able to decide what is best, and therefore are required to accept what is deemed to be best by the general will – in other words, by the state.

The implications of this aspect of Rousseau's thinking are enormous. If individuals are unable to challenge the 'general will', a state can carry out the most drastic action (decapitating the aristocracy, eliminating whole classes of people in state purges) on the basis of carrying out the 'general will'. In the twentieth century, the examples of Stalin's Russia, China under Mao and Cambodia under Pol Pot all illustrate the power of the state to claim to act for the benefit of all, while actually perpetrating state terror.

Key idea for life

In a properly functioning democracy, executive power is held in check by representative bodies. In the USA, a president may sign executive orders, but they can be challenged and revoked by the judiciary, and laws need to go before Congress, which alone has the authority to decide financial matters, and which has power of oversight over the executive. In the UK, a government can only enact laws that are scrutinized and approved by the Houses of Parliament, and they still require the assent of the monarch and may be challenged by the judiciary.

In theory, democracy enacts the will of the people; in practice establishing that 'will' is far from straightforward. Yet, however complex, that process needs to ensure that it does not frustrate its original intention, namely to provide the means of providing a truly representative democracy.

Marx and materialism

Karl Marx (1818–83) has been an enormously influential thinker. Indeed, one cannot start to describe the history of the twentieth century without reference to Marxism and the communist regimes that sprang from it. Born in Germany, he moved to Paris when the newspaper he was editing was forced to close. Expelled from both Paris and then Brussels, he finally settled in London. His most important book, *Das Kapital* (1867), predicts that capitalism has within it the seeds of its own destruction and will give way to socialism.

Marx argued that religion, morality, political ideas and social structures were fundamentally rooted in economics, particularly the production and distribution of goods. People have basic needs, which must be fulfilled in order for them to live, and society becomes more and more sophisticated as it seeks to produce the goods and services to meet those needs. He interpreted history in economic terms, as shaped by the struggle between different social classes. The bourgeoisie confronts the proletariat: employers facing employees as once landowners faced their peasants. Individual actions are judged by the way in which they contribute to the class struggle, and the actions of a class as a whole is seen in a broader context of the movement of society.

In terms of the history of philosophy, Marx was influenced by Hegel (1770–1831) who saw individuals as bound up with the tide of history, which itself was unfolding by a rational process. Like Hegel, Marx saw reality as working itself out through a process of change. Hegel had introduced the idea of a 'dialectic': first you have a thesis, then in response to this you have the opposite (an antithesis), and bringing these two together you get a synthesis. For Hegel, this process was non-material, leading to a harmonious awareness of the *Geist*, or spirit of the age, in which everyone freely accepts the interests of the whole of society. For Marx, by contrast, the process of dialectic is material. It is the economic conditions in which the classes live and work that produce the urge to change, as a result of which the existing economic system is overthrown through a revolution and a new system is set up, but that, in turn, leads to further class confrontation, and so on.

Marx looked towards the achievement of a classless society, where there would be no more confrontation, but where working people would own the means of production and distribution. This classless society would therefore be characterized by economic justice, in which each benefited from his or her own labour.

This was linked to his view of the fulfilment of the human individual. Marx argued that, in a capitalist system, an individual who works for a wage, producing something from which someone else is going to make a profit, becomes alienated from that working situation. He or she cannot exercise true creativity or humanity, but becomes an impersonal 'thing', a machine whose sole purpose in life is production, a means of making 'capital'. Marx saw this process leading to more and more wealth being concentrated in the hands of a small number of 'bourgeoisie', with the working proletariat sinking into poverty. This, he believed, would eventually lead to the overthrow of the capitalist system by the workers acting together. He believed that, with the advent of the classless society, each individual would be able to develop to his or her full potential.

Marx has things to say about the nature of history, of work, of the self, of political institutions and of social classes, but he is also a prime example of the way in which a philosopher can influence the course of history. It is difficult to study Marx without being aware of the global impact of Marxist ideology in the twentieth century. The decline of communism in the last decades of the twentieth century, and capitalism's failure to self-destruct in the way he predicted, will obviously be taken into account by anyone who studies his political philosophy. Contrariwise, it is difficult to overestimate the general impact of his thinking, particularly, perhaps, in the view that politics is rooted in economics.

> ## Remember this
>
> Although Marx's main work was *Das Kapital* (1867), it may be easier to approach him first through his earlier works, particularly *The German Ideology* (1846) and *The Communist Manifesto* (1848).

Notice that Marx (following Rousseau and, indeed, Hegel) saw the individual as subsuming his or her interests for the benefit of the wider group. The individual acts as a representative of his or her class or nation, and those actions are judged by whatever is deemed to be right by that larger social group. This is in contrast to the tradition, stemming from Hobbes and Locke, where emphasis is placed on the individual. We shall see in the next section that this divide is still found in political philosophy, as reflected in the differing views of justice taken by two modern philosophers, Rawls and Nozick.

Justice

The concept of justice is fundamental to political philosophy. If people are to band together for mutual protection, enter into social contracts and set their own interests aside for the greater good, they need to be persuaded that the society within which they live is based on principles that are just. But what constitutes political justice?

We shall look at ideas of justice presented by three philosophers, one ancient and two modern.

PLATO

The question 'What is justice?' dominates one of the greatest works of philosophy, Plato's *Republic*. In this book (presented as a dialogue between Socrates and the representatives of contemporary schools of thought), various answers are proposed and rejected, as, for example, the popular but rather cynical view that justice is whatever is in the interest of the stronger. Plato recognizes that human nature can be deeply selfish, and that – given the opportunity to act with absolute impunity – people will generally seek their own benefit rather than that of others, or of society as a whole; he also explores the idea (later to be developed by the 'social contract' theory) that people's appetites need to be restrained for the good of all. But what is the value of justice in itself?

Plato seeks to root his answer (presented through the mouth of Socrates) in a theory about the elements that make up a human individual and their equivalent in the political society of his day, the 'polis' or city-state. He considers the various classes of people that make up the city, and argues that each class offers particular virtues, but that justice is found in the fact that each class performs its own task. In the same way, the individual soul is divided into three parts – mind, spirit and appetite – and justice for the individual consists in achieving a balance, with each part performing its own task for the benefit of that individual. However, he insists that the rational element should control, and thus that – for the state – it is important for rulers to be philosophers.

Plato sees justice in terms of the harmony and proper functioning of each part of society, and he wants the rulers of his *Republic,* through their philosophical training, to be sufficiently detached and rational to seek a just balance of interests throughout the polis, rather than serving their own self-interest. This, he argues, will be necessary if justice is to be established for *all* rather than in the interests of a particular section of the population.

Every philosophy needs to be seen against the background of its particular time and society, and Plato is no exception. His concept of a state ruled by philosophers, seeking a balance between elements in society and in the self, with priority given to the intellectual faculty, is not easily translatable into a modern political context. What is clear, however, is that justice (for Plato) is seen neither in equality (he never envisaged a society of equals) nor in sectional interests (he rejected the idea that it was in the interests of the stronger), but in a balance in which different people and classes, each doing what is appropriate for them, work together for the common good.

Key idea for life

It is impossible to think that, looking around the world today, Plato would not have some astute comments to make about contemporary politics. Like Aristotle, he argued that the politician should rise above narrow self-interest and achieve a balanced view of the needs of society as a whole. It is frustrating that such an obvious requirement is so seldom found in the day-to-day operation of politics, where sectional influences, whether national, class, racial or economic, exert an often unquestioned hegemony.

RAWLS (JUSTICE AS FAIRNESS)

In *A Theory of Justice* (1972), John Rawls considers (as a thought experiment) a situation in which a group of people come together to decide the principles upon which their political association should operate. In other words, they set about forming a social contract. However, he adds one further important criterion: that they should forget everything about themselves as individuals. They do not know whether they are poor or wealthy, men or women. They do not know their race or their position within society. They come together simply as individuals, nothing more. He therefore seeks, by this means, to establish principles that...

> ... free and rational persons concerned to further their own interests would accept in an initial position of equality as defining the fundamental terms of their association.
>
> (p. 11)

By not knowing who they are, Rawls hopes to achieve an idea of disinterested justice, for people will seek to legislate in a way that will benefit themselves, whoever they eventually turn out to be.

Rawls argues that such a group would require two principles:

1 **Liberty:** Each person should have equal rights to as extensive a set of basic liberties as possible, as long as that does not prevent others from having a similar set of fundamental liberties.

2 **Distribution of resources:** Given that there are social inequalities, Rawls argues that the distribution of resources should be such that the least advantaged in society receive the greatest benefit.

This is justice based on 'fairness'. Rawls argues that it is fair to grant everyone equal freedom and opportunity, and that, if there is to be inequality at all, it should only be allowed on the grounds that it benefits those who have the least advantages in life. The task of society (in addition to the basic protection of individuals who have come together to form it) is, according to Rawls, that it should organize the fair sharing out of both material and social benefits.

Not all philosophers would agree with Rawls' desire to reduce inequalities. In the nineteenth century, Nietzsche's view was that the strong should not be restrained because of the needs of the weak. His views were that democracy and Christianity had a negative effect, weakening the human species by seeking special advantage for those who are weak or poor and handicapped in some way. By contrast, he looked towards an *übermensch* – an 'over-man' or 'beyond-man' – expressing the idea of striving to be something more. For Nietzsche, man is something that has to be overcome: a starting point from which we move forward and upward.

Key idea for life: Evolution and justice?

Natural selection suggests that competition, rather than fairness and consideration for others, is the basis of evolutionary advance. Applied to human society, this evolutionary perspective has a sad history, from Spencer's 'survival of the fittest' to eugenics, ideas of *racial* superiority, ethnic cleansing, and – under the Nazis – to genocide. In the economic sphere, however, free-markets operate a form of natural selection that is seen by many people as perfectly just.

There is, however, a more general criticism of his approach. Earlier in this chapter we contrasted those who give priority to the individual, with a minimal role for the state, and those who give priority to the state, so that it is only in the context of society that individuals come to their full potential. Let us examine Rawls' theory from this perspective.

By making the people who come together to establish the principles of society forget who they are, they also relinquish all that they might naturally have gained and achieved. The successful person, unaware of his or her position, plays safe and opts for an equal share of the pooled resources. That may be fine as a thought experiment, but could it work like that in the real world? All actual legal systems, and all ideas of justice, are framed within, and grow out of, a historical context. That's life!

Another criticism of this approach is made by Ronald Dworkin. He argues that, before you can ask 'What is justice?' you need to ask the prior question 'What kind of life should men and women lead? What counts as excellence in a human being?' He argues that the liberal position, as given by Rawls, does not take this into consideration. Rawls' treatment of individuals does not depend on *anything about them as individuals*.

Key idea for life

If every inequality is allowed only on the basis that it benefits the least well off (Rawls' view), there is little chance that excellence will be developed, as every facility offered for the development of excellence is likely to increase rather than decrease the gap between the most able and the least able. How can such a theory avoid bland mediocrity?

NOZICK (JUSTICE AS ENTITLEMENT)

If the purpose of society is to protect the life, liberty and property of individuals, then each person should be enabled to retain those things that are rightly theirs. A society which, in the name of establishing equality, redistributes that wealth is in fact depriving an individual of the very protection which led to the formation of society in the first place.

This approach to the question of justice is taken by Robert Nozick in *Anarchy, State and Utopia* (1974). He argues that it is wrong for the state to take taxes from individuals or force them to contribute to a health service that benefits others. It infringes their liberty to gain wealth and retain it. For Nozick, it is perfectly right to give what you have to another person if you so choose, but not that you should be required to do so. On this social theory, voluntary contributions are welcomed, but enforced taxes are not. He argues that justice is a matter of the entitlement of individuals to retain their 'holdings' – wealth that they have gained legitimately.

An important feature of Nozick's case is that, at any one time, the actual wealth that a person owns is related to history: that of the individual (through having worked for years, for example) or that of his or her family (through inheritance). In practice, however, it is not always easy to establish that all wealth has been gained legitimately. Land that has been in a family for generations may originally have been acquired by the most dubious of means. Nozick also argues, against those that seek equality, that even if people were made equal, they would immediately start trading, and would quickly establish new inequalities.

Key idea for life

In *The Examined Life*, the mature Nozick looked back on his life as a philosopher and admitted to being rather embarrassed by the youthful ideas for which he had become well-known.

Philosophers are human, and integrity requires that they should be able to change their minds and arguments. To maintain exactly the same argument over decades may suggest a) that you got it absolutely right first time, b) that you have given up on original thought, or c) that you have grown defensive of your ideas and position. Honest philosophers always recognize that they are, in Nietzsche's words 'Human, all too human'.

A fundamental choice:

▶ Private property is theft! (This implies that all property should belong to the state, or ultimately to the global community.) Justice demands redistribution on the basis of need.

Or

▶ Redistribution is theft! (This implies that each individual has the right to that which is lawfully gained.) Justice demands that each should develop to his or her potential, unhampered by false notions of equality.

In the name of liberty, it is tempting to suggest that politics should be morally neutral. In other words, there should be equal scope and equal respect for all views, values and beliefs, and politicians should keep out of issues of personal choice and morality. The danger with this is that it fails to address the moral question about what constitutes the good life.

Where fundamental values differ, agreement on political ends is very difficult to establish. Politics should therefore remain open to moral discussion and debate. This is argued strongly by, for example, Michael Sandel, who teaches a course on 'justice' at Harvard, and who is concerned that politics should not lose sight of the fundamental questions about what it means to lead a good life. His argument that political argument today is morally impoverished is set out in his book *Justice: What's the Right Thing to Do?* (Allen Lane, 2009).

It is on the question of values and virtues that Sandel differs radically from the approach taken by Rawls, as outlined above. For Rawls, and for many if not most politicians today, government should be neutral with respect to values, allowing people to make their own decisions, and should simply create a neutral space within which people can sort out their own agenda. Sandel, however, returns to the traditions of the Greeks, particularly Aristotle, in seeing the role of good governance to get involved with the moral questions. Politics is about understanding and promoting the good life, and that will always involve becoming engaged with moral and spiritual questions.

AYN RAND (1905–82)

Questions of justice and fairness usually assume the Enlightenment perspective in which, in an ideal society, every individual would be treated with respect and given equal status. Against this there stands a philosophy of selfish competition, where the weak should not be protected from the effect of the advance of the strong. Seen to some extent in Nietzsche (see page 268), it is found particularly in the writings of Ayn Rand, a philosopher and novelist, who has inspired right-wing politics, especially in the USA. She argues that what counts most is the individual ego and sees altruism as going against human flourishing. As an ideal, she holds that you should only do that which is in your own interest, and in the political sphere promotes the idea that taxes should be lowered, government should be minimal (mainly law enforcement and protection) and that aid to the poor should be reduced. Her philosophy, which she termed objectivism, thus argues for 'ethical egoism' and for a general laissez-faire, or free-market, capitalism based on individual ambition. She argues (particularly in her novel *Atlas Shrugged*, 1957) that, without the efforts of the most productive people, the world would fail to make any progress.

Every writer and philosopher responds to his or her own situation in life. Rand was born in Russia but lived for most of her life in the USA. She was critical of the Soviet system of rigid social and economic control, contrasting it with the freedom of American capitalism.

However, as Matthieu Ricard points out (*Altruism*, p. 305), her reasoning was faulty:

> ... Rand clumsily sets in place the cornerstone of her intellectual building: man's basic desire is to remain alive and to be happy; *therefore he must be selfish*.
>
> That is where the logical fault lies. Rand reasons in the abstract and loses contact with lived experience. The latter shows that a selfishness as extreme as the one she advocates is much more likely to make the individual unhappy than to favour his or her prosperity.

My own comment on Rand's view is that, even if one were to set aside all humanitarian and religious views about the value of individuals, it is difficult to see how such a competitive world could be sustainable long term. In a limited and interconnected world, survival requires co-operation. It is not that the most creative go on strike against a society based on welfare (Rand's view in *Atlas Shrugged*), but that, in an increasingly unequal society, those who have nothing to lose by doing so will eventually rebel against the establishment that neglects their interests.

The banality of evil

In looking back at the totalitarian regimes of the twentieth century, we see both the scale of suffering caused, and the banal way in which people became complicit in the most terrible atrocities. This is brought home in its starkest form by the work of Hannah Arendt (1906–75), in her books *The Origins of Totalitarianism* (1951) and, particularly, *Eichmann in Jerusalem: A Report on the Banality of Evil* (1963). Influenced by the work of Husserl (see page 50) and Heidegger (see page 51), whose lover she was until Heidegger became a member of the Nazi party and her situation, as a Jewish student, became unsustainable. She experienced totalitarianism first hand, having been interrogated by the Gestapo, and having to flee, first to France and later, after escaping from an internment camp, to the United States.

In contrast to the sometimes rather pessimistic view of life presented by Heidegger, and by Sartre's existentialism (see above page 51), Arendt emphasized the positive fact that we are all born free. Our natural state is one of freedom, but we grow to work alongside others and to engage politically. For her, love is the defining feature of the individual, and it stands in stark contrast to her work on examining the way in which the totalitarian regimes were able to gain ground and become established in Germany and the USSR. It included the recognition that terror was used as a means to an ideological end – whether that end was the 'dictatorship of the proletariat' (in the USSR) or a racially pure nation (in Germany). In contrast to all this, Arendt sought to recognize people as individuals who choose to come together for social or political action.

In observing the trial of Eichmann, she coined the phrase 'the banality of evil' to describe the way in which he had simply seen himself as a functionary and done what was asked of him. He had no special hatred of Jews, but just worked within a system that made the Holocaust possible.

Key idea for life

Two features of Arendt's thought particularly strike me as utterly relevant today. One is that totalitarianism thrives where an underclass feels that it has no stake in society and does not bother to vote (or votes merely to protest), and the other is the general relativism that sees all views as of equal worth, however destructive they may be long term. Both remain threats to civilization and require to be balanced by a thoughtful analysis of what actually constitutes the good life and a non-partisan approach to examining how it may be achieved politically.

Homo economicus

In *The Wealth of Nations*, Adam Smith set out his economic theory, which included the idea of an 'invisible hand' by which everyone in society would benefit from the operation of free-market capitalism. He did so against the background of the eighteenth-century Scottish Enlightenment, but since then this idea has developed into an often-unquestioned assumption behind economics and politics, namely that, with minimal interference from government, market forces and competition will ensure the success of the most efficient, and as a result of the 'trickle-down' effect (whereby the wealthy are able to spend their wealth and give employment) a fair distribution of goods throughout society.

In such a perspective (now part of what is termed 'neo-liberalism'), people are seen as consumers or entrepreneurs, motivated by self-interest – *homo economicus*. Companies are not formed to benefit society, but to maximize profits; consumers play the game and try to secure maximum benefit for minimum outlay. The world works, not by co-operation or the desire for mutual support and benefit, but through the markets. The political and economic implications of this view were starkly expressed by Milton Friedman in *Capitalism and Freedom* (University of Chicago Press, 1962, p. 133):

> Few trends could so thoroughly undermine the very foundations of our free society as the acceptance by corporate officials of a social responsibility other than to make as much money for their stockholders as possible.

In an earlier book, *Theory of Moral Sentiments* (1759), Adam Smith saw the perfection of human nature as the ability to restrain selfishness and promote benevolence. Unfortunately, he decided that responsibility for the welfare of everyone should be left to God, and that individuals were better suited to taking care of their own welfare and that of those closest to them. Hence it was the promotion of the 'invisible hand' of the markets, based on self-interest, that became the main thrust of his philosophical and economic legacy.

Key idea for life

One might assume that utility companies exist in order to offer a social benefit – the supply of gas, electricity or water – but, within neo-liberal, free-market capitalism, those companies exist in order to maximize their profits. People are expected to switch from company to company in order to get the best deal for themselves; companies make offers in the attempt to retain customers. It's economic cat and mouse! The unquestioned assumption here is that society *should* be driven by economic competition, rather than regulated politically. Pure Adam Smith. But who loses out in this competitive game, and is it a fair way to supply the fundamental necessities of civilized life?

It is commonly assumed that an economic perspective which works well for a small business or family may be scaled up to national (or international) level. So, for example, it makes sense, if income is fixed, to live 'within one's means', and this is then scaled up to justify a policy of austerity in terms of social provision at national level. However, at national level, expenditure may always be balanced against taxation and borrowing, and the choice of how to balance the books reflects the values and moral assumptions of society. A decision to maintain a low level of taxation, while applying austerity, shifts resources from the poor to the relatively wealthy. To say that funds for public services are to be restrained is, in a developed country, a matter of political choice, not of necessity.

Beware the 'naturalistic fallacy' (see page 222). As Hume and Moore pointed out, you cannot derive an 'ought' from an 'is'. The attempt to do so takes place in many spheres of life, including the economic. Watch closely, and you see many values and choices being presented as being based on facts. In politics and economics, whether domestic or national, you generally have more choices than you realize.

It is often interesting to trace ideas back from one philosopher to another. Today's obsession with the provision of material goods – from both ends of the political spectrum – owes much to Karl Marx, who saw the means of production and the provision of the basic necessities of life, observed through the prism of class confrontation, as a fundamental agent of change. Those who reject Marxism, seeking a neo-liberal future of unfettered free markets, still tend to measure success in terms of economic output and increases in the standard of living. Marx believed that the task of philosophers should be to change the world, rather than simply interpret it. But who did Marx study for his doctoral thesis? None other than Epicurus – the thinker whose philosophy was based on a lifestyle focused on taking pleasure in the simple necessities of life and rejecting the insatiable desire for more and more goods.

It is Epicurus who links happiness with the adoption of a simple lifestyle, and the rejection of the short-term promises of consumerism. *Homo economicus*, indeed, but with a goal of economic self-sufficiency and simplicity.

Take it back one step further and you come to Aristotle, who in *Politics* argued that a truly democratic statesman must seek to ensure that the multitude are saved from extreme poverty and is concerned to limit the excessive greed of a wealthy elite, seeking a way of establishing social justice, arguing that redistribution of wealth would be, in the long run, to the benefit of the whole of society. The Greek term he used for this – *oikonomia* (from which we get our term 'economics') concerns household management, rather than a means of gaining wealth. Unlike the current neo-liberal view that the task of government is to provide security and then get out of the way and allow market forces to control social provision, Aristotle saw the first aim of government as promoting the good life, and to regulate the market when necessary in order to make that possible. I sense that Aristotle would have plenty to contribute to the economic debates of the twenty-first century.

Key idea for life

Step back more than 2,300 years, and you find issues of wealth and poverty, equality and social justice that are much like those of today. Everything changes, but nothing changes. Aristotle's arguments are utterly relevant today, challenging our assumptions about the role of government and finance.

Freedom and rights

Freedom in this context means something rather different from the 'freedom/determinism' debate outlined earlier. In that case, the determinist argument was that everything depends on prior causes and may (in theory) be predicted scientifically. Hence we are never free to choose what we do, even if our lack of understanding of the determining causes means that we retain the illusion of freedom.

Here, the debate is about the degree of freedom that the individual has a right to exercise within society, given the impact that such freedom may have upon the freedom of others: freedom to act within certain parameters set out by the law. Once a person acts outside those parameters, society, through the police and the courts, can step in and impose a penalty on the 'outlaw'.

But how much liberty should we seek?

John Stuart Mill's *On Liberty* is one of the great works of political philosophy. Published in 1859, it sets the liberal agenda, arguing for radical freedom in matters of morality and economics, and promoting the 'harm principle', namely that in the case of any private matter, where an action and its consequences affect only the individuals concerned, there should be absolute freedom. In other words, you should be free to do whatever you choose, provided that it does not harm anyone else. Problems occur with this approach when there is doubt about whether an action is entirely private or affects others.

Case study

If smoking cigarettes were a private activity, with consequences, however harmful, suffered only by the person who chose to smoke, there would be no need to legislate against it. However, on the 'harm principle', the law may step in to prohibit smoking in public places if:

* it constitutes a fire hazard or
* non-smokers want to be free to breathe air that is not filled with smoke and thus avoid the dangers of passive smoking.

Legislation can then be justified on a simple utilitarian basis. The law protects other people from the effects of an individual's action.

Should society as a whole, however, through its medical services, be required to pay the price for an individual's decision to smoke, take drugs, or practise a dangerous sport? Here the law has to balance a utilitarian moral position with the preservation of individual human rights.

The idea of individual liberty has been of fundamental importance in modern political thinking, responding perhaps to the experience of horrific excesses of twentieth-century totalitarian systems in Nazi Germany, the Soviet Union and elsewhere. Karl Popper's book *The Open Society and its Enemies*, published in the 1940s, made the issue of freedom central. In the 1960s, much political debate centred on how to maintain social order and yet allow maximum freedom. Rawls' theory of justice may be seen as an attempt to justify liberal views of society, in which the redistribution of wealth is a logical choice of free individuals. Rawls took the view that, provided all the essentials of life were met (a presupposition of his theory), people would choose freedom rather than, for example, the chance of getting more wealth. This view has been challenged by Ronald Dworkin and others, who think that some people would rather gamble that they would win, rather than play it safe and follow the liberal and egalitarian views of Rawls.

This observation is actually in line with a key theme of Mill's *On Liberty*. His intention, in maximizing freedom, was to allow people to develop and shape their lives as they chose, rather than simply to follow what others prescribed for them. This is in line with the liberal agenda and neo-liberal economics – where the possibility to develop and shape the future is what gives colour and enthusiasm to life, rather than the stifling conformity of imposed social order.

HUMAN AND LEGAL RIGHTS

> We hold these truths to be self-evident, that all men are created equal, that they are endowed by their Creator with certain unalienable Rights, that among these are Life, Liberty and the pursuit of Happiness.
>
> The American Declaration of Independence (1776)

The view that individuals have rights that should be upheld by law follows from a basic sense of justice and equality. However it is not always 'self-evident' how you can establish a fair balance between the rights of the individual and the political requirements of the state.

In an ideal society, the law would always be framed on the basis of the agreement between free individuals, and every person would be equally free to enjoy basic human and legal rights. There is, however, a difference between having a set of rights and being free to exercise those rights. In general, even though rights are given irrespective of age and capacities, it is sometimes necessary for the exercise of those rights to be curtailed:

▶ **On grounds of age.** Children have rights, and are protected by the law from exploitation by others, but cannot, for example, buy cigarettes or alcohol, drive a car or fly a plane. These limits are imposed because below the relevant age the child is considered unable to take a responsible decision and parents, or society, therefore impose a restriction on the child's freedom.

▶ **On grounds of insanity.** Those who are insane and are liable to be a danger to themselves or to others are also restrained.

▶ **On grounds of lack of skill.** Flying a plane or driving a car (other than on private property) without a licence is illegal. This can be justified on utilitarian grounds, as others in the air or on the roads could be in danger. Equally, to pose as a surgeon and perform operations without the appropriate qualification is illegal. Without the public acknowledgement that a person has the required skills, many such tasks would endanger the lives or well-being of others.

Rights are also taken from those who break the law, for example:

▶ Through prison sentences

▶ Through legal injunctions to stop actions being carried out or to prevent one person from approaching another, or visiting a particular place. This may be taken retrospectively, if a person has already broken a law, or proactively, for example, to stop publication of a potentially damaging story in a newspaper.

In all these cases, a person retains his or her fundamental rights, but cannot exercise them, on the basis that to do so would be against the interests of society as a whole. This approach is based on the idea of social contract, where the laws of society are made by mutual agreement, and the loss of certain freedoms are exchanged for the gain of a measure of social protection. It may also therefore be justified on utilitarian grounds. It also reflects Article 21 of the United Nations Declaration on Human Rights which states that: 'The will of the people shall be the basis of the authority of government.'

But Dworkin argues that a 'right' is something that an individual can exercise even if it goes *against* the general welfare. After all, there is no point in my claiming a right to do something, if nobody would ever want to challenge it. A right is something that I can claim in difficult circumstances.

This means that (at least in the immediate context) rights cannot be justified on utilitarian grounds. They do not necessarily offer the greatest good to the greatest number. Rights are claimed by minorities. Rights are established by social contract (for example, within the US Constitution or the United Nations) and represent a basic standard of treatment that an individual can expect to receive by virtue of the social and legal system within which those rights are set down.

However, in considering the social contract basis of rights, we need to be aware of a distinction made by Thomas Paine (1737–1809), a political campaigner who shot to fame through the publication of a pamphlet entitled 'Common Sense', in which he called for independence for the American colonies, throwing off the British monarchy and establishing a new republican government which would provide a more equal distribution of wealth, getting rid of the privileges of the gentry. In his book *The Rights of Man*, he distinguished between 'natural rights' and 'civil rights': the former concern what an individual requires for his or her own comfort and happiness, the latter what an individual can expect as a member of a society.

Key idea for life

A key problem in considering rights today is to know how to strike a balance between an individual-centred approach, and one that takes into account the responsibilities that an individual has towards society as a whole. If everyone claims their own individual rights, but without accepting any social responsibilities, the result is likely to verge on anarchy, because it no longer depends on an implied 'social contract' that individuals have to work together for their mutual support.

The philosophy of history

In order to understand the present, it is necessary to know something of the past, if only to avoid repeating mistakes. So, just as ethics always needs to be informed by facts, values and arguments, so political philosophy needs to be informed by the history and the historical contexts of political thought.

But what is history? We might be tempted to say that history is the account of what has happened in the past. That will not do, however, for a theoretically infinite number of events have already taken place and, even if they could all be remembered and recorded, it would take an infinite amount of time to construct history out of them. In other words, history would unfold faster than it could be recounted.

History is therefore *selective*; most things are ignored. Without such selection, the sheer number of events in the past would smother any attempt to get an overall view of what happened. And this is a crucial point: history involves an interpretation of events, and that interpretation depends on the ideas and assumptions of the historian. *History cannot be an objective account of facts.* It is an interpretation of the significance of particular things that have taken place in the past.

More than one layer of interpretation may be involved; a modern historian examining ancient texts brings his or her own views to that study but, equally, the original authors of those texts were also interpreting the events they recorded. Much of the study of history is historiography, the study of historical writing.

This has led some postmodernist thinkers to argue that texts are simply based on other texts (the process called 'intertextuality') rather than on external 'facts'. The truth of a document is therefore related to the authority of those who wrote it, rather than to events it claims to describe. The American philosopher, Hayden White, in his book *Metahistory* (1973) put forward the view that the historian is actually producing a creative literary invention, rather than dealing in facts. *Some of the information that the historian uses may be factual, but it only becomes 'history' once it is part of a story.*

The postmodernist approach raises important issues for historians. How do you judge between conflicting interpretations of the past? While no historian would claim that his or her account of an event is totally objective, there is a professional interest in gathering evidence in order to illustrate past events as clearly as possible.

THE MECHANISMS OF CHANGE

Part of the fascination of history is trying to understand the process by which change comes about. The German idealist philosopher Hegel (1770–1831) thought that it was possible to discern a particular 'spirit', or *Geist,* unfolding in the historical process. The process through which this unfolding took place is described as a 'dialectic': each age has its particular feature (its 'thesis') which then produces a reaction ('antithesis') which is then resolved (in a 'synthesis'). This process then repeats itself, always aiming towards a rational ideal and absolute.

Karl Marx was influenced by Hegel's theory of historical change, but he argued that the basis of society was economic and material. In Marx, you therefore have a political philosophy which is also a philosophy of history, and you have a philosopher whose expressed intention is to change things rather than simply understand them.

One key feature of the philosophy of history is the recognition that as soon as events are described, they are interpreted, and as soon as they are interpreted, they are set within an overall pattern of understanding. The philosophy of history seeks to reveal that process of interpretation, and to relate it, as closely as it may, to the events that it seeks to present.

Enframing in a complex world

The problem with political philosophy (and perhaps with all philosophy) is that it works with abstract and generalized concepts that seldom match the actual situation in which people find themselves.

Political philosophy examines the principles upon which legal and political systems are founded. Rights, justice, fairness, social contract, democracy – it is important to clarify what these terms mean and imply because, once you get beyond Hobbes' view that society is constructed for mutual protection, once you say that it is *right* to organize society in a particular way, not just that it is *necessary for survival* to do so, then what you organize implies ideas of justice, of freedom, of equality, of the valuation of human life, and of the place of human life within an understanding of the world as a whole.

However, Heidegger pointed out (see above page 247) that we tend to 'enframe' our understanding of things; we see them in terms of the value they have for us and the way in which they fit with the basic assumptions we have about life. If we assume that individual freedom is paramount, and that government is basically an evil to be tolerated or resisted, then every piece of legislation will be viewed in terms of whether or not it limits personal freedom. What one person may see as the protection of worker's rights, or the minimum wage necessary for civilized living, another may see as an unnecessary interference in the freedom of employers to maximize profits within a capitalist system. Your 'frame' may decide whether, on reading the previous sentence, you naturally sided with one side or the other. Is it ever possible to present a question that is not enframed?

The world is complex. Concepts, and the popular use of 'thought experiments' in philosophical debate, try to simplify and make the complexity of life manageable. But beware any philosophy that does not bring with it its own disclaimer, admitting its own particular 'enframing' of the questions being discussed.

Key idea for life

The greatest wisdom is to know the limits of all knowledge and the fallibility of all views and arguments. The world remains complex, even if – in order to grasp it and make decisions within it – we are forced to enframe and simplify it. Nowhere is this cautionary note more relevant, and its neglect more potentially dangerous, than in the area of political philosophy, as the newspapers daily testify and the debate between what constitutes real news and 'fake news' amply illustrates. All news is enframed, but fake news is presented merely to promote its own frame.

10

The Philosophy of Everything

In this chapter you will:

▶ *Take a brief look at the range of issues and topics considered by popular philosophy today*

▶ *Examine some developments within academic philosophy and their relevance to life*

Why?

The range of popular books on philosophy today is quite astonishing, covering all aspects of life, challenging us to think again about things we may have taken for granted, and encouraging us to develop and shape a 'wise' view of life, its meaning and its significance. But at the same time, academic philosophy is broadening to take into account some of the key questions that face the world in the twenty-first century.

Popular philosophy can take you from the cradle to the grave. At the end of 2016, *The Philosophers Magazine* featured a forum on how many children one should have, and in the *Art of Living* series published by Acumen there are books on *Middle Age* (Christopher Hamilton), *Illness* (Havi Carel) and *Death* (Todd May), to say nothing of the way in which our characters are shaped as we go through life in *Me* (Mel Thompson). Then there are philosophy titles on the less attractive sides of human behaviour, including *Bullshit and Philosophy* (Gary Hardcastle and George Reisch) along with a book about how to avoid it *Believing Bullshit: How Not to Get Sucked into an Intellectual Black Hole* (Stephen Law), through to its most positive side with *Altruism*, a hugely important book by Matthieu Ricard, which has already been referred to in this present volume, and one that illustrates the way in which a philosopher can give a serious and substantial study (849 pages) without being long-winded.

When it comes to other species, there are plenty of books considering our relationship to animals, including the influential *Animal Liberation* (Peter Singer). More broadly, philosophers have tackled questions related to the environment and global warming.

For those who have a taste for it, there are books on food, such as *The Virtues of the Table: How to Eat and Think* (Julian Baggini) and a good range on wine, including *Questions of Taste: The Philosophy of Wine* (ed Barry Smith) with hints of aesthetic and spiritual insight via *The Philosophy of Wine: A Case of Truth, Beauty and Intoxication* (Cain Todd) – showing that *in vino veritas* still holds true – and *Wine and Philosophy: A Symposium on Thinking and Drinking* (Fritz Allhoff), and

Roger Scruton's *I Drink Therefore I Am*, finally sobering up with *Coffee* (ed Scott Parker and Michael Austin) in the 'Philosophy for Everyone' series.

After all, food is not just a necessity of life, as it is for other species, but provides food for thought. What we eat (vegetarianism, the treatment of animals bred for food, the distribution of the world's supply of food), how we eat (over-indulgence as compensation for dissatisfaction in other areas of life, fasting as a religious discipline) and with whom we eat (the table as providing the setting for social interaction, hospitality and so on) all provide material for philosophical reflection.

If you assume that philosophical books require you to chew your way through page after page of difficult text, you could always dispel that myth by trying Nigel Warburton and Noel Edmunds' *Philosophy Bites* books, taken from their brilliant set of podcasts, which, over a period of ten years (and over 28 million downloads) have recorded philosophers talking clearly and perceptively about... well... just about everything, in digestible bite-sized pieces. In addition, if you fancy philosophy chopped up into tasty morsels for holiday reading, there's *The Philosopher's Beach Book* (Mel Thompson), which invites you to 'wiggle your toes in the sand and think'.

Key idea for life

Even the wisdom of ancient philosophers may be applied directly to life. Who would have imagined, 50 years ago, that one would open a book on philosophy to find a chapter entitled 'Zeno of Citium on the psychology of shopping', but this appears in Mark Vernon's *Plato's Podcasts: the Ancients' Guide to Modern Living* (Oneworld, 2009).

There is huge interest in the philosophy of film, where visual intuition can make a convincing philosophical case. You have only to listen to Slovoj Zizek in full flood to realize how a philosopher can explore and use the impact of the cinema on the development of ideas.

Clearly, there can be a philosophy of just about everything. However, if you think this is parallel to a physicist's 'theory of everything' you'd be wrong – the latter is pure metaphysics, an attempt to integrate all that we know at the most general and basic level of reality, a level at which there can emerge a theory that then explains everything else. That, of course, is where this book started, and what many people assume philosophy is about. By now, though, it should be clear that, however important it is to ask fundamental questions, it is certainly not the whole of philosophy. We can philosophize on any aspect of reality – from the nature of the self, to the experience of drinking wine – looking at it clearly, asking relevant questions of it and exploring its significance.

All this has blossomed within the sphere of popular philosophy, represented not just by books but also by magazines and journals whose articles are frequently written by academic philosophers, but which address the interests of the general reader rather than the specialist.

Academic philosophy itself, however, continues to fight its corner, and gradually develops as it does so. During the twentieth century, a number of movements in philosophy attempted to reduce it to some other discipline. The positivists wanted philosophy to follow science, throwing out all that did not conform to empirical criteria of meaning. Then the linguistic analysts insisted that the whole task of philosophy was the unpacking of statements to clarify their meaning. Marxists wanted everything reduced to its social and political matrix and postmodernists saw everything in terms of cultural and literary metaphors or signs, strung together. One might imagine that philosophy would be shaken radically by such drastic criticisms and reinterpretations of its task, but this has not been the case.

For anyone coming to philosophy at the end of the 1950s, however, at least in university departments featuring the Anglo-American analytic tradition, the task and scope of philosophy was precise but narrow. Still dominated by linguistic analysis, it aimed to examine problematic sentences and, through their elucidation, clarify meaning. In effect, it offered its clarification services to all other subjects, rather than offering anything distinctive of its own.

Over the last 50 years, however, philosophy has seen remarkable growth, both in its popularity as a subject and in the range and relevance of the topics it covers. One impetus for change came initially within the area of applied ethics. In the days of linguistic analysis, everything was focused on the meaning or otherwise of ethical propositions, and it was quite reasonable for a philosopher to claim to have nothing to say about moral issues themselves. However, there came increasing demand for ethical guidance from professionals, particularly in medicine and nursing, in order to develop and implement standards for dealing with the many difficult moral questions raised in their everyday work. Questions about abortion and euthanasia, the use of drugs and the conduct of medical research, all needed to be answered by sound moral arguments.

At the same time, the rise of the cognitive sciences, information technology and artificial intelligence raised questions about the nature of mind. International politics grapples with concepts – democracy, human rights, self-determination, national sovereignty – to direct and justify its action or inaction in various crises. Political philosophy is therefore utterly relevant to the human agenda. Issues concerning the philosophy of art – censorship, copyright, what distinguishes valid erotic art from pornography, what constitutes 'taste' or blasphemy, the nature of artistic expression – come to the fore when the Turner or other prize is judged, or when artists produce images that some find inspiring and others want banned. Relevant here also are legal debates about the ownership of intellectual property, about who should be paid royalties or claim copyright on ideas and words. Social awareness brings with it issues of feminism and of race, of inequality and the dynamics of free markets.

With the internet comes a whole raft of issues about self-expression, privacy, international controls, exploitation and the nature of communication. In a complex world, something more is needed of philosophy than the mere clarification of meaning. Even beyond the obvious area of ethics, philosophy is increasingly becoming 'applied'. It is therefore also becoming more obviously relevant to everyday life – it is *the* subject for dealing with big questions. The nature of status, or love, or justice, or commitment, or work – in fact all the elements that go to make up the art of living – benefit from sustained and thoughtful reflection, and philosophy provides the discipline for doing just that.

This is where we return to a distinction made in the introduction to this book – between philosophy as a skill and philosophy as the history of ideas. Informed by the great thinkers of the past, we have the opportunity to explore and use the skills of good argument to sift through the huge amount of information and comment that arrives daily through the media. We make decisions about which issues to address – which tweets to re-tweet, which Facebook groups to join, which blogs or websites to follow. In each of these small decisions – I like the sound of that, I'll follow this, I'll mark that as SPAM – we are (consciously or unconsciously) expressing the cumulative effect of all that has influenced us in the past, and at the same time shaping our philosophy for the future. The question with which we are faced is whether or not we will take the trouble to think and reflect carefully on that process – in other words, whether or not we will engage in philosophy.

In two major political decisions of 2016 – the election of Donald Trump as president in the USA and the decision of the UK to leave the European Union – there was a general revolt against the assumed authority of political establishments and the role of experts. Many people chose to act – and saw it as in their best interest to act – in a way that went against the received wisdom of a majority of professional advisers. It was an affirmation of the right of each individual to play an equal role in decision-making, and to do so in the light of one's own intuitions, rather than simply conforming to an established view. Whatever the implications of the US election and the Brexit vote – and there have been numerous arguments used on both sides of both democratic choices – one thing is clear: people want to make up their own minds, to establish their own values and to become more autonomous. They no longer want to be taken for granted by those in power. Perhaps that is where philosophy is usefully broadening out from the professionalized academic discipline to recognize that, informed by the best academic thinking, it is also a skill from which everyone can benefit; *not philosophy for its own sake, but philosophy for life*.

My guess is that part of the reason for the growing popularity of philosophy outside the world of academia is the frightening range of issues with which we are confronted today, and to which serious thought and reflection needs to be given. Consider, for example:

- The impact of neo-liberal economics, and the long-term sustainability (on economic or social grounds) or otherwise of capitalism.

- Globalization in products and services, and its impact on employment.

- War/violence/terrorism.

- Poverty in a connected world, where we are all aware of how others live.

- How to create a humane environment in which to live.

- Climate change and sustainability.

- How to find political structures that enable people to engage and make a difference rather than succumb to social and political impotence.

These are not simply moral issues (although they all have a moral component) but also philosophical ones. We need clarity and insight as well as determination if any of the current range of issues is to be resolved.

So where does all that leave us? Clearly, there are two very different views about what philosophy is for:

- One view – sometimes described as 'quietist' – suggests that philosophy is a self-contained, fascinating set of questions and an activity that is valuable in itself, perhaps sharpening up our intellectual faculties but having very little impact upon ordinary life. Like David Hume, who was accustomed to regaining his composure by going out and doing something practical when consumed by serious philosophical issues, we set philosophy aside when we engage with normal life. Philosophy does not change anything – it looks, examines but leaves life exactly as it is.

- The other view – typified by existentialism – sees philosophy as a force that can shape and reshape our lives, giving us insights into ourselves and our situation that enable us to strive for self-fulfilment, grasping the essence of what life can offer, and using our new philosophical perception to enhance our chances of achieving success and happiness. One thinks of Nietzsche's view that one should do philosophy with a hammer, or Kierkegaard's quest for existential meaning, or Marx's view that whereas formerly philosophers had only sought to understand the world, his task was to change it.

The truth is probably somewhere between those two extremes, but it also reflects a shift in academic philosophy over the last couple of decades. Through much of the twentieth century, the world of philosophy was divided between the two extremes, with the 'analytic philosophy' of the English-speaking world largely taking the quietist position and 'continental philosophy' taking an existentialist and more culturally based approach. Now, that simplistic division is past, and with it the need to choose one or other option. That leaves us free to explore the whole range of questions about philosophy and life: what it can offer and what difference it can make.

In a world where rhetoric, brute force, instant news, fake news and a general view that emotional appeals may simply become the norm in a post-truth society, there is a growing need for serious, popular philosophy: serious because it can address the major issues of life; popular because it is not confined to the academic department, but to the global mix of ideas that shape our lives.

Perhaps the last word should come from a traditional metaphysical philosopher, writing early in the twentieth century. In *Modes of Thought* (1938), A. N. Whitehead set down very clearly the value of the whole philosophical enterprise:

> The sort of ideas we attend to, and the sort of ideas we push into the negligible background, govern our hopes, our fears, our control of behaviour. As we think, we live. This is why the assemblage of philosophical ideas is more than a specialist study. It moulds our type of civilization.

If that is so, there is nothing more important than developing and maintaining an interest in *philosophy for life*.

Glossary

The following is a selection of terms used in this book, gathered here for quick reference. For more information on each of them, please refer to the relevant index entry.

agnosticism The view that one should only believe that for which one has adequate evidence. In the philosophy of religion, it expresses the idea that we do not have sufficient evidence or other means of knowing whether or not God exists.

atheism The view that there is no God. This may be taken in the narrower sense of the rejection of the theistic concept of God, or as a broad rejection of all religious ideas. It should be noted that some forms of Buddhism and Hinduism are atheistic, in that they promote a religious and spiritual path without requiring belief in God.

behaviourism The view that the mind can be understood in terms of observed physical activity.

blik A particular way of seeing something, used especially of religious language.

casuistry The process of applying general rules to specific cases; often used in a pejorative sense of an insensitive rejection of particular circumstances in favour of strictly applied rules.

categorical imperative A sense of unconditional moral obligation; used particularly in Kant's ethics for his general principles of morality.

category mistake (as used by Ryle in *The Concept of Mind*) The attempt to treat a collective term as though it were one of the particulars of which it is made up (e.g. right-hand glove/pair of gloves; university/colleges).

cosmological (arguments) Arguments for the existence of God, based on observation of the world.

deconstruction The process of examining a text in the context of the linguistic and social structures within which it was put together (see also **structuralism**).

deductive argument An argument based on logical principles, rather than on the assessment of evidence.

deism The view that God created the world and exists external to it, but is not (or no longer) involved or active within the world itself.

dualism The view that mind and matter are distinct and separate (of importance for the mind/body problem, but also for epistemology).

empiricism A theory of knowledge based on sense experience.

enframing The observation (made by Heidegger) that our understanding of things is 'enframed' by the use they have for us and the particular way we choose to regard them.

epiphenomenalism The theory that the mind is a product of complex physical processes.

epistemology The theory of knowledge.

existentialism The branch of philosophy concerned with the experience of meaning and purpose (or lack of it) in human existence

foundationalism The attempt to find an indubitable fact as the basis, or foundation, for a theory of knowledge.

functionalism (as used in cognitive science) The view that the mind has a functional role in examining the input it receives from the senses and giving an appropriate response. Hence, the mind is not so much 'over and above' the brain, but is a way of describing the functions that are being performed by it.

fundamentalism Used in a religious context for the attempt to eliminate the superficial and return to the fundamental features of religious belief. Frequently associated with a radical and literal interpretation of doctrine and scriptures.

hedonism The view that pleasure, or human welfare and happiness, is the goal of life.

hermeneutics The study of the way in which texts are interpreted, used particularly for the examination of religious scriptures.

idealism The claim that the world, as we experience it, is fundamentally mental, or (within the theory of knowledge) that we cannot know things directly, but only as they are made known to us through sense experience.

inductive method The process of coming to a conclusion based on the assessment of evidence.

interactionism The general term for theories of the mind in which mind and body are distinct (dualism) but interact.

intuitionism The view that 'good' is a fundamental term, which cannot be defined in terms of anything else, but which is known intuitively; also used of the theory that all moral claims are based on intuition.

intuitive knowledge Direct knowledge that is not the result of conscious reasoning or experience.

materialism Reality is material (for example the 'self' is a way of describing the body and its actions).

metaphysics The study of theories concerning the nature, structure and general characteristics of reality.

modernism A general term for the self-conscious approach to philosophy and the arts, developed particularly in the first half of the twentieth century.

Natural Law The rational interpretation of meaning and purpose in nature, used as a basis for ethics.

natural selection Darwin's theory of evolution, by which only the strongest examples of a species survive to breed.

noumena Used by Kant for 'things in themselves' as opposed to things as we experience them.

numinous The 'holy', beyond rational definition (term used by Rudolph Otto).

ontological (argument) Argument for the existence of God, based simply on a proposed definition of God and independent of evidence.

panentheism Belief that everything exists within God (implied by theism, but not the same as pantheism).

pantheism The idea that God is identical with the material universe.

phenomenology The study of what people actually experience (a theory developed by Husserl).

postmodernism A modern, 'continental' approach to philosophy and the arts, rejecting the modernist concept of a self-conscious, authentic, creative self in favour of a direct appreciation of symbols and texts in their cultural context (see also **structuralism**).

postulates Those beliefs that are implied by the experience of unconditional moral obligation (as used by Kant).

pragmatism The idea that a theory should be assessed according to its practical use, its implications for other areas of knowledge and its coherence with other beliefs.

rationalism The theory that all knowledge is based on, and shaped by, the process of thinking.

realism The view that scientific theories are capable of giving a direct description of reality.

reductionism The tendency to reduce everything to its component parts; the 'nothing but' view of complex things.

scepticism The view that all beliefs are equally open to critical examination and challenge and that none should claim absolute or permanent truth on the basis of authority alone.

schema A cluster of rational terms by which the 'holy' is understood and described (the process is called 'schematization').

situation ethics The ethical view, as expounded by Joseph Fletcher's *Situation Ethics*, 1966, that the right thing to do is that which is the most loving, and therefore that general moral principles may sometimes be set aside in favour of the needs of particular situations.

solipsism The view that we cannot know other minds directly, but have to infer them from our experience of people's physical bodies, words and actions.

structuralism An approach to philosophy, developed within the 'continental' school in the second half of the twentieth century, which interprets the meaning of a text, a word or an idea in the context of the structures of thought within which it is found.

syllogism A logical sequence of statements, leading from two premises that have a common term to a conclusion that does not have that term.

teleological Describes a theory or view based on the end or purpose of something, used particularly for the argument for the existence of God based on the idea that the world shows signs of purposeful design.

theism Belief in the existence of God.

utilitarianism The ethical theory that evaluates actions in terms of their predicted results ('the greatest good to the greatest number').

verification Checking the validity of a statement, used especially of logical positivist and other empirical approaches to language.

Index